The Hunt
for the Engineer

The Hunt for the Engineer

How Israeli Agents Tracked the Hamas Master Bomber

Samuel M. Katz

THE LYONS PRESS
Guilford, Connecticut
An imprint of The Globe Pequot Press

The Lyons Press is an imprint of The Globe Pequot Press.

First U.S. Edition, 1999

First Lyons Press Edition

Manufactured in the United States of America

10 9 8 7 6 5 4 3 2 1

Library of Congress Cataloging-in-Publication Data is available on file.

To Special Agent Thomas V. Gallagher Jr. and Special Agent Donald P. Morris, U.S. Department of State, Diplomatic Security Service—two "super cops" who helped guide me along an arduous journey

Contents

Preface

In a part of the world where time is measured by the amount of blood spilled, Yehiya Ayyash was a standout of the terrorist trade. The master bomb-builder from the West Bank managed, in a remarkable three years of terror, to have his hand in the deaths of 150 Israelis and the serious wounding of nearly 500. His creations shattered lives and dictated political will. He presented the security services of the state of Israel, once considered invincible, with an adversary unlike any they had battled before. He was, according to a counterterrorist police officer charged with bringing him to justice, "the definition of danger wrapped in a time bomb." He was smart, secret, cunning, and cold-blooded. His craft depended on simplicity and reliability—the evasive aspect of his operation depended on stealth and safe houses, mastery in the art of masquerade, and fearless followers. He was Palestine's first cult icon—a legend.

Israel had faced formidable terrorists before, of course. In the fifty years that Jews and Arabs have been killing one another

over the real estate between the Jordan River and the Mediterranean Sea, Israel has battled bombers and gunmen, hijackers
and assassins. They have worn ski masks; spoken German and
Japanese; and killed with both indiscriminate glee and premeditated discipline. These terrorists, men trained in Libya, the Soviet Union, and the Beka'a Valley, were professional killers
executing assignments under the guise of promoting their political agendas. Many of these "freedom fighters" were carica-
tures, outlandish in their propaganda and lifestyles, sometimes
acting in foolish disregard, as if they were nothing more than
extras working on the set of a bad B movie.

Yehiya Ayyash was different. He was smart, low-key, unassuming, and enigmatic. Perhaps he embodied evil to so many
because he was so good at what he did, and so devout in his
beliefs. To the men and women of the Israeli intelligence and
military communities, Yehiya Ayyash was the one Palestinian
terrorist whom they did not dare slur, dismiss, or underestimate.
He dictated the rules of the game on his terms. He was respected
and feared, and he was loathed. To them he wasn't "that fucking
Arab." He was "The Engineer."

When I embarked on writing this book, I looked at the Israeli
campaign to hunt down Yehiya Ayyash as the classic story of
good versus evil. But nothing involving Yehiya Ayyash can be
defined in terms of black and white. After nearly two years of
research and interviews, I find there are still more mysteries
about this man than concrete facts.

The Engineer's reign of terror sparked one of the most dramatic, unnerving, unimaginable, and unforeseeable periods in
the history of the Jewish state. His vengeful war against Israel
can be traced to the historic handshake between Israeli prime
minister Yitzhak Rabin and PLO chairman Yasir Arafat. It en-
compassed a massacre in Hebron and a peace treaty with Jordan, and culminated with the assassination of Rabin and the

Engineer's own brilliantly choreographed killing, an event that would result in bloodshed and great political turmoil. Yehiya Ayyash's campaign of bus bombings had helped change the political landscape in the area. It altered a nation's course toward peace. Yehiya Ayyash was the embodiment of evil because, in the end, he was the terrorist who had won.

This book tells the story of several of the most painful years in the history of a nation that is no stranger to pain. During this period, the state of Israel became platonic partners with old and once-hated enemies; internal divisions festered into cancerous lesions that latched onto the Israeli psyche with a trigger's pull; fear and mourning became a way of life. So much happened in those bloody years of scorched bodies that Middle Eastern leaders still have not fathomed the repercussions. In many ways, Ayyash's bombs managed to shatter perhaps the Middle East's only chance for a peaceful future.

Writing a book of this nature is never a solo effort. It would have been impossible to present this slice of covert and cutthroat history without the help, support, and friendship of some remarkable men and women—in offices in New York, Washington, D.C., Tel Aviv, Amman, and beyond. Many, for the most obvious of reasons, have requested anonymity. I wish to thank those spies, soldiers, statesmen, and super-cops for their trust, insight, and courage.

My warmest words of appreciation go to my agent, Al Zuckerman. This book would have never happened without Al's insight, perseverance, tolerance, editing skills, and faith, and I will always be grateful to him for his assistance, support, and generosity. I would also like to thank my partner in crime (and a few wild parachute jumps in Israel and Jordan), Steve Hartov, for his guidance, friendship, and some invaluable suggestions. I would also like to thank two unique women for their kind assistance: Nikki Schilling, for her generous technical support on the psychological side, and Sharon Elyakim, for her kind and unrewarded assistance—many of the logistics of assembling the material in this book could not have been obtained without her tireless efforts. I would like to offer special thanks to my current "rabbi," NYPD Deputy Inspector Ralph Pascullo, and to my former "rabbi," NYPD Lieutenant (Ret.) Bob Sobocienski, for their invaluable expertise, guidance, and friendship—these guys are the best! I'd also like to thank Officer "Evil Ed" Caneva, Officer "Mo" Smith, and Officer John Murray of the Miami-Dade Police Department, and their elite Special Response Team and Bomb Squad for their friendship and support.

Finally, I would like to thank my wife, Sigi, for her incredible love, devotion, and "tolerance." It's not easy being a writer's wife, especially one married to this writer.

The Hunt
for the Engineer

Introduction:
Pioneers of Death

It rarely rained in Israel on Passover. Rainy days were always considered welcome luxuries in the parched Middle East, and cool temperatures this Passover were symbolic of a nation in pain. Passover is the holiday celebrating the deliverance of the Jewish people from slavery in Egypt, though most in Israel would have been grateful just to have God deliver them now from the fear and foreboding. For eighteen long and bloody months, Palestinian terrorist attacks and suicide bombings had shattered Israelis' sense of security. The attacks were perpetrated by Hamas and Islamic Jihad, as well as forces inside the Palestinian Authority, including Yasir Arafat's own security services. The weapon of choice was the suicide bomber. Buses, banquet halls, cafés, restaurants, and shopping malls were all targeted. Israelis were afraid to go out to eat, or to take their families shopping.

The bone-numbing drizzle that refused to subside on the night of Wednesday, March 27, 2002 was reflective of the dour mood inside Israel. However, life continued on the eve of what was usually a festive holiday.

In Netanya, a resort city some twenty miles north of Tel Aviv, the hotels were filling up with family gatherings flocking to the coastal city to celebrate the holiday. Inside the Park Hotel at 7 King David Street, all ninety of the eight-story building's rooms were booked solid throughout the holiday.

The dining room, lavishly decorated for the festivities, was filled to capacity with diners from all over Israel and from around the world. The sounds of children asking the four questions to start off the Seder meal resonated throughout the dining room, as did the sounds of cutlery clanking against plates, and of wine being poured into Italian crystal. Even in an Israel under siege, the mood inside the Park Hotel was grudgingly festive.

Security was at an all-time high during the holidays, even though Palestinian terrorists had traditionally refrained from attacks on holidays or religious gatherings. Police and security personnel were on a heightened state of alert throughout the country. Roving police patrols, both uniformed and in plainclothes riding in unmarked vehicles, converged on potential targets.

Abdel-Basset Odeh, the son of a greengrocer, was also preparing for the Passover celebration. Odeh, a lanky twenty-four-year-old petty thief from the West Bank town of Tulkarem, was wearing his holiday best when he crossed the invisible no-man's-land separating Israel from the Palestinian Authority and met the car—parked near an orchard—that would ferry him to his target.

Odeh wasn't selected for this mission because of his intelligence or skill. He was fair-skinned, which meant that with the proper clothing and haircut, he could pass as a Jew. This was the only requirement needed for the mission at hand. And his Hamas handlers knew that the young West Bank native would not hesitate to kill himself along with his victims when he set off his bomb.

The cadence of the rain had slackened as the dining hall swelled with men and women in their finest clothes, and filled with the sounds of children giggling at their elders. No one paid notice as Odeh walked into the hotel at 7:15 P.M., through the lobby, marching briskly toward the tables in the banquet hall.

No one there remembered what Odeh was wearing, or what he looked like, before the burst of orange light and the cloud of suffocating black smoke. But after the blast, few could forget the destruction and devastation. Odeh's bomb was wrapped in a cocoon of nails and screws, some dipped in rat poison, which acted as toxic shrapnel, slicing through the bodies of those not killed outright by the heat and fire. Windows blocks away were shattered by the blast. Bodies and body parts were hurled down the street.

Police in Netanya, as well as the specially trained, elite counterterrorist Border Guard units on standby in the region, knew that if Palestinian terrorists were to launch an attack on the holiday, it would be in a town close to the West Bank. Netanya was only six miles from Tulkarem, a large West Bank town and a Hamas stronghold.

Police units rushed to the scene when the first chaotic emergency calls were broadcast, and they were followed by scores of ambulances and emergency medical personnel. As medics worked to save lives, policemen with automatic rifles ringed the perimeter, wary of being "double-tapped." This is a favorite Hamas tactic that involves sending one suicide bomber into a target, followed by a second bomber whose mission is to take out the rescue personnel.

The bombing, dubbed the Passover Massacre, killed thirty men, women, and children, and wounded more than 150 others. Less than forty-eight hours after the attack, the Israel Defense Forces invaded the West Bank.

There was a time when seeing the crime scene of a suicide bombing in which thirty people were blown to bits and over 150 were critically wounded would have sparked shock and outrage. But suicide bombings have become all too common.

In a world forever changed by the September 11, 2001 attacks against New York City and Washington, D.C., when Osama bin Laden's al-Qaeda terrorists targeted America itself, suicide attacks no longer seem unthinkable.

The central conflict in the Middle East has dragged on for decades and has cost thousands of innocent lives snuffed out on both sides of the Arab—Israeli equation. Peace appears elusive, only reinforcing fears that the terrorism will continue for another fifty years.

There have been many 9/11s in Israel's brief and bloody history. The names of towns and sites such as Avivim, Munich, Country Club Junction, and Nahariya have become small-scale landmarks to the orchestrated killing of innocents, much like Ground Zero where the World Trade Center once stood in lower Manhattan. And, for Israelis, there have been many Bin Laden terrorist masterminds whose names and deeds evoke the dictionary definition of evil.

The Palestinian terrorist war against Israel has lasted more than fifty years. Eventually, this war was no longer designed to seize hostages and publicize a cause. Instead, the terrorist attacks, perpetrated by zealots eager to die in a frightening act of condoned religious sacrifice, were designed to kill and maim as many people as possible.

The man who became the leader of this terror campaign was an enigmatic and introverted commander in the military wing of Hamas named Yehiya Ayyash. Nicknamed The Engineer by the Israelis, Ayyash masterminded a two-year reign of terror that killed hundreds and wounded scores more. As buses and cafés in Israel were incinerated by the human bombs he dispatched, Ayyash earned a cult following in the West Bank and Gaza, because he seemed to be the one terrorist the Israelis couldn't capture or kill. For two remarkable years of cat-and-mouse, Yehiya Ayyash was Israel's Osama bin Laden.

The Israelis finally got their man. But this act of revenge was at best a fleeting victory. The Middle East hasn't really been the same since. As long as there are men like Ayyash willing to massacre worshippers in a mosque or coldheartedly send confused teenagers into restaurants wearing explosive belts, future generations will be cursed with a legacy of hatred, death, and hopelessness.

Chapter 1

The Chess Match Begins

Police work has been described as years of routine punctuated by seconds of unimaginable terror. It is never boring, and the most mundane duty can sometimes erupt into heart-stopping madness. The midnight shift in the Dan Area just north of Tel Aviv promised to be routine for police officer Aharon Bin-Nun and his partner Leon Cahalon, a volunteer in the national police Civil Guard program.

The objective of Civil Guard patrols was to be the eyes and ears of the regular patrol force, and to summon help if trouble was spotted. Trouble was generally considered to fall under the category of what the Israeli defense establishment called HTA, or hostile terrorist activity. Usually, however, Civil Guard volunteers and the cops who rode shotgun with them ended up stopping car thieves, arresting burglars, or breaking up a domestic argument that spilled onto a neighborhood street. As they drove through the industrial zone of Or Yehuda, a town southeast of Tel Aviv, the two officers checked factories for signs of break-ins and cruised the deserted streets and alleys hoping that the women of the evening were safe from harm. All was quiet.

In the early morning hours of November 19, 1992, the two men driving in their beat-up blue-and-white van came across a Fiat van whose rear lights weren't working. Civil Guard patrols almost never handed out traffic citations, but the vehicle looked suspicious, as did the three Arabs inside who appeared to be nervous about the appearance of police. Using the loudspeaker, Bin-Nun ordered the van to pull over, but the driver floored the gas pedal and quickly disappeared in a cloud of black smoke that reeked of smoldering rubber. Radioing the dispatcher with the license plate number, Cahalon and Bin-Nun engaged in the last thing the two men thought they'd be involved in that November night—a high-speed chase.

The chase proceeded north along the desolate No. 4 highway leading toward Tel Aviv's middle-class suburbia. Other police units joined the pursuit. The Fiat van swerved from northbound lane to southbound, racing through red lights and almost crashing at several intersections yet to be cordoned off. Police attempted to stop the van with snake-teeth spikes rolled out across the roadway, but the driver managed to avoid several such obstacles as the van headed into the exclusive community of Ramat Efal.

On Rimon Street, as sleeping residents were summoned out of their slumber by the sounds of police sirens and tires screeching, the van entered a one-way street. Had the driver been fluent in Hebrew, he would have realized that the sign bearing the words DERECH LE'LO MUTZAH was warning of a dead end. Backed into a corner, the three men leaped out of the vehicle and attempted to flee from the oncoming gauntlet of blue-and-white patrol cars. Two of the men were captured before they could escape; the third man was arrested an hour later as he attempted to break into a nearby home. The three men were Palestinians.

The plates of the van, number 19-380-54, came back as stolen, but the cops who responded had a hunch that the three men were not run-of-the-mill car thieves. Indeed, inside the van the cops discovered something ominous. Five twelve-kilogram gasoline tanks, filled to capacity, were bound together by duct tape and wired to a battery and what appeared to be a crude timer. Acetone and store-bought detergents served as the explosive nerve center.

Sappers from the bomb squad rushed to the scene. Many had handled improvised devices before, from hand grenades to booby-trapped paint cans crammed with explosives, but never something so big and precarious. Police used loudspeakers to roust residents out of their homes and into bomb shelters just restocked with food and water after the Gulf War; they were told to sit tight until it was safe for them to return to their homes. The van stopped in the middle of Rimon Street was a classically designed, soundly constructed car bomb that had the potential to rain death and destruction over an area of two thousand feet.

As police helicopters hovered overhead, members of the bomb squad maneuvered a small tracked robot toward the van. The sappers wanted to neutralize the device and then assemble the intact elements, to be used as evidence later on. The robot, an indigenously produced automaton named "Bambi," was to fire a twelve-gauge round into the central mechanism of the detonator, thus rendering the device inert.

As the sappers crouched for position, guiding Bambi by remote control, the chief bomb-disposal technician flipped a toggle switch to fire the round. Instead of neutralizing the device, however, the pellets detonated it. The explosion bounced the van like a child's toy as a fireball singed the overhanging trees. A cloud of thick, acrid black smoke shot into the crisp autumn air.

The blast was a monstrous one. Windows throughout the neighborhood shattered, storm shutters were ripped off their hinges, and several parked cars were sprayed with smoldering shrapnel. Bomb squad officers surmised that either the device was booby-trapped or it had been predetonated by the timing mechanism. They were sure that if it had exploded in a crowded area, hundreds would have been killed.

By the time dawn arrived at the crime scene, now crowded with investigators, journalists, and curious onlookers, the two men captured first were inside a soundproof room illuminated by a single fluorescent light. They had already been interviewed, had been introduced to the unpleasantness of what incarceration is like for terrorists. Already they had learned that they could either relinquish straight away all information the investigators would demand, or end up enduring hours, weeks, or even months of what was known as "pressure." Most never made it through the deprivations and humiliations of that unnerving pressure; they gave in as their physical and psychological envelopes were breached. After the third terrorist was in custody, and after several days of intense scrutiny, the investigators knew all that the three could tell. It was enough to paint a daunting portrait of what possibly lay ahead.

Israeli Prime Minister Rabin was informed of the averted disaster in a closed-door briefing. Ya'akov Perry, the head of the General Security Service, Israel's counterterrorist and counterespionage intelligence agency—better known by its Hebrew acronym of Shin Bet—told Rabin that the powerful device detonated in Ramat Efal was not a remote-control bomb, the type that had killed so many in other parts of the world: in Bogota, Belfast, Colombo, and the Basque lands. Rather, this was intended to be a suicide attack.[1] According to information extracted from the Shin Bet interrogations, the terrorists were planning to drive their vehicle to the Dizengoff Center shopping mall, park the van in the underground garage, and then, after a prayer and a surge of adrenaline that would stiffen their frames, they'd initiate the blast that would topple the massive mall, kill scores, and bring them martyrdom and paradise.

The attempted bombing was the work of Hamas, Rabin was told. The men captured had not built the device, nor had they planned the operation on their own. They had been dispatched by a twenty-seven-year-old commander in the Izzedine al-Qassam Brigade who, coincidentally, had also built the bomb. The man was married, a devout Muslim, and a longtime Hamas activist who had earned a Bachelor of Science degree from Ramallah's Bir Zeit University in electrical engineering.

A week later, the Israeli Army magazine *Bamachane* published a cover story titled "Living in the Shadow of Terror" in which Brigadier General Shmuel Arad, the head of the operations brigade in the IDF General Staff, warned, "Terrorists in the territories are receiving instruction and training from commanders who were trained abroad." In fact, there was a sense of foreboding in the minds of many intelligence service and police commanders following the Ramat Efal incident. They feared that a bloody winter lay ahead, and that car bombs had replaced stabbings and machine-gun attacks in the Hamas repertoire. They also began to fear the man who had dispatched the bombers, the man who became known in the Shin Bet vernacular as "The Engineer."

Rivkah Toledano was unaware of the trepidation that had overtaken Israel's counterterrorist community, nor had she ever heard of the mysterious individual known as "The Engineer." She did know that she rarely had the opportunity to watch her husband of six years, Nissim, dress for work. Often he was showered, shaved, and ready to go by 5:00 A.M. She made sure his lunch was ready the night before, and Nissim said good-bye to his wife before dusk, kissing her on the forehead after he had done the same to his pride and joy, his two children—Shai, the boy, who was five, and Natalie, who was two and a half. Their home was a comfortable apartment in a modest, single-story stucco block, with a neat garden shaded by a dangling eucalyptus tree in the town of Lod, just a few minutes from busy Ben-Gurion International Airport. The Toledanos lived on a modest Israeli income, the salary of a career policeman serving with the Mishmar Ha'Gvul, the Border Guards. Although service in the "Green Berets," as the Border Guards are known, could have sent him to the Lebanese border, to the international port of Ashdod, or even to the madness of the Intifadah in either Gaza or the West Bank, Nissim Toledano worked only two kilometers from his home, at Border Guard headquarters on Ha'Chashmonaim Street in Lod. He liked it that way. He wasn't in the job for danger and thrills—his family was his life.

To the Palestinians, the Border Guards were known as the Men of Kfar Qassem, a reference to the massacre of thirty-three civilians in the town of that name along the border with Jordan as a curfew was being enforced in the days prior to the 1956 Sinai War. The tag was inaccurate and unfair over the course of time, but privately many Border Guard commanders relished the idea of the Arabs thinking of them as brutal and "different" from the average Israeli soldier. Indeed, the Border Guards, part of the Israeli police, had always been something of an enigma in Israel's security service scheme of things—half army, half police, they were the perennial outsiders even though their skills as policemen, guards, and even troopers were internationally renowned. The average Israeli did not identify with the Guards, since most members were either Jews from the Arabic diaspora who spoke Arabic and understood the Arabic mentality, or Druze, Circassian, or Bedouin. Still, they were citizens of the Jewish state and served with Jews as comrades-in-arms, as professional policemen. Nissim Toledano had grown up with Arabs, Lod being a mixed city. He lived with them as neighbors and friends.

At 5:15 on the morning of December 12, 1993, Master Sergeant Toledano left his house for work. He kissed Rivkah and the kids good-bye, nestled his Beretta pistol into a brown leather hip-holster, and grabbed his green parka. Israeli winters are brief, but the cold and the dampness can chill to the bone. Morning rain greeted the border policeman as he headed out the door to the darkened pavement of Shlomoh Ha'Melech Street and the long walk toward Border Guard HQ on the eastern end of Ha'Chashmonaim Street.

Nissim Toledano never made it to work that morning. He was such a creature of habit that his commanders were immediately alarmed by his absence at the 6:00 A.M. roll call. They knew enough of the man's domestic situation to realize that he wasn't having the cursed problems that tend to afflict cops with too many years on the job—marital pressures, divorce, depression. In fact, Toledano was the envy of many in the Guard. By 8:00 A.M., Toledano's commander phoned Rivkah and, without trying to raise any flags, asked if her husband was ill or at home. "Isn't he at work?" she asked nervously. The commander, a veteran of the terrorist wars in southern Lebanon and the West Bank and Gaza, was alarmed; a sixth sense hit him in the gut like a hammer. He immediately ordered the Lod police precinct to send all available personnel to find the missing border policeman. Foul play had to be blamed—the officer suspected there could be no other explanation.

By the time the patrol cars began combing the streets of the city for Nissim Toledano, he was already across the Green Line, in the Occupied Territories, far removed from the security of Lod. In one well-planned move, three men had ambushed the twenty-nine-year-old police officer by running him down and knocking him to the ground, and, following a brief struggle, forcing him inside a white sedan with stolen yellow Israeli license plates that took him to a safe house somewhere in the West Bank.

Frantic with anguish, Toledano's family commenced a search for Nissim. One of Rivkah's sisters, following her brother-in-law's daily route to work, found a gray and red skullcap laying in a ditch. It belonged to Nissim. It was an ominous sign of the tragedy that would be confirmed hours later. Just after 10:00 A.M., two young men, their faces concealed by checkered kaffiyehs wrapped around their heads, walked into the lobby of the Red Cross building in the West Bank town of Ramallah, a suburb of Jerusalem referred to as the Beverly Hills of the West Bank because of its luxurious villas. The men, nervous though cocky, approached the attractive receptionist, a young student named Suha, and said abruptly, "We are members of the Hamas, from the Izzedine al-Qassam Brigade. We have kidnapped an Israeli officer, and we demand the release of Sheikh Ahmed Yassin in exchange for his life."[2] Before leaving abruptly, the two dropped off an envelope on Suha's desk with their demands and a photocopy of Nissim Toledano's laminated Border Guard ID. Suha, stunned by what had transpired, called her boss, who upon reading the neatly typed page contacted the local Israeli military commander.

The kidnapping of Nissim Toledano sparked a frenzy throughout Israel. At army checkpoints throughout the Occupied Territories, soldiers were placed on high alert. Leaves were canceled and additional units dispatched to roadblocks and villages known to be "problematic." The Israeli intelligence community dropped most of its routine tasks and began an all-inclusive search for the kidnapped cop. Commando cops from the Ya'ma'm, the Israeli National Police counterterrorist and hostage-rescue unit, were summoned to barracks at their base in central Israel and placed on immediate deployment status. Hostage-taking opened the door for a commando operation, and Israel wanted all its assets ready for action.

By noon, Israeli Prime Minister Rabin, somber and determined, had summoned his cabinet for an emergency meeting. The room inside the Knesset was uncharacteristically silent under a fog of cigarette smoke, as ministers read the Hamas communiqué that had now been quickly translated by Shin Bet Arabic-language specialists, photocopied, and highlighted.

> In the name of Allah the merciful and beloved
> Decree No. 2
> Message issued by the "Special Unit" in the martyr company of Izzedine al-Qassam, the military arm of Hamas. On 13/12/92, the sixth anniversary of the founding of the Islamic Resistance Movement carried out the abduction of an officer in the Occupation Army who is being held in an undisclosed location and the operation was carried out according to and as ordered. We are now informing the Occupation Forces: We are holding the officer, and we demand from the Occupation Army and the Occupation Government to free Sheikh Ahmed Yassin in exchange for this officer. The authorities have ten hours, no later than nine this evening. The release will take place under the following conditions:

> 1. Keep to the timetable, otherwise we will immediately kill the officer after the end of the ultimatum.
> 2. The release of Sheikh Yassin will take place under the supervision of the International Red Cross, the Egyptian Ambassador, the French Ambassador, the Swedish Ambassador and the Turkish Ambassador. These ambassadors will guarantee that Israel does not return Sheikh Yassin to prison following his release.
> 3. We warn the Occupation Authorities that we will respond immediately and harshly to any attempt to harm our Sheikh.
> 4. We must free the officer immediately after the release of Sheikh Yassin, in the way that we see fit.

5. Israeli Television will film the process of Sheikh Ahmed Yassin's release and will broadcast, live, him being turned over to the foreign diplomats.

"The Special Unit"
Izzedine al-Qassam Company
Military Arm/Hamas Movement[3]

A deafening silence descended upon the cabinet. Hamas was no longer a splinter group on the religious fringe of the Palestinian revolution, nor were its members amateurs. They had kidnapped before; but these were usually spasms of opportunity masked by mystery—there were no demands and no challenges to the Israeli political leadership. This, coming on the heels of the thwarted Ramat Efal bombing, was clear and present proof that Hamas had raised the ante of violence.

The manhunt was the largest in Israeli history. Thousands of soldiers and policemen raced against time to find any trace of Toledano or his abductors. The Border Guards, eager to save one of their own, worked double shifts. Israeli soldiers, policemen, and counterterrorist agents from Shin Bet frantically searched the villages and towns of the West Bank and Gaza. Informants were tapped, suspects brought in for questioning, and the message put out on the street that something bad would happen to Hamas supporters if Sergeant Toledano was harmed. Although the Israelis had no intention of releasing Sheikh Yassin, the crippled spiritual guide of the movement, they did convince him to make a plea for the sergeant's life on Israeli TV. On the night of December 14, thousands of troops conducted a house-to-house campaign, literally rousting a population of 1.3 million out of their beds in search of the abducted Border Guard sergeant.

At a cave east of Rafat, in hills that were treacherous in the pitch black, one of the many men wanted by the Israeli task force was watching the Israeli search operation with a pair of binoculars and eyes trained by years of the Occupation to notice threats from a distance. Yehiya Ayyash, Israeli ID No. 932116239, had an inkling that there would be an operation that night, and he had left his home just after midnight with his trusted Israeli Army issue assault rifle. Ayyash was a survivor, and survival in the Middle East required luck.

What transpired in Rafat also took place in Gaza, in Ramallah, in Nablus, Hebron, Jerusalem, and a few dozen small villages so small and innocuous that most senior commanders had never heard of them. A combined police/IDF/GSS sweep during the night of December 14-15 was the largest dragnet ever mounted by the Israeli security apparatus. In the West Bank and Gaza, 1,129 Hamas activists were rounded up. But there was no trace of Toledano—and time was running out.[4] Israeli officials had no doubt that Hamas would carry out its threat to murder the kidnapped Border Guard. Guard policemen had turned the courtyard of Toledano's home, at 65 Shlomoh Ha'Melech Street, into an open-air synagogue as they prayed for their comrade, but privately, many feared the worst—they had come across Hamas handiwork in the past and had taken crime scene photographs of the mutilated bodies of its victims.

On the morning of December 16, 1992, Fatma Abu Dahuk, a twenty-five-year-old Bedouin girl from the Abu Dahuk tribe, left her family's tent near Kfar Adumim in the West Bank halfway between Jerusalem and Jericho to search for a camel that had strayed during the night. The desert hills and wadis, peppered with green patches of grass where rainfall had been completely absorbed, were deep and cavernous but easy terrain for an experienced Bedouin. During her search through the majestic beauty of the cavernous valleys, Fatma came across something that appeared misplaced in the tranquil desert setting. In a ravine turned colorful by the growth of winter flowers, Fatma came across the body of a man wearing military khaki and a green parka covering his face. His hands were bound and he was lying in a pool of dried blood.

The tribe's *Muchtar* was summoned to the grizzly scene and he immediately realized who the man was. News of the Toledano kidnapping had been the sole topic of conversation in the village, and it was impossible to escape the impromptu roadblocks, hovering air force choppers, and Border Guard jeeps maneuvering slowly through the village. By the time the Muchtar returned to his village, hundreds of Shin Bet agents, forensic pathologists, soldiers, high-ranking officers, politicians, and newspaper reporters had congregated in the desert. Israel Air Force helicopters flew overhead looking for clues, any signs of the killers. Border Guard and police units, searching in the area, arrived shortly thereafter and apprehensively entered the wadi to make a positive ID.

Nissim Toledano had not just been murdered, he had been butchered. There were signs of strangulation around his neck and mouth, and he had been stabbed repeatedly throughout his entire body. "This is a murder carried out with hatred and a lust for barbarity," uttered one Border Guard policemen on the scene, "cruelty like this is animalistic."[5] Toledano's body was transported to the national pathological forensic lab in Abu Kabir, just south of Tel Aviv. Meanwhile, Border Guard commander Chief Superintendent Meshulam Amit, along with a police rabbi, made the dreaded knock on Rivkah's door. It was an emotional moment for a wife turned widow and two children robbed of their father.

For the police, there was an investigation to conduct and the thankless task of making sure that Jews in Lod and elsewhere did not make private gestures of revenge against Arab civilians. For the IDF, the kidnapping and murder of Toledano meant that the war that they had just begun to fight against Hamas had entered a new and bloody stage. Shin Bet agents tasked with tracking down Toledano's killers knew that they faced a difficult hunt for the men responsible for the abduction, torture, and execution of the Border Guard. Hamas was a secretive, highly compartmentalized organization. There was genuine fear that the terrorists had already fled across the Allenby Bridge into Jordan[6] and then possibly on to Egypt, the Sudan, Iran, or even the United States.

A bold and politically resonant move was needed, and for the Israeli government, the choice was clear: massive deportation. For a Palestinian, no punishment could be worse. It was permanent and therefore particularly painful for those ferried across the frontier under armed escort who would leave family behind. There was no glory in deportation, just distance from everything held sacred. Better to die in battle a *shaheed*, or martyr, then to be handed one's walking papers on a windswept Lebanese mountain road. Among the 1,129 Hamas operatives that the security forces picked up during the sweeps of Gaza and the West Bank, GSS agents assembled a list of the most dangerous, the most senior, the most capable ringleaders. In all, 415 names were recommended for possible deportation.

On December 17, 1992, a rainy winter's morning, the suspected terrorists were loaded onto a convoy of buses for the two-hour drive into Lebanon. The buses left the detention facilities in a slow and deliberate motorcade. The mood onboard the buses was somber and bleak as the men sat cuffed to bars and one another. The military policemen overtly escorting the convoy—and the counterterrorist commandos riding a covert shotgun—were perplexed. Their charges looked meek and benign. They were, according to one man involved in the operation, "so innocent looking, so unmenacing, that thinking that such men could torture and kill sent a shiver up my spine."

Israel had always attempted to keep its war against the Palestinians from turning into a religious struggle of Judaism versus Islam. The conflict over the strip of land between Lebanon and

Egypt sandwiched by the Jordan River and the Mediterranean Sea was more complex than two religious elements battling each other for righteous supremacy. In fact, in the course of Israel's many wars and battles, the Druze, Circassians, and Bedouins— all Muslims—had fought and died defending the Jewish state. At the same time, many Palestinians were Christians, and their goal of bringing about the creation of an independent Palestinian state had nothing to do with the preachings of the Prophet; in fact, Dr. George Habash, the founder of the Marxist Popular Front for the Liberation of Palestine (PFLP), was a Greek-Orthodox from Bethlehem. Some of the most notorious individuals that the Israeli military and police had ever come up against were Christian Palestinians. Their struggle, and the war waged by virtually all the Palestinian guerrilla factions who were nurtured by regimes in Cairo and Damascus, were socialist in nature, pro-Soviet in indoctrination, and void of any true Islamic identity and influence.

Hamas, the acronym for *Harakt al-Muqaqama al-Islamiya* (Islamic Resistance Movement), meaning "zeal", was not a terrorist phenomenon born out of the ideology of a few Marxist followers wishing to set up camp in the hills, quote Engels and Mao, and wear khaki fatigues their entire lives. It wasn't fueled by the political desire to overthrow a wealthy ruling class. The movement had nothing to do with the Cold War, the Soviet Union, or the Warsaw Pact's generous assistance to fledgling revolutionaries waging their little wars throughout the world. Hamas had virtually nothing to do with the Arab-Israeli conflict either, as the organization and its violent branches could have—and might still—declare war against a secular Arab regime with the same ferocity and effectiveness as it strikes the Jewish state of Israel. Hamas is exactly what its name says—an Islamic resistance to the evils of the Jewish state in Palestine and, in a campaign waged with unbridled brutality, against fellow Palestinians who would subvert Islam. A ballistic and benevolent empowerment of Islam's sole claim to the Palestinian soul and the Palestinian political landscape, Hamas is a rejection of the Jewish state and the PLO (and later Palestinian Authority), it is a scourge and a social entity that looks out for its own.

Although it has become a terrorist group worthy of the infamous reputation inspired by Black September and the Abu Nidal Faction, few of Hamas's senior operatives began their careers in the classrooms of Patrice Lumumba University in Moscow or in the Stacie's training centers in East Berlin. Nor were they sent by a patron superpower to the sugar fields of Cuba or to the gritty fields north of Pyongyang. Hamas operatives learned their tradecraft from one of the most violent, secretive, and effective terrorist undergrounds ever to operate in the Middle East: Egypt's Muslim Brotherhood.

The Muslim Brotherhood Society was founded March 1928 in Ismailia, Egypt, by Hasan al-Banna, a firebrand cleric who would quickly build one of the largest political parties in Egypt by proposing a society based solely on the *shari'a*, or Islamic law. The Egyptian branch of the Brotherhood Society was in essence a movement of national liberation, in that it worked to free Egypt from Western control and non-Islamic influences. British forces in Egypt soon found themselves the target of random and violent hit-and-run attacks. The society reached Mandate Palestine in 1935 when Hasan al-Banna's brother, Abdel Rahman, visited Jerusalem and the city's ultranationalistic and vehemently anti-Jewish mufti and head of the Islamic Council, the controversial Haj Amin al-Husseini.* When the notorious riots broke out in Palestine in 1936—the harbinger of worse to come, instigated in many ways by the mufti—small bands of armed Brotherhood

*For his support of the Nazis during the Second World War (Husseini was a guest of Hitler in Berlin for much of the war), especially his role in recruiting Bosnian Muslim volunteers for the foreign division of the Waffen SS, Husseini was indicted as a war criminal.

supporters entered Palestine and participated in attacks against Jewish settlements and installations throughout the Mandate. Following the Second World War, Brotherhood operatives from Egypt returned to Palestine to help spread the *da'wa* (the call to Islam) among the various factions preparing for the inevitable struggle against the Jews of Palestine and the remnants of Europe's Jewry, seeking to establish a Jewish homeland. By March 1948, four months after the U.N. decision to partition Palestine and well into the bloodletting that shocked the departing British garrison, a proud and empowered Hasan al-Banna claimed to have 1,500 Brotherhood volunteers in Palestine.

The Egyptian military, originally wary of the threat the Brotherhood posed to the regime of King Farouk, had authorized the training of volunteers to wage a Jihad in Palestine. Camps were established along the border near Gaza, and contacts made with local fundamentalists—better to have the seditious forces out of the country where they could get killed in action than inside the slums of Cairo and Alexandria plotting revolution. Following the war, Egypt annexed the Gaza Strip and took under its control the approximately one million Palestinians living there, subjecting the local populace to a repressive occupation. Gaza then was the definition of misery: crowded, poor, unsanitary and underdeveloped to the point of malicious neglect. There was no industry, no hope for work, and therefore often no hope at all. The power and promise of Islam became the sole hope to many, and the only true means by which the refugee population could vent their rage.

In the towns and villages of the West Bank, however, Islam did not catch on with such intensity. Palestinian residents were offered Jordanian citizenship, Jordanian rights, and Jordanian opportunities. As a result, the Muslim Brotherhood became more of a political entity than a subversive force; the principal issue that united the Brotherhood in Jordan was not the organization's desire to drive Israel into the sea but rather the divisive presence of British officers in the Jordanian Army and the demand for their ouster. The Muslim Brotherhood, in fact, has always viewed the struggle, their struggle, not as Arab versus Jew but rather as East against West.

In Egypt, the Brotherhood's fortunes improved briefly following the Free Officers Revolution of July 23, 1952, which brought Colonel Gamel Abdel Nasser to power. But their support quickly deteriorated when Brotherhood operatives from the "Secret Organ" attempted to assassinate Nasser on October 26, 1954. The plot was an impudent failure. In less than two weeks, the organization was crippled to the brink of dissolution. Members were arrested and tortured, confidential lists of leaders obtained through coercive means, and six leaders hung in public displays; in all, it is believed, five thousand supporters were placed in hastily set up concentration camps throughout Egypt. The Brotherhood was banned in Egypt and in the Gaza Strip, and the movement headed underground, becoming the voice of spiritual opposition and a source of considerable violence.

Even before the ban, the Brotherhood was extremely popular among the Palestinian refugees in Gaza and was most active in the United Nations Relief and Works Agency (UNRWA) schools and facilities throughout the Strip's refugee camps, as well as among the Palestinian students fortunate enough to have been permitted to study in Egyptian universities. In Cairo, for example, the League of Palestinian Students, a precursor to the revolutionary groups that would one day rock the Middle East with violence and subversion, was led by sympathizers to the Brotherhood, including one of the most vocal fundamentalists in the group, a young engineering student named Yasir Arafat.

Much of the Brotherhood's financing came from the Saudi royal family and rich sheikhs still angry about Nasser's socialist revolution of the Egyptian monarchy, but the group's politician strength was limited, and meetings were held in great secrecy. Nasser's Muchabarat (secret service) agents were ruthless, and they routinely infiltrated the mosques and Islamic universities of Cairo and the surrounding Nile Delta. Mere mention of the Brotherhood was dangerous talk, and clerics and believers were regularly rounded up and imprisoned. The situation was worse in Gaza. When the Muchabarat went after the Brotherhood in Cairo, they did so with a vengeance against the Palestinians in the Strip. In 1965, following a bungled attempt by the Brotherhood to seize control of the Egyptian government, the Egyptian military arrested hundreds in Gaza, including a young crippled cleric named Ahmed Yassin who had permanently injured his spine while frolicking on the beach with friends and who now dedicated his life to the study of Islam.

Muslim fundamentalists viewed the Arab defeat in the 1967 Six Day War as the divine realization of what they had been preaching for years: revenge by Allah, particularly against the Egyptian regime, for the imprisonment and persecution of the Brotherhood's leadership. The defeat was so profound, so striking, and so humiliating for many Arabs—from Damascus to Gaza and Amman to Alexandria—that many turned to Allah for forgiveness and direction. In fact, when the Egyptians and Syrians launched their counterbalance to the 1967 defeat, the 1973 Yom Kippur War, their top-secret plan to cross the Suez Canal was given the code name Operation Badr, a reference to the battle of Badr in the Islamic year 632 when an army of Muslim warriors, led by the prophet Muhammad, fought against idolaters and achieved a rousing victory. The Brotherhood would later claim that Egypt's performance in the conflict had been significantly improved because Allah had forgiven the Egyptian military when commandos had shouted "Allahu Akbar!" as they crossed the canal.

For the Palestinians, again following behind the Egyptian branch of the Brotherhood, the watershed mark for the explosion of fundamentalism inside the Occupied Territories was the Islamic revolution in Iran and the Camp David Peace Accords between Egypt and Israel. The Shiite resurgence in Iran was a precedent to be admired and possibly copied. The Khomeini revolution indicated to Islamic movements throughout the world, from Indonesia to Rabat, that they too could prevail over tyranny and repression, and that a true Islamic state could be established anywhere in the world. The appeal of fundamentalist Muslim preachings was particularly strong at the onset of the peace negotiations and subsequent treaty signed between Egypt and Israel. The Camp David Accords proved to many that secular Arab regimes, in Cairo, Amman, Damascus, and even the PLO Beirut, were simply out to bankrupt their principals and the faith of their people and cut the best deal they could arrange with the infidel Jewish state. Egypt, the beacon of Arab military might and political thought, had capitulated. No other political system could be trusted to deal with the Israeli problem, it was argued in the mosques and religious centers of Gaza, Heron, and Nablus. Only Islam held the key. Only Islam could liberate Palestine.

It was during this resurgence that had been sparked in of all places Iran that the number of mosques in the West Bank nearly doubled and the number in Gaza more than tripled. In 1978, the Islamic University, considered by many to be a headquarters of operations for the Brotherhood, was opened in Gaza. At the same time, immigration laws in Europe and the United States were relaxed; an increasing percentage of those allowed entry to America were Muslims from the Asian subcontinent and the Arab world. Many were Palestinian. Some of these newcomers had opted to leave their homes to escape religious persecution. They established a series of mosques and cultural institutions throughout the United States—many in large urban areas such as New York City, Chicago, and Los Angeles. A good number of these immigrants would establish successful businesses and excel in various professional and academic careers.

Back home, following the Six Day War the Brotherhood had set up several charitable associations that provided religious education and daycare—nurseries and kindergartens were attached to neighborhood mosques throughout the Gaza Strip. Libraries and social clubs were established for youths; sports clubs, hobby centers, and free health clinics opened overnight. The Brotherhood was becoming known as purely benevolent, while the various PLO factions were seen as corrupt.

The Brotherhood had another advantage over the PLO in wining the hearts and minds of the residents of the Strip and the West Bank. Because the PLO was at war with the Israeli authorities, the ranks suffered greatly in battles against Israeli forces and from the counterintelligence efforts of the Shin Bet. The Brotherhood suffered no such repression. Their members had displayed no hostile moves against Israeli institutions or security personnel and had not engaged in politics. When Brotherhood clerics preached from the mosque, they did so without fear of Shin Bet surveillance. Even after the Muslim Brotherhood had staged the assassination of Egyptian president Sadat on October 6, 1981, the Israeli authorities refused to look at the group as a political entity—instead opting to view them as purely religious.

As a result of being allowed to operate freely, the Brotherhood expanded its presence throughout the Territories. Islamic societies were created in virtually every large town and city. The organization used the charity fund known as the Zakat to provide assistance to thousands of poor families. Medical clinics were opened offering free medical and dental care to thousands of families who for years had been denied treatment. Parents were allowed to enroll their children in Islamic schools for minuscule fees or for nothing at all, and student loans were provided for college tuition. Small-business loans were made to craftsmen and merchants eager to expand their businesses. The Waqf, Arabic for religious endowment, controlled a sizable chunk of the real estate (both residential and commercial) in the Gaza Strip and the West Bank, and these holdings were used to wield influence. It was also the largest single employer in the Occupied Territories.

In 1978, Sheikh Ahmed Yassin founded a small and tightly structured group called Hamas. Officially registered with the Israeli authorities under the name al-Mujama (The Assemblage), Hamas advertised itself as the Palestinian branch of the Muslim Brotherhood. Yassin was a charismatic leader whose handicap only reinforced his mystique as a courageous warrior of Islam, though publicly he preached solely on educational and social issues. As a result, he became a popular figure among the poor and needy of the Strip for his benevolent organization's pledge to help, and also among the Shin Bet and the Israeli authorities for his apolitical stance. The Israeli authorities, in fact, welcomed a counterweight to the growing Pan-Arabist Marxism being preached by the PLO and the various "Popular Liberation Fronts" and "General Commands" that at the time dominated terrorist activity and recruitment in the Occupied Territories. They allowed Yassin to open more schools, clinics, and social institutions throughout Gaza. In turn, membership in Hamas grew with each passing week of rousing sermons promising religious salvation from the poverty and pervasive misery of life under the Israeli gun. Secretly, hard-core followers of Yassin established small groups, or cells, that gathered intelligence and sought out weapons.

The creation of Hamas coincided with yet another Islamic quest to liberate Palestine in the name of Allah. The onset of the Jihad in the Occupied Territories was a uniquely profound phenomenon, one both the Israelis and the PLO failed to appreciate. It was a militant Sunni movement, laced with Sunni tradition and

yet inspired and propelled by the actions of Ayatollah Khomeini's meteoric rise to power in Iran. The Islamic Jihad was a
stepchild of the Brotherhood.

It is believed that in late 1979, the first cell of the Jihad in the
Territories became operational in the Gaza Strip. It was led by
Fathi Shiqaqi, a physician from Rafat who had learned the art
of terrorist compartmentalization and covert tradecraft during
his days in Egypt's Zaqaziq University (a hotbed of Brotherhood
activity).[7] Following the example set by the Egyptian Brotherhood, the Islamic Jihad would operate in small, secretive cells,
usually consisting of five to ten (at the very most) operatives
that are known in the local vernacular as families. Cell members
might know others in their own inner circle but would be unknown and not know other operatives working in other cells
throughout the Occupied Territories.

Both Hamas and the Islamic Jihad came about before revolutionary Islam would erupt throughout the Middle East. The
Camp David Peace Accords had been a painful, nearly mortal
blow to the Arab world opposed to any accord with the Jewish
state. Yet the Islamic revolution in Iran had sparked hope that
the West—and Israel—could be defeated.

In December 1979, the Soviets invaded Afghanistan in a
lightning-strike assault. The Soviet army that crossed the snow-
covered border was one of the most powerful military forces in
the world, but rebel Afghan forces, spurned by hatred toward
the atheism of Communism, gave as good as they got. In fact,
the Soviets were soon stopped in their tracks by *Mujahadeen*, the
fighters for Jihad, who not only put up a determined resistance
against the invading forces but began to counterattack with silence, stealth, and tenacity. This ragtag army of peasants (and
vengeful victims) fought with century-old carbines and
Peshawar-produced Kalashnikovs in a life-and-death struggle
against the high-tech Soviet war machine. The Central Intelli-

gence Agency found great use in the robe-wearing rebels who humbled even the mightiest of military powers.

In Saudi Arabia, Islamic insurgents making the *Hajj* (pilgrimage) seized the Grand Mosque in Mecca with more than fifty thousand worshippers inside for the true followers of Islam. It took the Saudi Army two weeks to dislodge them; victory came only after French counterterrorist special forces were invited by the Saudis to commit sacrilege and trespass inside the Grand Mosque of Mecca to systematically terminate the rebels. One year later, an offshoot of the Egyptian Muslim Brotherhood, the Takfir wa-Hijrah, assassinated Egyptian president Anwar as-Sadat as he stood on a reviewing stand in Cairo commemorating the eighth anniversary of the October 6, 1973, crossing of the Suez Canal. Many of those involved in the plot to assassinate Sadat, including blind cleric Sheikh Omar Abdel Rahman, had worked closely with Sheikh Yassin years earlier. The time seemed to have come to bring the successes of Iran, Afghanistan, and Egypt to the streets of Gaza.

For the Shin Bet, whose intelligence apparatus in Gaza rivaled the British intelligence operation in Northern Ireland in scope and scale, support of Sheikh Yassin and his movement was a necessary evil of classic tradecraft. "The enemy of my enemy is my friend" has long been a code of conducting business in the Middle East, and the ethics of alliances based on temperamental dislikes and vendettas was the accepted practice in Gaza. All of Yassin's organizations, foundations, and Islamic undertakings were supported by the Israeli military authority—from the sports clubs to university seminars, which meant that the Shin Bet provided a leg up to all of the activities. And why not? In 1981, Sheikh Ahmed Yassin was a popular interviewee on the Arabic-language broadcasts of Israel Radio. He never attacked the Israeli occupation but rather hurled abusive accusations at PLO chairman Yasir Arafat.[8] Some security operatives privately viewed the potential for conflict between the PLO and the Islamic fundamentalist as pennies from heaven.

Shin Bet commanders and A'man officers assigned to Gaza realized that playing the Islamic card was a gamble—one former officer serving in Gaza at the time referred to it as playing Russian roulette with an automatic weapon. Many feared that the genie would come flying out of the bottle in a violent spasm. Indeed, Yassin's followers vented their rage one spring day in 1982, when a mob of men from the Shati Mosque attacked non-Islamic sites, such as places that sold beer and arac, and beat known narcotics users and prostitutes.

The promise of the Islamic Jihad struck a popular chord among those flocking to hear Sheikh Yassin's sermons. Islamic liberation seemed a viable alternative to the stagnated revolutionary status quo of Arafat and his cohorts. Yassin ordered his most trusted associates to begin stockpiling weapons and ammunition in well-hidden arms caches throughout the Gaza Strip. Weapons were easy to come by in Gaza, from Egyptian machine guns abandoned in caves to brand new IDF-issue Galil assault rifles purchased from Israeli organized crime contacts. So too were explosives.

Many of the new recruits to al-Mujama had served in Jordan and Lebanon with Arafat's Fatah; some had attended guerrilla and special-operations training courses in Egypt or Syria, or in the Soviet Union, Poland, Czechoslovakia, Hungary, or Romania (some had even been trained by the North Koreans and Cubans). These graying veterans of the struggle, now working for a new paymaster, were revered for their experience, and Yassin called upon them to draw up operational blueprints that singled out Israeli targets for attack.

Al-Mujama volunteers adopted the principles of Jihad: martyrdom (*shahada*) and self-sacrifice (*istishhad*).[9] Dying in the name of Allah was a blessing, a privilege, and all those who joined al-Mujama and the Jihad were prepared mentally, physically, and spiritually to surrender their lives in the struggle against the Zionist enemy. They also identified the crux of their struggle—of Palestinian versus Jew—as an Islamic and not as a national (*wataniyaa*) problem.

By early 1982, Shin Bet surveillance of Yassin's modest home in Gaza's Sabra neighborhood was no longer restricted to intelligence reports and possible protection against vengeful Palestinian terrorist cells acting on the order of Arafat, Habash, Jibril, Hawatmeh, or any one of the other half-dozen PLO and PLO rejectionist front warlords who might have wanted Yassin removed. The "enemy of my enemy" was becoming dangerous.

In the wake of the Israeli invasion of Lebanon, Hamas founded a military section that was independent though allied with the Moslem Brotherhood. The Mujahadeen A-Falestin was formed to execute strikes against Israeli military and civilian targets inside the Territories. In 1983 the Shin Bet, operating on an anonymous tip, raided Sheikh Yassin's home and uncovered a telltale cache of AK-47 assault rifles and Egyptian-produced "Port Said" 9 mm submachine guns, along with explosives, grenades, and, ominously, intelligence-gathering material.

The authorities could not ignore this obvious affiliation as a hostile terrorist organization. Yassin was arrested, tried, convicted, and sentenced to twelve years behind bars. He continued preaching from prison and running al-Mujama, but the Jihad would have to wait. Israeli commanders in Gaza had feared the outbreak of rioting and possibly full-scale civil war over the conviction of Yassin, but there was an unexplained quiet that veteran intelligence operatives in the Strip found unnerving. It was an eerie calm of acquiescence—the separation that follows a battle, during which the defeated party gets up, dusts himself off, and winks at the victor, suggesting that he will be stronger and crueler the next time around.

In the early evening hours of May 19, 1985, Yassin was informed by senior officers of the Israeli prison service that he was to be released the next day in an astounding exchange engineered by master terrorist Ahmed Jibril, warlord of the Popular Front for the Liberation of Palestine General Command (PFLP-GC). Jibril recognized the power of Islam and the potential it had to explode deep in the Israeli psyche. The former Syrian Army captain may have commanded only a small gang of gunmen, but he was the true chess master of the Palestinian revolution. He was able to accept losses and setbacks, never tipping his hand that he was biding his time while ingeniously backing his opponents into a corner. A technocrat, Jibril was considered something of a renaissance man in guerrilla circles. He had designed and perfected barometer bombs that were triggered by an atmospheric timer and could bring down passenger jets. He specialized in military assaults on civilian targets— school buses were his favorite.

Jibril was holding three Israeli soldiers kidnapped in Lebanon in 1982. A master of the Byzantine human bazaar—of seizing and then bartering off hostages—he was willing to relinquish his charges if the Israelis would surrender 1,150 terrorists wasting away in high-security installations throughout the country. Among those Jibril demanded be released was convicted killer Kozo Okamoto, the infamous surviving gunman from the June 30, 1972, Lod Airport Massacre, and Sheikh Ahmed Yassin. Jibril knew that Yassin was no ordinary gunrunner and far from the image of the average cleric clutching a copy of the Koran in his Gaza mosque.

If Yassin had learned anything in prison, it was that Israel was an enemy that could be defeated. Observing the who's who of Palestinian terrorists behind Israeli bars and barbed wire, the wily cleric discovered the shortcomings of the armed struggle. Many of the Palestinian inmates in Israeli prisons were corrupt, incorrigible, even psychopathic. Wanting to kill Israelis was a good excuse for joining the ranks of Fatah, the PFLP, the Democratic Front, or one of the other dozen or so groups represented by P.O.-box mail drops in Damascus, Baghdad, and Tripoli. These thugs would murder for profit or mere pleasure. Hopelessness had overtaken much of the Gaza Strip and the West Bank because the Palestinian leadership in exile, busy assembling private armies and untold fortunes, lacked the fundamental—and moral—necessities to bring the Palestinian people out of Occupation. Yassin realized that Islam was Palestine's way out.

Upon his release from Israeli custody, Yassin promised to refrain from politics and hostile terrorist activity. Yet he was determined to transform his organization into a more militant, polarized, and lethal entity. The al-Mujama became Hamas. To move the brains and financial nerve center of the organization far away from the Shin Bet, Yassin ordered emissaries to set up an operations center in Amman, where the Moslem Brotherhood had made considerable political gains. Branch offices were opened throughout the world, to raise funds and support from the sizable Palestinian and Islamic communities that were well established in Europe and North America; the European headquarters became London, and the U.S. headquarters was Arlington, Virginia.[10] The organization received donations from Saudi Arabia and even Shiite Iran in those first few years of Hamas, funds totaling as much as thirty million dollars. Once again, communications networks were established and weapons and explosives cached.

Still not considered a true terrorist group, Hamas organizers were free to move about much of Israel and the Territories unhindered. Members were virtually invisible to Shin Bet cameras and surveillance devices. All that would change in November 1987.

Just before midnight on November 25, Ahmed Jibril launched one of the most spectacular, successful, and historically significant terrorist attacks in the history of the Arab-Israeli conflict. A lone terrorist, pumped-up on amphetamines and armed with explosives and automatic weapons, silently flew across the frontier with Lebanon on a motorized hang glider and landed at a crossroads separating the northern town of Qiryat Shmonah and a small infantry unit's base. In a significant break from his orders and tradition, the terrorist opted to attack the soldiers instead of the sleepy town. In a mad charge with guns ablaze, the terrorist stormed the hilltop base, aided by the element of surprise and the sudden fear of the gate guard, who ran away from his post. Before the terrorist was cut down by Israeli fire, he managed to kill six soldiers and wound nearly a dozen. It was one of the most humiliating episodes in the history of Israel's defense forces, and it had repercussions that are felt throughout the Middle East to this day.

On the streets of Gaza, Tulkaram, Jenin, Hebron, and Nablus, the Night of the Hang Glider, as the attack became known, forever changed the image of the Israeli soldier in the eyes of the Palestinians. Revered as virtually superhuman, the Israeli soldier had been considered an icon: super fighter, super patriot, a uniform and weapon not to be crossed. The Night of the Hang Glider showed that he was not only human but as vulnerable to failure as the Arab armies had been for so long. The respect that had been shown the Israeli Army now seemed undeserved and unwarranted. In effect, it too was killed in that flurry of gunfire in northern Israel. The Israeli defense forces had been proven vulnerable, human, and now became the target of the rage felt by Palestinians frustrated over the failure of the leadership in Tunis and still dumbfounded by the defeat in Lebanon that had ousted Arafat and his court-in-exile to North Africa. This frustration warranted a change. It called on Islam for answers, and Islam, in the minds of Sheikh Yassin and his lieutenants, warranted Jihad. The Intifadah, the war for Palestinian self-determination and the bloody soul-search for the Palestinian political and religious identity, had begun.

Almost immediately after the Night of the Hang Glider, violence broke out in Gaza. It began when rumors of a truck accident—an Israeli driver supposedly running down Palestinian women and children—spread through the refugee camps and Gaza City center. Much of the baiting and rumor-mongering was the work of Hamas supporters. Youths threw rocks at Israeli patrols and soldiers. Unaccustomed to containing massive unrest, the Israelis fired live ammunition into the mobs to disperse the crowds. The resulting loss of life led to an escalation of the crisis. Outlawed Palestinian flags were displayed boldly in the streets. Teenagers set fire to tires to block off vital crossroads, and old women and children, many wearing kaffiyeh masks, threw stones, Molotov cocktails, and just about anything that would fit in the palm of their hands at long rows of young Israeli soldiers whose veil of invulnerability had disappeared overnight. This David-and-Goliath scenario was played out in front of millions around the world every night on the evening news. The upstart Palestinians were gaining public sympathy and support for their popular struggle against the IDF.

Hamas activists, in their characteristic black ninja outfits and masks, initiated much of the violence in the Gaza Strip and the West Bank. The Night of the Hang-Glider had presented Hamas with an explosive invitation to the fray, and Sheikh Yassin was not about to allow the opportunity to pass quietly. Yassin was determined from the inception of Hamas as an *armed* movement in 1987 to make it a completely different creature than the then most powerful political and military force in the Occupied Territories, Yasir Arafat's Fatah. Many of those initially attracted to the fundamentalist promise of Hamas had become disillusioned with Fatah and the overall political portrait of the PLO leadership in exile. The PLO had been beaten more times than could be counted; the leaders were corrupt, lazy, and living in exile; they provided only the most basic limited and frugal services to their constituents and seemed more interested in lavish spending in the plush hotels of Tunis than in the dustbowl hell of a Gaza camp.

Seizing on this unrest, Hamas leaders entered a new phase of organizational and philosophical self-construction. In Gaza, for example, quarters, neighborhoods, and streets where Muslim influence was already strong were soon transformed into Islamic enclaves and fortresses—there were some areas in the Strip where even heavily armed Fatah gangs feared to enter. Palestinians considered Hamas to be safe—after all, the organization was new and relatively clean from the compromising hand of the Israeli intelligence services.

The success of Hamas to develop into a powerful political and military force depended on its ability to be covert. In prison, Yassin had seen first-hand how some of the most hardened Palestinian inmates, veterans of Lebanon and KGB-training camps, would trade information for perks and privileges. Yassin knew that operatives in prison were susceptible to coercion and to being turned, and the exchange of information—whether it was in order to get back at someone in another faction or to buy a weekend visit to a family member—became the currency of day-to-day dealings. Yassin saw the aftereffects of this intelligence bartering on the streets of Gaza—how Fatah commanders were picked up off the streets, how DFLP safe houses were raided by the Shin Bet, and how PFLP-GC arms caches were uncovered and destroyed. These organizations, financed by Arab governments and Eastern-bloc intelligence services, were compromised and rendered ineffective by bloated egos and poor security. Hamas, however, developed into a highly compartmentalized entity drawing a clear and sometimes publicly irrefutable distinction between its political, charitable, and social operations and the covert missions in the field against the Israeli occupation. Loosely structured, Hamas operational units were made up of no more than four or five volunteers organized into cells. If the Israeli Army, or the Shin Bet, managed to arrest one cell member, the greatest amount of damage that could result from an interrogation was the arrest of the remaining three cell members. Cell members did not know anyone in the organization outside of their own well-contained community. All operatives were extremely dedicated, highly motivated, and screened for any potential Israeli connections.

The liberation factions, although supposedly covert and illegal, suffered from a strong central system and a highly structured rank system. On the contrary, the Hamas structure in the Gaza Strip and West Bank was, by revolution standards, irregular. It was based on parallel and identical frameworks operating in regional commands. The Dawa, or infrastructure, engaged in recruitment, the distribution of funds, and political and military appointments. An entity known as A-'Alam routed information throughout the Territories, from coded messages to leaflets, propaganda messages, and press support. Military operations in the organization fell to the Al-Majahadoun Al-Falestinoun, the underground army that Yassin began to build in the late 1980s. The Jehaz Aman, or security section, gathered intelligence on suspected collaborators with Israel as well as interviewed and conducted backgrounds checks on Hamas operators who volunteered for the organization. The kneecapping and throat-slicing work in the movement was the responsibility of the security section's Majd, the acronym for Majmouath Jihad u-Dawa (Holy War and Sermonizing). Most Majd unit members were young, poor, and devout. They had been recruited in the mosques and Koran learning centers, and they were selected for missions based on their complete lack of fear. Violence was a message of the resistance, and the more brutal, the more effective.

At first, Majd cells concentrated their efforts on fellow Palestinians—suspected collaborators, known informants, drug pushers, newsstand owners who sold pornography, pimps and prostitutes. Although these low-level criminals were targeted because they supported anti-Islamic values, Israeli military and police officials were concerned because the criminal underworld of Gaza and the West Bank were often their best sources of intelligence. Men and women who peddled in flesh and fantasy were also experts in the Byzantine art of peddling information, and when many began turning up dead, often hacked to death in the most brutal of manners, Shin Bet officials took notice. They feared that the Islamic movement was turning violent, and that it would shortly turn against the Israelis.

Yassin was able to build a strong network courtesy of cash—a lot of it. Initially, most of the Hamas financial assets came from donations made by wealthy businessmen in Saudi Arabia and the Gulf states. According to conservative Israeli intelligence estimates, Hamas networks in the West Bank alone operated on a stipend exceeding one million dollars a year. The funds were filtered through foundations and charities—laundered, in the classic sense of the word—until they made it to the cells and operatives in the field. "It was a money-laundering operation that the Mafia in Sicily and the Yakuza in Japan would be proud of," claimed an Israeli police investigator commenting on the elaborate and completely legal means by which funds from abroad were financing what Israeli officials knew was a hostile terrorist operation.

Yet charity was an essential pillar of the movement's ideology. Yassin placed great importance in the distribution of zekath—not only was charity one of the five basic principles of Islam, it was also a public relations dynamo that endeared the movement to many in Gaza and the Territories and also brought accolades from sympathetic bodies overseas. In fact, charity served as an ideal cover for Hamas when working closely with the movement's leadership abroad—in Amman, in Damascus, in Europe, and later in Iran. By investing much of the money into mosques, schools, unions, clinics, and other socially worthy endeavors,

Hamas was able to conduct legitimate social services while shielding its acquisitions of guns, explosives, safe houses, and forged documents. Still, Hamas wasn't assembling a war chest simply to act as an Islamic Salvation Army. It was gearing up for the onset of a full-scale guerrilla conflict.

The first Hamas military operations were directed against Israeli forces in the Gaza Strip. The attacks were indiscriminate, small in scale, yet virtually always directed against military and security personnel. Hamas field commanders realized that by hijacking a bus, or tossing a grenade into a crowded cinema, the movement ran the risk of becoming yet another one of the many cookie-cutter liberation movements that had achieved nothing in a twenty-year campaign against the Occupation. For Hamas to make a difference, it needed to strike boldly and go for the jugular.

On February 15, 1989, a young Israeli soldier, Avi Sasportas, was doing what many Israelis soldiers do when trying to get from point A to point B—he was hitchhiking. Motorists regularly ferried soldiers to and from wherever they wanted to and needed to go, and hitchhiking was quick, cheap, and convenient. Israeli field security officers had warned soldiers thumbing rides to be extra careful—regulations prohibited soldiers from entering into cars bearing blue Palestinian plates, and soldiers were also prohibited from hitchhiking in cars bearing diplomatic, United Nations, or Multi-National Force Observer vehicles. It was because of these regulations that Corporal Sasportas, waiting for a ride at Hodiyah Junction on his way home to Ashdod, felt no qualms about entering into a white Subaru bearing yellow Israeli plates and occupied by three Orthodox men wearing skullcaps. It was a tragic play of fate. The three men were Hamas gunmen—masquerading as Orthodox Jews. Once inside the car, Sasportas was beaten and shot point-blank in the head with a

.22-caliber pistol.[11] His mutilated body was dumped at the side of a road in a shallow grave.

Three months later, on May 7, Corporal Ilan Sa'adon was looking for a ride at the Mesima Junction near Kiryat Malachi to his home in Ashqelon. Investigators later assessed that Sa'adon was approached by a white car bearing Israeli plates, and that the driver and passengers were dressed as Orthodox Jews. Sa'adon, like Sasportas, disappeared from the face of the earth after his abduction.

The abduction and murder of soldiers was something new in the Arab-Israeli equation; usually the only real threat soldiers felt when hitchhiking was on the part of female soldiers who were preyed upon by Israeli sexual predators. These kidnappings and murders were the turning point in Israel's war against Hamas—a point of no return.

The disappearance of the two Israeli soldiers sparked the largest manhunt in the history of Israeli law enforcement. Thousands of volunteers, ranging from soldiers to Shin Bet investigators working in their spare time, combed every inch of land between the point of kidnapping and the soldiers' homes. The parents of the two soldiers manned passionate, though tragic, vigils, hoping that their sons would return home—alive. Days after Sa'adon's disappearance, investigators from the Shin Bet and the Israeli police's major crimes unit uncovered the badly decomposed corpse of Sasportas.

Israeli security officials realized that they had to act decisively and forcefully. Sheikh Yassin and some 250 Hamas activists both known and suspected were rounded up in an early morning Shin Bet and IDF operation. There was vigorous debate concerning the bhandling of Yassin—the Israelis did not want him to die in custody and become a martyr, thereby inviting violence that could last for generations. Yet they also realized that the handicapped cleric presented a visible challenge to Israeli authority and security.

In November 1989, Yassin and his alleged supporters were indicted by a Gaza military court. Charged with some fifteen counts, ranging from membership in an illegal terrorist organization to financing acts of terror, Yassin was convicted and sentenced to fifteen years behind bars. His imprisonment marked the first salvo in the war that Hamas and the state of Israel waged over the next ten years. In a nation marked by wars and bloodshed, it would become one of the bloodiest wars in Israel's history.

On December 12, 1990, the IDF, the National Police, and the Shin Bet declared full-scale war against Hamas. In a joint sweep of the Occupied Territories, seven hundred Hamas supporters, representatives, and field agents were apprehended. It was the largest Israeli operation against Hamas up to that point. The Israeli authorities realized they could never defeat the soul of the organization, so they went after the brains—the most senior Hamas commanders.[12] The arrests capped what the Israelis believed was a successful campaign against the holy warriors who had stolen center stage from Fatah in the Intifadah. From December 1987 to the seven hundred arrests, fifty-eight Hamas cells had been destroyed throughout the Occupied Territories (twenty-five in 1990 alone). Some Israeli security officials, confident about the number of arrests, believed that with Yassin behind bars and so many of his bosses in detention, they had broken the back of Hamas. They were wrong. Hamas had taken great pains to establish an international headquarters and operational infrastructure outside of Israel in order to secure its leadership and the very composition of the organization out of the reach of the Israeli military and counterintelligence forces.

Hamas was a hydra: with one head removed, it grew ten more, and the new minds taking over were just as cunning if not more so than those languishing behind barbed wire at Ansar

2, the city-sized detention center near Gaza. Yassin's conviction and the arrest of so many of his aides did little to slow down the fledgling terrorist group.

Israeli generals, spymasters, and analysts all realized that Hamas presented a serious security threat—one made even more acute by their ability to achieve maximum damage with the most unsophisticated of means. The kidnappings, the stabbings, and the drive-by shootings were cruel and barbarous acts, and virtually all were aimed at security forces personnel. This tactic differed markedly from the other Palestinian groups, who dedicated their efforts mainly in attacks against civilian targets. For example, the men who had kidnapped Nissim Toledano, unable to get hold of a gun, simply ran over the Border Guard sergeant and broke his legs. He then was beaten, tortured, and murdered, and his identity papers, badge, and side arm stolen. Such primitive execution was of grave concern to Shin Bet director Perry and Prime Minister Rabin, especially because the planning and preparation behind each strike was impressively sophisticated.

Separating the spiritual heads of Hamas from the secretive cells of fearless gunmen in the Territories was a stopgap measure, a way to buy time for a country embarking on a most serious political gamble. When Rabin won the June 1992 election, returning to power on the promise of peace, he entered into difficult and extremely precarious negotiations with the Palestinians. The negotiations, which had begun with the Madrid Peace Conference between the regional players—willed by the United States following the Gulf War—had already entered a critical phase, with backdoor and top-secret negotiations with Arafat's PLO in Oslo. Rabin had even ordered that several deportation orders issued by the administration of former prime minister Yitzhak Shamir be rescinded and the individuals returned to the Gaza Strip and the West Bank. Yet as the new year approached, Rabin found himself faced with a national security and political crisis he did not know how to neutralize—in the first ten months of 1992 alone, Hamas was responsible for some 192 acts of terrorism, including the murder of twenty Israelis and fifty-three Palestinians.[13] All Prime Minister Rabin could do was hope that the 415 deportees shivering for the cameras in the no-man's-land of southern Lebanon would be unable to issue orders and directive to their legions in the Territories. All Rabin could do was to buy time.

Winter comes with a vengeance to the vanquished hills of southern Lebanon. The winds, winding down from the north, accelerate as they cross the Turkish plains and the valleys of Syria's jaggedly carved frontier with Lebanon. It is an ironic injustice that a land so hot in the summer can be so bone-biting cold in winter. The days are often sunny but not warm, and the nights are blank and frozen with silence, aside from the distant bark of stray dogs and the roar of Pratt and Whitney engines propelling Israeli fighter jets freely across the star-filled skies. It snows in the mountains of southern Lebanon, and it rains. Legend has it that the minuscule showers of rain, in a state hovering between flake and droplet, are a test of a man's worth: weaker men are overwhelmed by the climactic hardships; the strong endure. That legend was written centuries before the 415 were dispatched into the frosted Lebanese hillside. The strong would become stronger. The determined would exact a hellish vengeance.

Notes

[1]Interview, Ya'akov Perry, August 15, 1998.

[2]Yedudit Yechezkeli, Roni Shaked, Danny Sadeh, and Tzvi Zinger, *"Lo Nadun A'd She 'Nekabel Ot Chaim,"* *Yediot Aharonot*, December 15, 1992, p. 4

[3]Ibid., p. 4.

[4]Danny Sadeh, Roni Shaked and David Regev, *"Zru 'ot Ha'Bitachon A'atzru,"* 1, 129

[5]Ronny Shaked, *"Ze Haya Retzach Achzari, Chayati,"* Yediot Aharonot, December 16, 1992, p. 2.

[6]Ronny Shaked and Doron Ma'iri, *"Ze Rak I'inyan Shel Zman A'ad She 'Nitfos Otam,"* Yediot Aharonot, December 16, 1992, p. 2.

[7]Elie Rekhass, "Khomeinism In Gaza," *The Jerusalem Post*, January 11, 1991, p. 8

[8]Khaled Abu Toameh, "The Sheikh's Progress," *The Jerusalem Report*, January 11, 1991, p. 8

[9]Ibid., p. 8.

[10]John Kifner, "Roots of Terror: A Special Report," *New York Times*, March 15, 1996, Section A.; Page 1.

[11]David Regev, *"Chipusei Aharei Gufat Sa'adon Ve'Matzu Et Gufat Sasportas,"* Yediot Aharonot, November 10, 1989, p. 3.

[12]Yoav Caspi, *"Ha'Matara: Jihad Miyadi Le 'Shichrur Palastin,"* Bamachane, December 19, 1990, p. 8.

[13]Steven Emerson, "Meltdown," *The New Republic*, November 23, 1992, p. 27.

Chapter 2

The Thin Blue Line

Across the no-man's-land separating the Israeli-occupied security zone in southern Lebanon from the rest of Lebanon, the small legion of Israeli intelligence officials watching the expulsion of the 415 Hamas leaders from behind fortified perches realized that the deportations were risky. Championing public opinion had never been an Israeli specialty, and attempting to gather sympathy for the murder of Nissim Toledano was impossible when CNN, the BBC, and networks from the four corners of the globe converged on men wearing donated coats and hovering over smoldering pots of lentil soup. It was a pitiful sight—and a public relations bonanza.

Senior officials in the Shin Bet, and in Agaf Ha'Mode'in, the IDF's intelligence branch known simply by its Hebrew-acronym of Aman, realized that Hamas would emerge from the ordeal having won the public relations battle, but Israel didn't care. The men were security threats—"ticking bombs," as one police official at the time said with, in retrospect, acute foresight—and

Israeli security was better served with the men out of the country than operating in the secretive and virtually impregnable cells inside Gaza, Hebron, Nablus, and Jenin.

Yet Israeli intelligence wasn't the only espionage group carefully monitoring the plight of the 415. During the day, when television news crews turned the hillside refuge into outdoor interview studios, the men who spoke Arabic with a distinctively Persian accent, and whose camouflage fatigues were always neatly ironed, stayed away from the deportees. But at night, when the journalists transmitted their footage from satellite links in Beirut or Damascus, they became the center of attention inside the makeshift tent city. They were both admired and feared, and to many of the Hamas officials deposited in southern Lebanon they were a symbol of Islam's global reach, and the force that it could deploy. They were the intelligence agents of the Jerusalem force of the Iranian Revolutionary Guards Corps (IRGC), and their task was the violent spread of Khomeini's revolution through terrorism.

In Lebanon, the Iranian mission has traditionally been the nurturing, supplying, training, and dispatching of Shiite guerrillas from both the Amal and Hizballah terrorist factions in a campaign of terrorism mounted primarily against Israeli military forces inside southern Lebanon. The first Iranian "teachers" were deserters from a particularly troubling and rebellious army battalion that the Shah quickly and "generously" volunteered to a U.N. peacekeeping effort that followed the March 1978 Israeli invasion of southern Lebanon.

Nearly half of Lebanon's Muslims were Shiites. They were certainly the poorest segment of the population, discriminated against by the ruling Christian and Sunni power base in Beirut and the target for cruel and often barbarous treatment at the hands of roving Druze militias or, worse, from the PLO. In June 1982, in fact, when the IDF invaded Lebanon, Shiite villages in the south greeted Israeli troopers as liberators. The repression, the poverty, and the chaotic political and military situation in the country made Lebanon an ideal litmus test for the export of Khomeini's firebranding return to fundamentalist Islam.

Lebanon's Shiites, now organized into well-armed militias of their own, not only embraced the Iranian revolution, but transformed the fundamentalist movement into one of the most feared terrorist phenomena in modern history. From the October 29, 1982, bombing of the Marine barracks in Beirut, to the 1992 bombing of the Israeli embassy and the AIMA building in Buenos Aires, Hizballah had proven its skills as one the world's most lethal terrorist factions. Its members had killed French paratroopers and Israeli Border Guards, and they had kidnapped and tortured to death a CIA station chief and American colonel serving as a U.N. military observer. They were a fearless bunch transfixed by a landscape stained by the blood of the stateless, the powerless, and the fearful. They had fought against Christians, Israelis, Druze, Palestinians, and even the most powerful military superpower in the world. And, in virtually all the battles they waged, they were victorious.

Yet Hizballah was nothing without its Iranian support—its Iranian training, its Iranian funding, and its Iranian intelligence officers. The Pasdaran is the intelligence entity of the Iranian Revolutionary Guards responsible for Lebanon. They are emissaries of the Iranian revolution who spread the word to agents, supporters, and proxies throughout the Middle East. Pasdaran agents, like their counterparts in the Mossad, the CIA, the British MI6, and the former Soviet KGB, are assigned to Iranian diplomatic missions, where they monitor dissidents and maintain links to underground and allied terrorist factions—especially in the Arab Gulf states. Iranian intelligence operations, funded by a virtually endless cash flow of counterfeit American dollars, paid for the establishment of Hizballah branches in Lebanon,

Iraqi Kurdistan, Jordan, and Palestine, and the Islamic Jihad in many other Moslem countries, including Egypt, Turkey, Chechnya, and the new republics in the Caucasus.

The *Qods* (Jerusalem) Force of the IRGC is responsible for extraterritorial operations, including terrorist operations. A primary focus for the Qods Force is training Islamic fundamentalist terrorist groups. Currently, the Qods Force conducts training activities in Iran and Sudan. The Qods Force is also responsible for gathering information required for targeting and attack planning.

Pasdaran influence over Hizballah was an unequivocal success. Lebanon's determined and highly motivated Shiite guerrilla army introduced such terms as *truck bombs* and *suicide bombers*. From Ba'albek, in the eastern approaches of the Lebanon's Beka'a Valley, to the mountain villages along the Marjayoun range in southern Lebanon, to fortresses such as Jibchit and Safi Jebel, the Iranians helped establish a small network of armed bases and training camps. Syrian president Hafez el-Assad, the true landlord of Lebanon, welcomed the Iranian-sponsored phenomenon with typical Middle Eastern one-upmanship. For a promise of not usurping Syrian policy and plans in Lebanon, Hizballah was allowed to wage its holy war against the Israeli occupation, and, for a small fee, Damascus Airport and military airfields throughout Syria could transport supplies and other necessities flown in on Iranian Air Force transports.

Hizballah's relationship with the rulers in Damascus was nothing short of pragmatic. Syria funded much of its economy via the poppy and hashish fields of the Beka'a, although the devout Party of God commanders, who despised the consumption of alcohol or narcotics, did not mind having their villagers cultivate fields and their soldiers protect stashes. Syria's Alawite hierarchy had also proven itself incapable of coming to terms with the zealous promise of fundamentalist Islam. In 1980, in

Aleppo, and then in February 1982, in the town of Hama, Syrian forces had massacred some twenty thousand men, women, and children as part of a brutal guerrilla war against the Muslim Brotherhood. Yet both Assad and Hizballah leaders understood the importance of their relationship and the strategic juggernaut it represented. The Iranians, too, appreciated the strategic benefits of investing—and investing heavily—in the Islamic Army fighting for liberation in Palestine.

In October 1991, as Israeli, Palestinian, and Syrian delegations were exchanging uncomfortable niceties at the American-imposed Madrid Peace Conference, the Iranians were hosting a conference of their own examining a solution to the Arab-Israeli question. The Iranians, however, spurned the idea of negotiation as a political tool and instead focused on an terrorist front to be opened in the war against Israel. The first links between the Iranian government and the Palestinian Islamic movements came courtesy of General Ali Duba, the wily spymaster in charge of Syrian military intelligence who arranged a meeting between Mohammed Nazzal, the head of Hamas in Amman, Hamas spokesman Ibrahim Ghosheh, and Iran's ambassador to Damascus and coordinator of Iranian policy in Lebanon, Ali Akhtari.[1]

General Duba was an old hand at the intricate world of cutthroat Middle Eastern espionage and counterespionage. One of his main objectives as commander of Syria's largest intelligence-gathering entity was anything within his power to destabilize Israeli national security. Duba had monitored Hamas and its meteoric rise to prominence, and he knew that Iranian assistance to the potentially significant regional destabilizing entity could reward Teheran with invaluable political dividends. Bridging a working relationship between the Iranian government, a Shiite theocracy, and the devout Sunni Hamas was something of a Byzantine miracle.

Iran's first overture to Hamas, the Muslim Brotherhood of Palestine and its offshoot, the Islamic Jihad, came at the lavish rejectionist conference hosted in October 1991. The Teheran gathering was a bit of a revolutionary swan song for organizations like Dr. George Habash's Popular Front for the Liberation of Palestine (PFLP) and Nayif Hawatmeh's Democratic Front for the Liberation of Palestine (DFLP). These Marxist, pan-Arab revolutionary movements had died a slow and insignificant death alongside their principal patron, the Soviet Union, yet they were in Teheran to help formulate strategy and opposition to Arafat and the PLO in response to what they perceived as his treachery of acquiescing to American pressure by having his representatives actually sit across the negotiating table from the Israelis.

The only true star with any military and operational significance at the conference was Ahmed Jibril. Since 1988, as a result of his role in the downing of Pan Am 103, Jibril's PFLP-GC had experienced something of a spiritual renaissance courtesy of Iranian cash and Syrian military support. The stalwart terrorist soldier was Syria's man, but he had undergone a return to Islam and allied himself with Teheran. Jibril, with a thousand-man army in Damascus and the Beka'a Valley, vowed to wage a Jihad against the Zionist enemy—and its Great Satan allies—anywhere and everywhere in the world. Hamas observers to the assembly were impressed by Jibril's rhetoric and by his zeal. Hamas was ready for interorganizational alliances and a strong political network spread throughout the Middle East.

Battling regional threats was nothing new to the Shin Bet. Even before the Jewish state was established, the Shin Bet and its forerunners had quietly and effectively kept tabs on Israel's enemies from within. The task of maintaining internal security has always been a demanding though manageable task. During the first twenty years of Israeli independence, the principal nonmilitary threat to the state of Israel had been the exorbitant number of foreign espionage agents operating within the nation's boundaries. In its formative years, the intelligence service scored numerous and sometimes quite impressive counterespionage victories, ranging from the arrest of deep-cover KGB spies serving in the ranks of the Israel defense forces to Czech and East German operatives. Through its coups in Europe and South America, and its success in seizing spies in Israel, the Shin Bet had developed a reputation as a ruthless though highly efficient counterespionage service.

The Shin Bet's legendary founding father, Isser Harel, was a spymaster who demanded unyielding dedication and discipline from his agents in the field. Secrecy wasn't just a professional requirement in Harel's Shin Bet—it was the agency's religion. The intelligence services of Lebanon, Syria, Iraq, Jordan, and Egypt found the Shin Bet to be a daunting and humbling foe.

Israel's lightning military victory in the 1967 Six Day War altered the geopolitical map of the Middle East and realigned the global focus of Shin Bet operations to precincts far closer to home. For the Shin Bet, Israel's acquisition of the Golan Heights, the West Bank, and the Gaza Strip increased their area of responsibility fourfold. For the Palestinians, Israel's capture of the West Bank and Gaza, filled with refugees from earlier wars, served as a call to arms for dozens of highly political and revolutionary Palestinian liberation organizations that emerged after the Arab defeat. Overnight, the Shin Bet went from a small and nondescript entity tasked with staking out spies and engineering elaborate false-flag operations to a proactive force engaged in the often brutal world of counterterrorism.

Shin Bet is divided into eight different departments or sections: Arab Affairs; Non-Arab Affairs; Protective Security; Operational Support; Technology; Interrogation and Legal Council; Coordination and Planning; and Administration. Much like the

Israel defense forces, it is subdivided into regional commands, with local field offices supervising operations in a particular stretch of territory.

Arab Affairs is the Shin Bet's largest and most important department, responsible for directing all counterespionage, counterintelligence, and counterterrorism operations against Arab-inspired sources; these range from tracking Syrian military intelligence operatives among the Druze villages of the Golan Heights to infiltrating a terrorist cell in the Old City of Jerusalem. Its agents, according to foreign sources, are mainly Arabic-speaking veterans of the IDF's elite units who undergo extensive counterintelligence and legal training. Nobody goes into the Arab Affairs department seeking a quick and uneventful twenty years of civil service. The agents are overworked, overstressed, and faced with waging a desperate war of nerves and guile inside hostile pockets so very close to home. Arab Affairs agents are rarely home, and then many don't have homes to return to when wives, incapable of competing for their husband's time in the service, decide to find a husband with a less glamorous but more stable means of earning an income. Arab Affairs agents smoke too much, live off drive and caffeine, and have been known to take out their anger and frustration on the hapless souls who are unfortunate—or guilty—enough to be sitting inside one of the Shin Bet's interrogation cells. They had thought they had fought the best the Palestinians had to throw at the Israeli security apparatus, and that they had won. Hamas would prove these unshakable spirits wrong.

Following the kidnappings of Sasportas and Sa'adon and the subsequent and massive Shin Bet sweeps of Hamas activists in the territories in 1989 and 1990, Hamas redefined and restructured its political and military leadership to meet the Israeli counterterrorist juggernaut. The clerics, most of whom were either in prison, awaiting trial, or awaiting deportation, were replaced by a ruling body of twelve men, all of exceptional intelligence and diplomatic skills, who spearheaded the movement's political wing while secretly preparing the military apparatus for a full-scale guerrilla campaign. Most important, perhaps, six of the twelve leaders resided abroad—ostensibly out of reach of the Shin Bet or Israeli special forces: Imad al-Alami, a thirty-year-old engineer deported by the Israelis from the Gaza Strip in 1990, set up the Hamas embassy in Teheran; Mohammed Nazzal and Ibrahim Ghosheh established Hamas offices in Amman; Mohammed Siam established a political liaison office in Khartoum; Abu Mohammed Mustafa set up the Hamas embassy in Beirut; and Musa Abu Marzouk, a man who achieve great prominence in the months to come, was the Hamas representative in Damascus.[2]

In October 1992, Musa Abu Marzouk led a Hamas delegation that traveled to Teheran to cement the logistical framework behind a full-scale partnership with the Iranians. According to the agreement signed during the two-week visit to Teheran, and various intelligence and terrorist training facilities throughout the country, the Iranian government pledged an annual budget of thirty million dollars to Hamas to support its international network and its war against the Jewish state.[3] More significant, however, was Iran's pledge to turn Hamas into another Hizballah. The framework for this support came through the ultramysterious Third Department of the Iranian Foreign Ministry, headed by the brother of Iranian president Hashemi Rafsanjani and dealing with what Iranian strategic planners termed the Jordanian Front. The Iranian Foreign Ministry, in fact, was affording Hamas "embassy status," abandoning any diplomatic contacts once maintained with Yasir Arafat's PLO.

According to the Saudi daily *Ashraq al-Awsat*, the Iranians viewed the alliance with Hamas as a genuine article of opportunity. Teheran predicted that U.S. President George Bush would lose the November 1992 general elections, and as a result

Middle East diplomacy would encounter a superpower vacuum that Hamas operations could conveniently exploit.[4]

The Iranians promised to train three thousand Hamas fighters in camps spread throughout Lebanon, Iran, and the Sudan. The camps included the Imam Ali barracks, situated north of Teheran; the Kranadanje camp, near the holy city of Qom; and the Beit el Makedes complex, inside Qom. In the Sudan, Hamas operatives would train in ten camps that the Revolutionary Guard had set up with the full backing of Sudanese strongman Hassan al-Tourabi's Arab Popular Islamic Congress. Iran had, since 1990, entered into a tacit alliance with the Muslim government in the Sudan and it was a marriage of great convenience to both sides. The cash-strapped Sudanese desperately needed Teheran's oil millions, and the Iranians found the African heartland a strategic staging ground for spreading the revolution to Egypt and Algeria to the north, and to Saudi Arabia and Yemen to the east, across the Red Sea.

Most of the terrorist training facilities built by the Iranians in the Sudan were meant for Egyptian radicals battling the Mubarak regime in Cairo. Hamas operatives were invited to train and set up camps at Jedid al-Hak, near Khartoum, in the annex to the notorious Kardi military prison, while Hamas special operations forces and intelligence personnel were sent to Umm Barbaita, south of Al Fasher, where Iranian instructors taught the A-to-Z's of terrorist and espionage tradecraft.[5]

For the very best Hamas talent inside the Territories, however, the Pasdaran would train spies and deep-cover intelligence officers at the Imam Hussein Institute north of Teheran. The Pasdaran would train Hamas operatives in intelligence-gathering, sabotage, hijacking, how to build covert and infrangible networks, how to run agents and double agents, and the art of false-flag operations and misinformation. Radio stations, such as the powerful al-Quds station beaming out of downtown Damascus, provided round-the-clock news and information to the faithful in the Territories, as well as coded orders emanating from the controlling desks in Teheran, the Syrian capital, and overseas.

The Iranian alliance was a turning point. Iranian support and investment came with a significant and specific Iranian demand: escalate the level of violence to disrupt the peace process. Teheran wasn't interested in sponsoring a paper tiger. It wanted blood, violence, acts of terror so brazen that not only would Israeli public opinion turn away from any potential negotiated settlement with Arafat and the PLO, but Israeli countermeasures would be so severe and so irreversible that Palestinian public support for the peace process would wane as well.

Rabin's deportation of the 415, and Lebanese Prime Minister Rafik Harari's refusal to allow them to enter the country, was exactly the type of response the spymasters in Teheran, downtown Damascus, and the Beka'a Valley were hoping for. World opinion, galvanized with sympathy by the sight of the wretched bearded men praying, eating, and (barely) living in the snowy squalor of a frigid no-man's-land, was vehemently anti-Israel. Westerners were outraged by nightly news broadcasts of the middle-aged men—all doctors, lawyers, clerics, engineers, architects, dentists, and accountants—wearing long johns and soiled overcoats, stranded without supplies or hope on the snowy banks of a Lebanese mountaintop. The U.N. General Assembly, never friendly toward Israel, condemned the flagrant violation of the Geneva Convention, while the U.N. Security Council issued Resolution 799 demanding that Israel return the deportees immediately.

Even in Israel, where a majority of the population supported the harsh measures taken against Hamas, the Supreme Court issued a ruling stating that the deportations could only be temporary and that some sort of process to return most of the men would have to be implemented. The Supreme Court declared that the mass deportation was illegal but upheld the government's right to expel the men on an individual basis. Prime Minister Rabin, following intensive mediation on the part of American president-elect Bill Clinton and promises that America would veto any threatened Security Council action against Israel, announced that Israel would allow back 100 of the remaining 396 Palestinians, and that the remainder would have their two-year banishment order cut in half.

Much of the crisis surrounding the deportees was, naturally, PR-driven propaganda of convenience. During the day, the deportees shivered on cue, professed their hunger and deprivations, and publicly prayed while news crews from Europe and the United States quickly got their sound bites and headed back to Damascus before dusk so they could transmit their stories via satellite and be at the bar at Le Meridian Hotel before happy hour began and the restaurant filled with Muchabarat agents. At dusk, according to Israeli and Western intelligence and diplomatic sources in the area, the deportees were visited by Hizballah operatives and Iranian intelligence agents who provided the deportees with food, hearty supplies, and a night's worth of terrorist training.

A frequent visitor to the no-man's-land encampment was Assadalah Haji Reza Asgar, the Iranian Pasadran commander in Lebanon. The owner of a fierce and violent reputation, Asgar viewed the deportation of the 415 as a golden opportunity to provide the top echelon of the Hamas political hierarchy with advanced terrorist and counterespionage instruction. According to some intelligence reports, deportees were whisked away to Teheran for additional instruction. The 415 became an ideal tool by which Teheran could direct the war of liberation for Palestine.

The failed bombing attack in Ramat Efal, Yehiya Ayyash's reason for coming out of the terrorist closet, was a Hamas modus operandi change stemming directly from directives emanating from Teheran, filtered through political offices in

Damascus, and faxed, via a third party, to cell commanders in the Gaza Strip and the West Bank. The planned suicide bombing, identical to past Hizballah successes in southern Lebanon, was meant to put the Israeli public on notice. The kidnapping and murder of Nissim Toledano was intended to place the crosshairs on the foreheads of Israel's security forces. In reality, Israeli security forces had already endured a year of being in the crosshairs of Izzedine al-Qassam.

In January 1992 a mysterious new terrorist entity emerged when the Izzedine al-Qassam Brigade began issuing communiqus taking credit for Hamas attacks against Israeli soldiers, policemen, and civilians. Izzedine al-Qassam was a martyr, although his battles had been fought some fifty years earlier. Born in Syria, in the port town of Latakia in 1882, al-Qassam learned the art of the Jihad as a teenager, studying Islam in Cairo's El-Azhar University. According to legend, he was a pious youth who had memorized the Koran by heart. Upon the completion of his studies he returned to his village near the Mediterranean and became a firebrand in the local mosque, preaching the virtues of Islamic solutions to everyday problems—including colonialism. He is reported to have fought the Italians in Tripoli prior to the First World War, and to have waged a determined guerrilla war against the French occupation of Syria and Lebanon after the Great War. His campaign was a thorn in French colonial plans but serious enough to warrant the military governor to set a price on al-Qassam's head.

In 1922, al-Qassam escaped the French Mandate and traveled to Palestine, where he set up shop in the port city of Haifa—preaching the virtues of Islamic nationalism and organizing resistance to the British and the wave of postwar Jewish migration. He joined an Islamic school, as a teacher, and after a while joined the Association of Young Muslims in Haifa—a cover for the small band of fighters he was assembling. Performing wedding ceremonies and sermons in mosques, he pressed the Palestinian communities not to sell land to the Jews, to resist the Jewish threat, and to openly attack British forces. In 1935 he was killed by British military units in a raging gun battle in the hills near Jenin. He was Palestine's first true *shaheed*.

Izzedine al-Qassam was the type of larger-than-life figure of resistance and courage that the young and the impressionable men of the Territories could aspire to emulate. Yet Izzedine al-Qassam was far more than a Paul Bunyon armed with a Koran and a British Lee Enfield rifle. He was a master organizer who, while Palestinian nationalist leaders squabbled over allegiance to Cairo, Damascus, or Baghdad, managed to assemble a highly secretive, extremely effective guerrilla army.

Izzedine al-Qassam's holy army was divided into secret units, each consisting of five soldiers and a commander. Another unit was responsible for coordinating activity among the forces in the field and maintaining secure communications with al-Qassam himself. The guerrilla army was divided into five principal groups: the combat element, tasked with hit-and-run attacks against Jewish targets and British forces; the preparation element, tasked with assembling the material and manpower for the struggle; the financial element, tasked with raising money and seeking donations to purchase weapons and look after the families of fallen soldiers; the preaching entity, tasked with spreading the gospel of Jihad to mosques and schools throughout Palestine; and the political entity, responsible for coordinating political and diplomatic contacts with other Arab leaders.

When the Hamas military apparatus adopted the title Izzedine al-Qassam Brigade to cover the regional combat cells operating in Gaza and in the West Bank in early 1992, the new force adopted the organizational structure of the original force that had waged a secretive war in Palestine some sixty years earlier. Divided into four regional commands, the brigade's basic operational unit was a five-man cell, independent of all other cells, that was linked to political officers and commanders faxing orders in from the political leadership abroad—primarily Syria, Great Britain, and the United States. The foot soldiers in this new entity were unlike previous Hamas gunmen who sniped at Israeli patrols or murdered informants. They were young, incredibly zealous, and in many cases psychopathically violent.

Although one needed to be devout to be a member of Hamas, the young brigade paid nothing more than lip service to the prison statements of Sheikh Yassin or the directives issued from the deportees in southern Lebanon. They followed the rule of the AK-47, or the Uzi taken from the dying body of an Israeli soldier or settler killed in an ambush. The young foot soldiers of the Izzedine al-Qassam Brigade cared little for sermons and speeches, and their worth wasn't measured by how much of the Koran they could memorize. Instead they were judged by their street-fighting abilities, their skills with explosives, and by being able to walk up to an enemy soldier, aim the barrel of a K'latch square, and revel in the explosion and the pink spray.

Unlike many of the Hamas leaders—men in their late thirties and forties who were raised under Egyptian and Jordanian occupation—the teenagers and young Turks in their early twenties who flocked to the brigade in 1992 were brought up under the Israeli gun. These kids were dirt poor and without the hope of gainful employment or political freedom. They had spent their formative years watching neighbors die or be arrested and struggling with their parents to put food on the table as well as cope with the frustrations of life under occupation. Like the kids in the inner cities of America who find safety in numbers and feel the glory of belonging by joining street gangs, so too did the young men of the Territories seek a violent alternative to life under Israeli rule by joining the Izzedine al-Qassam Brigade. Yet these young men armed with assault rifles and pistols did not sell crack, nor did they rob old ladies or convenience stores. Their form of release was to wage a Jihad. Rage and religion, tossed in with geopolitical considerations, had produced a most volatile mix.

Although the young guns of the al-Qassam Brigade weren't schooled in the art of guerrilla warfare in the camps of southern Lebanon, they worried senior Israeli commanders. The al-Qassam volunteers were brazen, brave, dedicated, and willing to die. They were fanatics, and formidable foes in battle. When confronted by security forces, especially special operations units, they rarely surrendered—even when surrounded and offered the chance to walk away with their lives.

On May 24, 1992, a strike force of commando cops from the Ya'ma'm—the Israeli National Police counterterrorist and hostage-rescue unit—served a high-risk warrant on a house in Gaza where three Izzedine al-Qassam terrorists were wanted for the killings of some twenty-nine Arabs and Jews. The raid was textbook: the Ya'ma'm, acting on behalf of intelligence obtained by the Shin Bet, had executed dozens of such raids in the past on Fatah and Popular Front safe houses and strongholds. Usually the Ya'ma'm would execute the dynamic entry with such speed and skill that the terrorists were literally caught with their pants down and unable to offer any resistance. Surprise was a Ya'ma'm calling card, although Hamas was learning the rules of engagement with uncanny skill.

The terrorists knew that Israeli units like the Ya'ma'm, who operate under strict guidelines in the use of deadly force, will not fire at women and children, so they used civilians, their own people, as human shields. When the Ya'ma'm task force reached the building early on the morning of May 21, the terrorists saw what was coming and quickly escaped up the building's stairs. One Ya'ma'm unit, led by twenty-six-year-old Sergeant Major Eran Sobelman, followed the terrorist up the staircase but hesitated momentarily when he saw the area crowded with old women and small children. Sergeant Major Sobelman was killed

by a point-blank gunshot to the head fired by one of the terrorists taking advantage of his humanness.

Chaos erupted. A hellacious firefight ensued, complete with
grenade fire. Israeli Air Force helicopters flew overhead, directing concentrated beams of light onto the battle zone, while supporting troops launched flares into the thick spring air. Two of
the wanted terrorists, Mohammed Kandil and Yasser Hassarat,
were cut down by a fusillade of Ya'ma'm fire; the third terrorist,
Marwan a-Zayegh, was killed by sniper fire as he attempted to
toss a grenade from the roof of the building. A-Zayegh, believed
responsible for the deaths of some sixteen men and women, was
only nineteen years old.

At Sobelman's funeral, Commander David Tzur, the commander of the Ya'ma'm, said, "Eran was one of our best, who
exposed himself to everyday danger of fighting terrorists who
are acting without any law or limits from within their population, who operate out of buildings filled with women and children, and they force us to adapt the fighting to this jungle in
which we find ourselves operating." The Ya'ma'm had fought
Arafat's elite Force 17, Jibril's men, and Hizballah, all in southern Lebanon. Yet Hamas was proving to be a lethal enemy;
many Israeli troops in the field feared that the upper echelons
had foolishly underestimated its power and resolve. Eran Sobelman was the first Ya'ma'm operator to be killed in the line
of duty since the unit was created in 1974. He wouldn't be the
last. The war against Izzedine al-Qassam had only just begun.

On December 10, 1992, the Shin Bet summoned the Ya'ma'm
into action for an immediate mission. A Shin Bet informant who
had provided reliable information in the past had told his handler that a wanted Hamas terrorist, Issam Barhama, was hiding
out in a safe house in the village of A'nza, notorious for Hamas
activity. Morale in the Israeli special operations community was
already at an all-time low. In August the commander of the

Border Guards undercover unit, the Ya'mas, was killed in a raid on a terrorist safe-house in Jenin. The commander, Eli Avraham, was a former Ya'ma'm officer and one of those rare natural-born leaders. According to a bomb-disposal officer who worked with him in Ramallah, "Men would follow him into a wall of fire!"[6]

The year 1992 had been a bloody one. Sobelman and Avraham were but two casualties. There were others in the special operations community who fell in battles against the al-Qassam fighters. There were IDF undercover squad soldiers, officers, and policemen also killed in running gun battles or point-blank executions.

Issam Barhama was a feared man—even by the battle-hardened men of the Shin Bet. But the mood was optimistic. Weeks earlier, an IDF undercover unit had ambushed and killed Imad Aqal, the young Turk commander of the Izzedine al-Qassam Brigade in Gaza in a fierce gun battle. Aqal was no ordinary terrorist. Conservative estimates made him the trigger-man in some twenty cold-blooded murders of Israelis and Palestinians alike. In fact he took special pleasures in the murders of fellow Palestinians whom he believed were supplying the Shin Bet with information.

Aqal didn't just murder his victims—he tortured them with grotesque and diabolical measures designed to get a confession. Fingers and extremities were sliced off one by one; battery acid was tossed down the throats of those unwilling to cooperate; skin was scorched with cigarettes, blowtorches, and even industrial glue set alight on the back and backsides of victims. He was reported to have reveled in the carnage, considering it his holy duty. Barhama was believed to be one of Aqal's many disciples.

The Shin Bet case officer met with the Ya'ma'm task force at the unit's home base somewhere near Lod, and briefed the officers about the mission in hand. The operators, lanky and thin, were veterans of late-night operations where the only sound heard was a terrorist talking behind a wall and the deafening cadence of one's beating heart. They were trained to assault hijacked buses, storm barricaded buildings, and—in the instantaneous eruption of a diversionary device—race through a room crowded with terrorists and hostages with weapons at the ready. It was difficult work that required absolute dedication. "We are all a bit crazy," claimed a retired Ya'ma'm lieutenant. "Who else but a crazy person would be the first through the door in order to go eyeball to eyeball with a fanatic pointing a gun at your head already resigned to an orgy of young virgins in paradise?"[7]

The operation in A'nza was supposed to have been routine—routine, that is, in a line of work where there are no definites, no absolutes. The Shin Bet informant was to go to Barhama's home, seek him out, and when the two men walked out of the front door, they would be pounced upon by the combined Ya'ma'm/Shin Bet/IDF task force that had assembled several kilometers away from the village entrance once darkness had shed its comforting cast of cover. The Shin Bet and the IDF placed great importance on stopping Barhama—a small who's who of military commanders, including future Mossad director and Central Command head Major General Danny Yatom, joined the mission as observers.

Yet as the Ya'ma'm operators slinked their way through the village, closing in on Barhama's house, a group of small children playing in the muddy unpaved road distinguished the masked figures crawling into position. Sensing an ambush, the preschool veterans of life in the Territories yelled *"a-Jaish,"* or "soldiers," warning all those inside the house of the impending operation. Murphy's Law had once again become the order of the day. A snatch-and-grab operation had suddenly developed into a volatile barricade situation with hostages involved. Shots were heard inside the building, the impact of the rounds absorbed by the crumbling walls.

The Shin Bet case officer and Ya'ma'm commander David Tzur realized that it was imperative to rescue the informant; he was a goldmine of information, and it was bad for the business if handlers let their men die in the field. A team entered the building in classic Ya'ma'm fashion, though they were met at the door by a hail of gunfire. An operator, Ronen Razieli, was shot in the eye and critically wounded. He was pulled out of the ricocheting hail of fire by the unit's bomb-disposal officer, Sasson Mordoch. Miraculously, the Shin Bet informant and the occupants of the house managed to slip out of the house during the melee, presenting the commanders on the scene with a convenient set of options: wait until the terrorist came out of the house with his hands up, or blow the one-story structure to hell. The Israelis opted for hell. Fifteen antitank rounds were fired into the structure; grenades and automatic-weapons fire followed. The building erupted into a fireball that burnt brightly for more than two hours. Surely nothing could have survived the inferno.

Major General Yatom, a veteran commando himself, had ordered a Ya'ma'm team inside the building to fetch Barhama's corpse. Ya'ma'm commander Tzur knew it was dangerous. No one believed Barhama was still alive, but there was the risk that several propane gas tanks in the rubble could still explode. Rather than argue with a major general, though, Tzur ordered a team inside the smoldering rubble. Sasson Mordoch entered the building with his bomb-sniffing Rottweiler Tiberias and a fire-support team, searching through what remained of the blaze, sifting through the living room and entering the kitchen to look for the dead terrorist.

But Barhama was still alive. Although suffering from terrible burns, he had managed to find his way inside an upper-level food pantry above the kitchen and lay in wait. When Mordoch entered the room, he took aim with his Carl Gustav 9 mm submachine gun and unleashed a murderous barrage of fire. Mordoch was hit by the volley; so too was his trusted dog. Another Ya'ma'm operator was seriously injured by the gunfire, and bullets whizzed past the face of Danny Yatom, who had followed the commandos inside. Mordoch collapsed on the floor in a pool of blood.

Although critically wounded, Mordoch managed to maintain constant radio communications with his commander. Ya'ma'm officers were poised to race in and retrieve their wounded comrade, but every time they creeped closer to the door, Barhama would fire from inside the wrecked home. Mordoch lay wounded for forty-five minutes as general, commanders, and operators debated on how to rescue him. Finally one of the unit's K-9 teams was dispatched into the building in the hope that the dog would act as a diversion. The plan backfired miserably. The dog attacked the wounded Mordoch, biting him with iron jaws. "The dog is biting me!" Mordoch screamed over his radio set in a confused and anguished plea. Barhama heard Mordoch's cries and closed in for the kill. Standing over the wounded Ya'ma'm operator, Barhama readied a fresh thirty-round ammo clip for the chamber of his Swedish-made gun, then locked and loaded the magazine. The last sound heard from inside the building before the ominous rip of 9 mm ammunition fired at point-blank range was Mordoch yelling, "He's killing me!"[8]

The Ya'ma'm operators, heartbroken and outraged, entered the location with weapons ablaze. Doron Madmon, an operator in the unit, was shot in the chest and seriously wounded in the final assault, but this time Barhama would be vanquished. He was cut down in a flurry of Ya'ma'm fire that, without any doubt, put an end to his reign of terror.

On one December's night in the heart of the West Bank, one Izzedine al-Qassam gunman had humbled perhaps the world's top counterterrorist team. Countless factors had led to the failures that night in A'nza, and fingers are still being pointed at the commanders for their lack of appreciation of the danger at hand, or their failure to rescue one of their own who lay bleeding to death in the charred remains of a Hamas safe house. Morale in the Ya'ma'm was never lower. Morale in the ranks of the al-Qassam Brigade was at a high. Two days after Barhama and Sasson Mordoch died in that smoldering hell in the West Bank, Sergeant Major Nissim Toledano was kidnapped and murdered.

Prime Minister Rabin, IDF Chief of Staff Ehud Barak, and commanders in the Shin Bet, military intelligence, and National Police had hoped that the deportation would, at least temporarily, slow down the Hamas blitzkrieg, but optimism was fool's gold in the Middle East. Hamas had been dealt a serious blow but it was far from immobilized by the expulsions. In fact, the banishment of the old guard and the new support from the Iranians had left the war in the hands of men determined to bring the conflict into one segment of the Israeli defense establishment that had, for years, been virtually untouchable.

On the night of January 3, 1993, twenty-nine-year-old Shin Bet agent Haim Nahmani, a soft-spoken and highly regarded case officer working in the Jerusalem field office, left his desk for a clandestine meeting with an informant. The meeting was routine. Shin Bet agents didn't uncover terrorist cells by listening to the radio or reading the newspaper. Intelligence work meant human contact—and intelligence agents rarely met people who were innocent, honorable, or 100 percent trustworthy. Intelligence gathering and counterespionage were the work of men who left their morality and sense of fair play at the door. Intelligence work is anonymous and unrewarding and dangerous as hell. Especially, as in this case, when the agent calls the handler requesting to meet, with the promise of "urgent information."

Haim Nahmani feared very little. The handsome former combat officer was a Jerusalem native who felt safe working in his

hometown. Although the meeting was with an informant providing information on rogue cells of the al-Qassam Brigade operating inside the Israeli capital, the debriefing was considered
routine—routine enough for the agent to use a Shin Bet apartment, at 14 Ha'Tivonim Street, a narrow and quiet corner in the
middle-class Rehavia neighborhood for the face-to-face encounter. The building was innocuous—especially in midday, when
most of the adults were at work and the kids were not yet home
from school. There were dozens of safe houses throughout Israel's major cities that the Shin Bet used for such purposes. They
were places where a young man wearing jeans and sneakers
could enter without suspicion, where the sight of an Arab would
not prompt neighbors to immediately call police.

Handling informants was deadly business, and the Shin Bet
agents knew the risks. In January 1973, Baruch Cohen, a Shin
Bet agent working on the hunt for Black September operatives
responsible for the Munich Olympic Massacre, was killed by a
double agent he was running in Madrid. In June 1980, Shin Bet
agent Moshe Golan was killed by a double agent he was running, as the two met in a Netanya safe house.

Nahmani arrived at the apartment early—just as he had
learned to do at his course at the grueling Shin Bet academy. It
was imperative to establish command and dominance when the
handler met the man whose life he literally controlled. It was
also important to check for listening devices, explosive booby
traps, or other signs that an ambush was imminent. The agent
arrived at the appointed time; but as Nahmani opened the door,
other men forced their way in. Maher Abu Srur, an operator
well known to Shin Bet, struck Nahmani on the head with a
hammer. Although Srur had an affection for the American-made
M-16 assault rifle, he came calling that frigid Jerusalem night
with knives and axes and two of his cousins. The killing would
have to be silent and, as a calling card, the carnage would have

to shock even the most seasoned Shin Bet agents. Nahmani put up a fierce battle for his life, but the massive blows were simply too much.

After finishing off Nahmani, the Srur cousins washed the blood off their bodies in the kitchen and then grabbed Nahmani's identification card and attaché case. A third cousin was waiting on the street below in a stolen Subaru sedan procured specifically for the killing. Making their way slowly out of the capital, the three headed south to a junkyard in Hebron where they torched the vehicle and escaped into the surrounding hills to avoid the dragnets and manhunts.

At around 4:00 P.M., a building resident called police after noticing bloodstains on the door; the man, a recent immigrant from Brooklyn, had thought he had escaped the urban madness of muggings and killings when he moved to Jerusalem. Police responding to the call were horrified by the butchery at the crime scene—until they realized that the murdered man was a Shin Bet agent. Within minutes, the entire Rehavia neighborhood was swarming with a legion of Shin Bet officials. Agents openly wept outside the apartment where Nahmani's body was photographed by investigators and fingerprints and other bits of forensic evidence gathered. Other agents openly vowed revenge.

The next day, reporters were kept far from Nahmani's funeral atop Mt. Herzl in Jerusalem—the national cemetery where Israel buries its war heroes. Nahmani left behind a twenty-two-year-old widow, and comrades in arms who were stunned by the murder. Shielded behind their sunglasses, the men and women of the Shin Bet realized that the struggle against Hamas had taken a turn that afternoon in Rehavia. The once untouchables were now fair game. The rules of engagement had dramatically been challenged. The murder of the Shin Bet agent was the first of its kind in the Intifadah, and it had undermined the Shin Bet's traditional veil of deterrence and intimidation. Agents would now act more cautiously, take fewer risks, and the intelligence work was bound to suffer. Senior Shin Bet officials viewed the killing as one of the major turning points in the war against Hamas, but many privately feared that agents would, in the months to come, view this period as the good old days.

Shin Bet officials were stunned by the killing of one of their own, but the mood in the Territories was festive. In southern Lebanon the deportees enjoyed their payback at the agency that sent them to the purgatory of the mountainside camp. "The killing of this Shin Bet agent has boosted the morale not only of the deportees," deportee spokesman Abdul-Aziz Rantisi was quoted as saying, "but of the whole Palestinian people."[9] In the Territories the ranks of Hamas swelled. Shin Bet investigations increased tenfold in Gaza and the West Bank; Palestinians who relied upon menial jobs inside Israel to support their families were barred from crossing the Green Line for weeks at a stretch while the Territories were quarantined. The poor were growing poorer, the hopeful were becoming disillusioned, and the hopeless were slowly making their way toward village and neighborhood mosques, seeking an answer and a means to exact revenge against the hated occupier.

At just after 2:00 A.M. on the night of March 30, 1993, at the Talmei-Eliezer Junction northeast of the town of Hadera, two Israeli highway patrolmen, officers Danny Hazut and Moti Yisrael, radioed their central dispatcher that they'd be taking a brief break. It had been a quiet night on patrol; there weren't too many speeders that time of night, nor had they spotted any stolen vehicles. The highway patrol, or traffic police as the Mishteret Tnu'ah was called, was something of a relatively new phenomenon in Israeli law enforcement. In a futile attempt to persuade Israelis to drive within the speed limit (and within the realm of human decency), the national police had created a traffic force to issue summonses and make arrests. The measures were needed; Israel had more traffic-accident fatalities than al-

most anywhere in the world. The patrol also attempted to slow
the meteoric rise in car thefts, perpetrated mainly by Palestinian
criminal gangs operating in the Occupied Territories. The
thieves stole brand-new cars, chopped them up in thriving all-
night factories, and then sold the parts back inside Israel for a
hefty profit. Many of those involved were part-timers who also
operated as full-time terrorists with Fatah, the PFLP, or Hamas.
Cars were more valuable than guns or explosives—especially
those with yellow Israeli plates, which were essential for operations inside Israel.

Traffic work wasn't glamorous but it was relatively safe and
routine. Officers Hazut and Yisrael knew that the middle of the
night was when the Arab car thieves attempted to sneak their
night's work back into the Territories, though the two parked
their blue-and-white Ford Sierra underneath a streetlamp. A terrorist alert was in effect for all Israeli security service personnel.[10] Rumors filtered through the hallways of Shin Bet offices
that Hamas would try something in the days to come. Most
veteran investigators believed that Hamas would attempt to kidnap an Israeli soldier, possibly a female, so that they could demand Sheikh Yassin's release. Other reports warned of the
potential onslaught of suicide bombers. One of the dangers of
police work is that the monotony of routine often lowers a cop's
guard, even for a split second, and lives are lost in less time.

Police officers Hazut and Yisrael weren't aware of the white
Peugeot 504 that had driven by their car once or twice, nor had
they seen the two Arab males inside the vehicle staring attentively at the target. Driving up alongside the patrol car, one of
the men in the Peugeot opened his window and took aim with
an Uzi submachine gun at the two napping cops. A thirty-round
clip was emptied into the heads and torsos of the two officers;
handgun fire followed for effect. Once the cops' shields and ID
cards had been stolen and their service weapons lifted, the white
Peugeot backtracked. The killers drove to Tel Aviv, where police

and Shin Bet investigators would never look, and then on to Jerusalem along the No. 1 Highway with the rush-hour traffic heading to the capital and listening to news reports of the double killings.

The following morning, before the Occupied Territories were sealed off, Hamas issued a communiqué claiming that the attack was the handiwork of the Izzedine al-Qassam Brigade. Contrary to Rabin's hopes, the deportations did not hamper operations. On the contrary, the action begged for vengeance. The stakes of the game had been raised.

In Teheran, in Damascus, and in Falls Church, Virginia, where Hamas political director Musa Abu Marzouk had been a resident for some thirteen years, the fax machines were kept busy sending cryptic messages to third-party relay stations in Europe where the messages could be faxed to the Territories. By the time the machines in Gaza, Jenin, Nablus, and Hebron were printing out the message, the copy was faded though just legible enough to be understood. The message was relayed to a political officer before being destroyed, and then passed on verbally to a runner so that it could be disseminated to a battalion commander in the field. It was a roundabout method of communication but it was secure.

Because of dragnets and operations in Gaza, the Hebron area, and Jerusalem following Nahmani's murder, the only Izzedine al-Qassam yet to make a name for itself operationally was the north battalion. The orders that spring were to escalate the Jihad. After the kidnappings, drive-bys, and intelligence-agent ambushes, escalation could mean only one thing: bombs. The man charged with initiating the offensive was a commander in the northern battalion, Yehiya Ayyash.

The twenty-seven-year-old Ayyash was very much an anomaly. Soft-spoken, meek, and brooding, he lacked the violent bravado of the thugs who led the battalions in Gaza, and he did not have a rap sheet and a trail of mutilated corpses as a calling card of his talents. Yet Islam was not the lone force that drove him to eventually become the most famous terrorist in the Middle East. He was a terrorist with a personal vendetta and that made him very dangerous.

Yehiya Abdal-Tif Ayyash was born on February 22, 1966, the eldest of three boys, to a family of field workers in the village of Rafat, at the western fringe of the old border that separated the Jewish state from the Hashemite Kingdom of Jordan. The elders of the village were no strangers to violence and guerrilla operations. Fatah units had used the area as a staging ground for hit-and-run attacks against Jewish agricultural settlements nearby. Israeli paratroopers often responded in kind on retaliatory strikes of their own. Rafat was the typical West Bank village—small, lower middle class, and beset by the politics and conflicts of Palestinian nationalism.

Many of the urban Palestinians from the large cities of Hebron, Nablus, Jerusalem, and Jenin looked down on the villagers as primitive. They were less versed in political reading than their urban counterparts and far too religious. Rafat was exactly such a village. With a population of three thousand inhabitants, Rafat looked nearly the same when Yehiya Ayyash began his career as a terrorist as it did when the Turks and British ruled the land. The Wali Mosque, the central nervous system of village life, is over eight hundred years old. Horses pull carts with hay and goods for sale in the market through the poorly paved main street in the center of the ascending village. Young boys wearing battered sandals guide flocks of sheep through the back alleys. By day, the smell of olive and beans adorn the village with a sweet and alluring bouquet, while at night trash is burned in the same manner as it has in Rafat for thousands of years. Many of the homes in the village still do not have running water or indoor facilities.

Ayyash's family was pious and close-knit; many of Rafat's natives were related to the Ayyash clan, though Islam was the bond that kept the family together. According to legend, religion was the cornerstone of Ayyash's life—even at an early age. He began studying the Koran and Islamic sciences at age six, and he received an award by the Islamic Trust in Jerusalem for his excellence in reading the Koran and memorizing its passages.

In 1985, Ayyash graduated the local high school in the village of Bidya, some three miles away from his home, with a high 92.8 percent matriculated average in nationwide examinations. After perfoming odd jobs around his village, he entered Bir Zeit University, just north of Ramallah, in 1987; there he studied electrical engineering. Bir Zeit University was long known in Shin Bet circles as a hotbed for Palestinian nationalism, and for the recruitment of upper-crust talent for the ranks of the liberation movements. Students talked politics, participated in low-level underground activity, and were either swept up in a movement or tossed aside for lack of political dedication. For years, Bir Zeit University was dominated by Arafat's Fatah faction. Fatah controlled the student body elections and the mood on campus.

Ayyash cared little for the political struggle or Fatah politics— village boys like Ayyash viewed the Fatah loyalists and their three-martinis-at-lunch commanders-in-exile as everything that was wrong with the Palestinian liberation movements. Hamas was a different story. Spiritual faith and the virtues of Islam were pure and honest. Hamas promised benevolence and salvation without corruption or nepotism. Getting an education in those tumultuous days of the Intifadah was no easy task. Bir Zeit University was often closed by student protests and Israeli closures. Students and faculty alike were often arrested and placed in administrative detention by the IDF and the Shin Bet. Nevertheless, Ayyash managed to complete his education in 1991, earning a bachelor of science degree with honors.

From the time he was a small child, Ayyash had a natural gift for tinkering and repairing anything mechanical. Family members brought him broken radios and TV sets, abandoning any hope that they'd ever work again, only to find that Ayyash was able to make the appliances work better than ever. During the Gulf War, for example, when the Iraqi SCUD barrages flew overhead en route to Tel Aviv and Ramat Gan and blackouts had cast the village in absolute darkness, the Ayyash home was with power. On a whim, Yehiya had rewired the house and hooked it up to a home-built generator he had put together from a discarded car battery and electrical odds and ends he had found while rummaging through the village garbage. Had he been born in a different place, or a different time, Yehiya Ayyash had the ability to become a star of Palestinian industry. But in the purgatory of the West Bank, where blood feuds were fought with religious fervor, genius and potential were commodities that men with guns and a price on their head rarely let out of their clutches.

Little is known of Ayyash's transformation from electrical engineer to "The Engineer." Information concerning his recruitment into Hamas and the Izzedine al-Qassam Brigade is sketchy. What is known is that Ayyash had long-term plans to escape the mindless violence and futureless existence of life under the Occupation. His dream was to travel abroad, earn his master's degree, and possibly work in Jordan or the Gulf states, where he could support his entire family and not have to worry about that knock on the door in the middle of the night that would place him handcuffed and hooded opposite a Shin Bet investigator.

Like any West Bank native, Ayyash feared and hated the Shin Bet. The *Shabakniks*, as the agents were known in the Territories, controlled every facet of day-to-day life. They could arrest on a whim, close down businesses and factories, and search people and homes without legal warrants. Anyone requesting a work permit or a building license needed military authorization, and all such requests were, in reality, approved or denied by the Shin Bet. When Yehiya Ayyash requested formal permission to study for his master's degree in Jordan, the Israeli authorities simply refused. There was nothing personal or security-related in the Shin Bet denial—Ayyash had never been arrested, nor was his family involved in subversive activity. Authorizing the request required nothing more than a rubber stamp and a preliminary background check. Refusal was nothing more than bureaucratic spite. In hindsight, that rubber stamp could have altered the course of Middle Eastern politics forever.

Ayyash's first known formal contacts with Hamas came after he received that fateful no from the Israeli military authorities. Withdrawn and depressed, Yehiya spent long hours at home reading and staring at the walls—too sad to be with others and too angry to work.[11] Vowing vengeance, he began to fuel his religious faith with the promise of retribution. Hamas leaders realized that Ayyash wasn't a natural-born killer. He wasn't psychopathic like many of the men who had achieved martyrdom in clashes with Israeli forces, and few believed he'd have the courage to pull the trigger in a running firefight with the undercover squads. Ayyash was highly intelligent with a chameleonlike appearance. He spoke fluent Hebrew and was well traveled. He was fair-skinned with a narrow face and average features; his teeth, unlike those of many of his fellow West Bank neighbors, were white and straight. Because of his electrical engineering degree, Ayyash was an obvious choice to become the al-Qassam's chief bomb builder. He could design circuits and produce reliable explosive devices from store-bought items that would not warrant undo attention from informants or the Shin Bet.

Most important, Ayyash was a teacher. The Brigade had dozens of men who could pull a trigger or toss a grenade, but men with the ability to disseminate knowledge, skill, and tradecraft was a missing commodity. "Charisma and intelligence," a retired Israeli special operations officer noted, "is a weapon system that can't be bought, smuggled, or assembled."[12]

As a Hamas cell, and later battalion, commander, Ayyash was an enigmatic leader. Unlike most of the other high-ranking officers within the al-Qassam apparatus, Yehiya married; his wife, Heyam, was a second cousin. In September 1992 he became a father when his son Bara'a was born. He possessed perhaps the most dangerous assets a man living in the shadows could own— links that could not be cut. His love for his family, his wife, and his newborn son were all-encompassing elements of his existence. Ayyash walked the fine line between military commander and dedicated family man. It was a conflict of enormous risk and emotional consequence. The young foot soldiers in his cells respected his sacrifice. Few among them, even those determined to die, would have forsaken the pleasures of a wife and the promise of a child for the struggle.

Ayyash managed to keep his Hamas ties covert, and few in Rafat knew of his work on behalf of Hamas or of his high-rank within the organization. Yet after the Ramat Efal incident he became a wanted man. Shin Bet visits to the village were frequent. Army attention to the village also intensified. Following the abduction of Nissim Toledano, there was no turning back. His life became a myriad of safe houses, caves, and the occasional late-night visits home to the one-story dwelling he shared with his parents for hurried intimate reunions with Heyam and the chance to play with Bara'a.

Ayyash's cell was, at first, delegated to minor operations and primitive strikes. One of the first operations he directed was the premeditated running-over of two Israeli men, Ofer Cohen and Ya'akov Bracha, on March 15, 1993, as they waited for a ride at a hitchhiking station and bus stop at Eli Junction halfway between Ramallah and Nablus near the ultra-right wing settlement of Kfar Tapuach. The driver, Shahar al-Nabulsi, had used his father's Mercedes to run over the two settlers and then escape to Nablus. At first, military and Shin Bet investigators working the incident were not sure if the double homicide was a terrorist crime or simply a hit-and-run accident—most Israelis killed on the roads, after all, were not killed by Hamas terrorists but by that lethal four-wheeled reality known as the Israeli motorist.

Following the murders of police officers Hazut and Yisrael, Ayyash received instruction to perpetrate a "large-scale" operation meant to drive home Israeli vulnerability. The murders of the two police officers was masterful according to Hamas planners. The front-page photos, showing the bullet-riddled police car and the two bloodied corpses covered by white sheets, had shocked many Israelis. The kidnappings, ambushes, and murders had penetrated the Israeli sense of security. Now that needed to be obliterated.

In a secret workshop somewhere near Nablus, Yehiya Ayyash worked on what he hoped would propel the name of Hamas to front pages around the world. Ayyash was just the man for the job, and his cell was just the group—they had yet to warrant full-scale interest from the Shin Bet and IDF. The plan was for the cell to perpetrate a massive car-bomb attack inside an Israeli city; according to intelligence reports gathered from Shin Bet interrogators months later the plan called for the crew to detonate a device in front of the Kirya, the sprawling IDF General Staff Headquarters and Ministry of Defense complex in the heart of downtown Tel Aviv, as well as attacks in Jerusalem's busy King George Street thoroughfare and the Beit Lid junction along the old Tel Aviv-Haifa highway.[13]

The bomb, built by Ayyash and attached to the fuel additional tanks inside a Volkswagen Transporter, was meant to kill scores. Built from explosives collected from grenades and other seized ordnance, it was connected to three large propane tanks and hooked up to a master control switch in the driver's control. One flip of the switch and an electronic charge completed the circuit that initiated the detonator and set off the device. If placed properly in a crowd of people, there was no telling what carnage such a device could produce.

Ayyash's plan was diabolical but failed to appreciate one important factor: reaching the intended targets would be impossible. Following the murders of the two traffic policemen, the territories were completely sealed off. The operation would have to be executed inside the Territories and Ayyash selected a target close to home. The Mehula Junction was one of those gas-station snack-bar landmarks that dotted the lengthy Jordan Valley Highway. It was a place where soldiers, settlers, and tour buses could stop, fuel up, and consume soft drinks and snacks. At times, hundreds of people were gathered in front of the road stop. It was a ripe target.

On April 16, 1993, Ayyash's faithful operative Shahar al-Nabulsi drove the booby-trapped Transporter west, from Nablus toward the desert hills of the Jordan Valley. Just after 1:00 A.M., al-Nabulsi swerved his vehicle in between two buses and initiated the explosive charge, detonating himself in a thunderous fireball of heat and shrapnel. The blast was so powerful that bits of al-Nabulsi's body were thrown a hundred yards away. The Transporter was obliterated in the explosion, but the force of the device was directed upward—and out—not in a 360-degree radius. Miraculously, the blast killed only al-Nabulsi and a young Palestinian who worked in the rest area. Twenty soldiers and a civilian were wounded in the attack.

To many of the Shin Bet investigators who raced to the Jordan Valley ground zero, it was déjà vu. They had seen suicide truck bombs in Lebanon, they had sifted through the remnants of the victims and the rubble in the needle-in-a-haystack search for the design of the device; and any bits and pieces of the bomber that could be identified in the crime lab. Suicide car bombs were a poor man's artillery shell, and they were used with great effectiveness in Lebanon by Hizballah. Lebanon was hell, however. It was a land void of human justice and morality. It was a land destined to be scorched by the fires of insanity.

Picking through the remnants of a suicide bombing was dirty and difficult work, and the fact that there was no suspect to question was frustrating to investigators sifting through the crime scene as was the fact that these men, used to field work and clandestine meetings with agents, were now picking through the pieces of carburetors, seat covers, and brain tissue. Suicide bombings were difficult for investigators—no motive, no clear and definitive answers to jot down in a report, and no confessions. Many of those searching the remnants of the Volkswagen Transporter were young, though the grim expressions and weathered faces made them look much older. They thought they knew the psychology of a terrorist—what drove a man to grab an AK-47 and rake a bus with indiscriminate fire. They couldn't comprehend the thought process behind a suicide attack. Was it cowardice or bravado? Fanaticism or desperation?

As one team of field agents illuminated bits of the twisted wreck in search for a wallet or an identity card so that a suspect file could be established, others enjoyed a fifteen-minute break, drank bottled water, and inhaled deeply with the soothing flow of nicotine racing through their veins. Paused amid the bloody mess and the search for an identity card for a quick drink of bottled water and the obligatory dose of nicotine, the agents did not talk to one another or share the required gallows humor that follows murder. Their mood was somber. Lebanon had come to Israel.

Israeli security officials downplayed the Mehula Junction bombing, and for good reason. The Israeli public was exhausted by the almost daily news reports of someone killed by Hamas. Creating panic over this new threat was not viewed as prudent— or politically wise for the Rabin administration. Peace talks with Arafat's Palestinians in Washington were proceeding slowly, though the secret backdoor channel in Oslo, through the mediation of Norwegian foreign minister Johan Jorgen Holst, was producing remarkable progress. For the first time in Israel's torrid history, the prospects for peace with the Palestinians appeared possible. Yet in order for the Israeli people to be able to digest the peace process—and digest making peace with Arafat—as something that most inside Israel could never even fathom; public opinion and the sense of public security was of paramount importance. Hamas would have to be humbled.

In Rafat and the surrounding villages, Ayyash moved about like a man with a price on his head. The Shin Bet had yet to turn the screws on Ayyash's family, though he knew that investigators were hauling more suspects to military compounds night after night. Men guilty of nothing would gladly confess to mass murder if it meant that the beatings and pressure would stop. Someone was bound to give up a name of someone who could give up a name, who might give up Ayyash. An interrogation was the peeling of layers from speculation and hunch until it became fact. How fast the layers were discarded depended on who was holding the information and who was trying to get at it. Ayyash knew that he was a wanted man after the Ramat Efal blast. He was now certain that the Israelis would not rest until he was arrested or eliminated.

Ya'akov Perry's Shin Bet was, indeed, on the trail of Ayyash, though the first priority was to arrest men with far more blood on their hands than the engineering student from Rafat. Some of the Izzedine al-Qassam foot soldiers and cell commanders on Perry's Most Wanted were mass murderers. They had killed cops and soldiers, Shin Bet agents, and even hookers. Spring was a busy season for the Shin Bet. Thousands of individuals were "interviewed"—some more seriously than others. Information was compiled, checked for authenticity, and rechecked. Undercover units mingled into town squares and city centers in order to eavesdrop on the local scuttlebutt. Perry received daily updates. Rabin was pleased by the pace of the ongoing investigations.

On June 6, 1993, on the twenty-sixth anniversary of the Israeli capture of Jerusalem, Prime Minister Rabin, Police Minister Moshe Shahal, and IDF Chief of Staff Ehud Barak convened a remarkable press conference. Rabin, never one to display emotion in public, especially a smile or any gestures of relief, seemed at ease and calm by being able to report on the massive sweep. The Shin Bet had arrested 124 hard-core Hamas operatives—most belonging to the Izzedine al-Qassam Brigade—in a night-long operation that, with speed and surprise, buckled the operational capability of Hamas.

Among those arrested was Mohammed Issa, a twenty-five-year-old newspaper editor from Jerusalem who commanded "The Secret Squad of Izzedine al-Qassam." The squad was formed in October 1992, weeks after Hamas signed its alliance with the Islamic Republic of Iran. It was designed to be a special operations unit of the Brigade tasked solely with targeting Israelis in uniform. Because the cell consisted of men from East Jerusalem, annexed by Israel a decade earlier, they all possessed "blue" Israeli identity cards, as opposed to the orange cards known by the locals as the *hawiyya* that residents of the Occupied Territories are forced to carry; these "citizens" were also entitled to yellow Israeli license plates. For nearly two months, the cell stalked Israeli soldiers in Jerusalem, attempting to monitor routines and select potential kidnap victims. The secret squad of Izzedine al-Qassam was responsible for the kidnapping and murder of Nissim Toledano as well as police officers Hazut and Yisrael. Their last act of bravado was the May 6 drive-by shooting of police Deputy Commander Shalom Guetta, at Bilu Junction near Rehovot, southeast of Tel Aviv. Although the cell emptied a magazine of 9mm ammunition into Guetta's car, he managed to somehow survive and provide investigators with a partial description of the vehicle involved.

News of the arrests was the sole story covered by television and radio broadcasts that evening—even the Arabic-language broadcasts dedicated aboveboard coverage to what some journalists called a fatal blow to Hamas. Yehiya Ayyash had heard of the arrests earlier, when a messenger left word with a contact that the garage in Nablus where the Ramat Efal and Mehula Junction bombs had been built had been raided by the Shin Bet. The Hebrew daily papers began publishing stories of the "Samaria Cell" and some of their exploits; several low-ranking members of the cell had also been picked up in the Shin Bet dragnet. A wanted poster bearing the likeness of some twenty Hamas commanders not arrested in the June sweep was posted at military checkpoints throughout the Territories. Soldiers were expected to memorize the faces on the poster and stop anyone bearing a resemblance. To many of the eighteen-year-old conscripts who disdained the police duty they were relegated to carrying out, it would have been impossible to identify Arafat himself had he driven up to them in a beat up Subaru heading into Israel. The same held true for the middle-aged reservists. Although wary of Hamas gunmen and other threats, they weren't detectives, and their thoughts drifted back and forth between their annual forty-five-day stints and businesses and families forced to leave behind. The checkpoints were porous funnels, and Ayyash made full use of them to leapfrog back and forth between Rafat and other safe houses, even though *his* photo was one of the clearest in the poster.

Ayyash knew that he would have to sit tight, avoid arrest, and await his next assignment. Rumors of a peace deal between Arafat and Rabin had filtered through the villages of the West Bank like news of a stock crash hitting Wall Street. Those who feared the end of the struggle panicked and those who vowed to fight volunteered. The ranks of the Izzedine al-Qassam were soon replenished by fresh new faces, electrified by the chance to fight the Israelis and the treacherous Arafat on one holy battle-field.

Notes

[1]"Hamas Secret Units," *Intelligence Newsletter*, no. 209, January 20, 1993.

[2]Ibid.

[3]Haim A. Raviv, *"Orvim Le'Hussein,"* *Bamachane*, February 10, 1993, p. 18.

[4]"Hamas Embassy in Teheran?" *Mideast Mirror*, October 7, 1992, p. 15.

[5]"The Ten Fundamentalist Camps," *Intelligence Newsletter*, no. 209, January 20, 1993.

[6]Interview, Ramallah, May 1992, with Lieutenant M., a Border Guard EOD officer.

[7]Interview, Lieutenant (Ret.) J., New York City, September 9, 1998.

[8]Nadav Ze'evi, *"Bizayon Be'Kfar A'nza,"* *Ma'ariv Weekend Supplement*, March 11, 1998, p. 14.

[9]Bill Hutman and David Rudge, "Search Continues for Agent's Killers," *The Jerusalem Post*, January 5, 1993, p. 1.

[10]Yuval Peleg, *"Nuru Be'Shenotam,"* *Yediot Aharonot*, March 31, 1993, p. 3.

[11]John Donnelly, "Israel's Most Wanted: The Elusive Engineer," *The Miami Herald*, December 23, 1994, p. 1A.

[12]Interview, September 9, 1998.

[13]Michael Rotem, "Arrest of Hamas Terrorists Foiled Massive Car Bomb Attacks," *The Jerusalem Post*, June 7, 1993, p. 1.

Chapter 3

The Other Sons
of Abraham

There were only so many claims that three of the world's top religions could stake on the narrow strip of barren and mountainous territory between the Jordan River and the Mediterranean Sea. Yet Christians, Jews, and Muslims all claimed exclusive rights over the land of Abraham, Isaac, and Jacob, the land of Jesus, and the land from where Muhammad ascended to heaven. Peace has always been a fleeting proposition in the Holy Land for that very reason: too many religions, and religious souls, claiming exclusive ownership of the same patch of earth. Yet in no city was this impasse more evident and more volatile than in the ancient city of Hebron.

Hebron isn't a center for commerce or the arts, nor is it a trading route perched conveniently on the banks of a mighty river. Hebron is a city of neither grand beauty nor particular comfort. Built on a series of hills some thirty kilometers south of Jerusalem, it is a twisting and crowded city, known for two diverse though intertwining facets of the human condition—religious zeal and ferocious hatred. Hebron is a pious ground zero where the disciples of two religions have declared a holy war on each another.

The name Hebron is derived from the Hebrew word *haver*, or "friend," referring to Abraham, who many consider to be the first mortal close enough with the Almighty to be considered God's friend. Abraham, in fact, is the focal point of much of the hatred and indiscriminate bloodshed that has plagued the city for the past two thousand years. As described in Genesis, chapter 23, the patriarch Abraham purchased the Cave of Machpelah from Ephron the Hittite for four hundred silver shekels as a family burial plot. Abraham, patriarch to both Jews and Arabs, secured the tomb for his wives, Sarah, Rebecca, and Leah, though Isaac and Jacob are also buried there. According to Jewish beliefs, Adam and Eve are buried under the cave, in Hebron. Hebron is mentioned eighty-seven times in the Old Testament; both King Saul and King David were crowned in Hebron. Part of the Kingdom of Judah that fell to the Babylonians in 586, it is the oldest Jewish city in the world.

Hebron is known by the Arabic moniker Al-Khalil, which also means "friend." Abraham was also the husband of Hagar and father of Ishmael, who is Isaac's half brother. Muslims have laid claim to the Machpelah cave as a holy site of *their* own. With both Jews and later Muslims claiming exclusive preference to the Tomb of the Patriarch's mourning rites, conflict was all but inevitable. This conflict over ownership and exclusivity of worshipping rights in the City of Friendship stems from an ancient feud of birthrights. To this day, Abraham's sons still have not learned to live as brothers.

There has always been a Jewish presence in Hebron, but following the Six-Day War, settlers pitched tents and bought property inside the city and in the surrounding hills. They built the town of Kiryat Arba and watched it grow from a few caravans in the early 1970s into a sprawling settlement of around six thousand inhabitants. It is now a suburb of Hebron, which is home to some 120,000 Arabs—a Palestinian city that has become a hotbed of nationalism and, during the Intifadah, Islamic fundamentalism. When five hundred Jewish settlers chose to live in the remnants of Beit Hadassah, in the center of town, they needed protection.

The Israeli soldiers who were charged with safeguarding the small Jewish community in Hebron were sometimes confused about the tour of duty they had pulled. Many felt that they were there more to protect the Arabs from Jewish violence than visa versa. The Jews of Hebron were boisterous and cocky as they strutted through the streets of the city. Men with plaid shirts, fringed prayer garments hanging out of their jeans, and skullcaps carried Uzis as they walked through the center of town toward the Avraham Avinu Synagogue at the Tomb to worship. To them, ownership was far more than nine-tenths of the law—it was God's will, and it was enforced with the cold blue steel of a submachine gun. Anyone who threatened them, looked at them the wrong way, or challenged their Wild West approach to the Occupation received an eyeball-to-barrel confrontation. Even pregnant women shepherding six and seven children through town carried a purse in one hand and an M-16 assault rifle in the other.

A good number of the Jewish residents of the city itself, and of Kiryat Arba, spoke poor Hebrew with a distinctive accent: many had come from the spiritual vacuum of Brooklyn, New York, where the revival of religious passions, combined with government grants for housing, made the return to Zion a convenient and spiritual practicality. Many of these transplants from Kings County were as foreign to the trials and tribulations of Middle East life as one could imagine, though the chance for the oppressed and the often misunderstood to suddenly be in charge held tremendous appeal. The Uzi brought power, prestige, and the chance for a role reversal. The victim was now the ruler, and any Arab transgression could spark the vengeance of those looking for an easy victim.

Because Hebron's history had been one of hatred and massacre, revenge was something of a passion in the city. In 1517 the Ottoman Turks conquered Hebron and marked their victory by raping and killing a good portion of the Jewish community. On August 23, 1929, an Arab mob perpetrated the notorious Hebron massacre in which sixty-seven Jewish men, women, and children were killed and dismembered; British forces, the new landlords of the city, watched in passive indifference. When the first settlers checked in to the Park Hotel in April 1968 in order to reestablish a Jewish presence in the city, "1929" was a motivating factor. They vowed never to let Arab sabers drive them out again.

The residents of Hebron and Kiryat Arba boasted that they feared very little. On September 13, 1993, however, their worst of all possible fears, an Israeli peace with the Palestinians, was broadcast into their homes live on national television from a sun-soaked garden in Washington, D.C. Hollywood couldn't have cast a more beautiful backdrop to one of history's most remarkable scenes, a snippet from a Greek tragedy that seemed to have finally found a conclusion. After fifty-plus years of warfare, hatred, terrorism, retaliation, massacres, and political double-dealing, the impossible had taken center stage.

Prime Minister Yitzhak Rabin, Israel's venerable old soldier, handled the stress of the job the way he had for most of his life: by chain-smoking cigarettes. It was a pardonable vice for a man who had dedicated his entire life to the establishment and security of his country. As a youngster he had fought in Israel's underground army, the Haganah, during the darkest hours of Israel's 1948 War of Independence. He had led a commando brigade in the bitter fight to reopen the treacherous mountain roads and passes leading to the Jewish state's besieged capital, Jerusalem. Rabin had fought many a battle—as a company commander, brigade commander, and, in 1967, as chief of staff of the Israel Defense Forces. He had fought in the trenches, with a Sten machine gun in one hand and a dagger in the other, and he had led campaigns, ordering men killed and sending others to their deaths from behind a mahogany desk, either as defense minister or prime minister. On this bright fall morning in Washington, D.C., Rabin was about to face perhaps his toughest test as a soldier.

Of all the remarkable events that have transpired during the Arab-Israeli conflict, few have been as exciting or bizarre as the signing of the Oslo Peace Accords on the White House lawn on September 13, 1993. The fact that Israeli Prime Minister Rabin and the Chairman of the Palestine Liberation Organization, Yasir Arafat, were committing themselves to peaceful coexistence between Israel and the Palestinians was mind-boggling. No one man symbolized terrorism, wanton murder, and revolutionary intransigence more than Arafat. When he ventured to the United States in November 1974 to address the General Assembly of the United Nations, his military fatigues, black-and-white checkered kaffiyeh, and "empty" brown-leather pistol holster bolstered his image as a rogue revolutionary.

Rabin and Arafat were sworn enemies, and both had tried, in their own ways, to have the other killed. In March 1985, Arafat sanctioned a large-scale seaborne terrorist assault on the Israeli Ministry of Defense in the heart of downtown Tel Aviv. The assassination of Rabin was the mission objective; but the raiders, traveling on a rusty Algerian freighter, never made it to the Israeli shore, and many were killed when their boat, the *S.S. Attavirus*, was sunk by Israeli Navy missile boats. In October of that same year, Rabin signed the orders unleashing a surprise air raid by Israel Air Force jets against PLO headquarters in

Tunis. The objective of the raid was, ostensibly, the removal of Arafat. Although the jets missed Arafat by minutes, more than eighty others were killed in the attack.

Arafat and Rabin were not in Washington that beautiful morning because old age had softened their political stances or ideologies. Nor had American president Bill Clinton managed to convince both leaders to, borrowing from the John Lennon song, just "Give Peace a Chance." Rabin and Arafat were prisoners of pragmatism and of the uncontrolled events following an instance of poor national judgment.

In 1991, Israel had been forced to the negotiating table by U.S. President George Bush. (Ending the Arab-Israeli madness had been a footnote to America's victory in the Gulf War and its leap to the forefront as the world's sole superpower.) Israel's governing Likud coalition, right-wing stalwarts led by the wily Yitzhak Shamir, had acted indecisively and without direction in the wake of Saddam Hussein's SCUD barrage on Tel Aviv; the Israelis had neither dealt with the Iraqi missile preemptively, nor had they retaliated once the missiles began raining down on Holon and Ramat Gan. Instead they permitted American and later European crews to fire Patriot surface-to-air missiles, effectively defending Israeli airspace from outside aggression—something Israeli leaders vowed they would never let happen. Full-scale American involvement in Middle East diplomacy was now unavoidable.

The PLO, for its part, submitted to a negotiated settlement with Israel for political survival. Arafat, in supporting Saddam Hussein, had led his liberation movement down the path of bankruptcy, disrepair, and insignificance. The Gulf state Arabs and the Saudis, Arafat's chief financial patrons, were outraged over his support of a conflict that the emirs, sheikhs, and sultans interpreted as a conflict of pure survival. Exacerbating Arafat's woes was the fact that the Kuwaitis, upon their own liberation, quickly expelled a majority of the Palestinians who had lived in the kingdom and had made it run. Arafat was less concerned with the personal plight of these professionals and their families, once again forced to become refugees in transit camps in eastern Jordan, than he was with the fact that the taxes that these men paid to the PLO was a significant source of funding for the organization's day-to-day activities. An end to the conflict with Israel—which meant accepting whatever was in Israel's best interest to offer—was Arafat's sole means of extricating himself and his organization from what was destined to become one of the bloodiest and least-successful national liberation movements in history.

Yet there was more than just the Gulf War to thank for the two years of secret negotiations and closed-door meetings that led to the highly charged ceremony on the White House lawn. There was Hamas. The Israeli public, the Israeli security apparatus, and Israel's leadership had been humbled and exhausted by the war against Hamas, and some solution, even a deal with the devil itself, was important. Hamas had the potential to rival the PLO for popularity and military prowess, and that daunted Israeli officials. Many in Rabin's inner circle, especially Foreign Minister Shimon Peres, realized that the time was right for a deal with Arafat. Cutting a deal with one's foe when he was down and desperate was sound business.

Arafat, too, had Hamas heavy on his heart and mind when he accepted the accords with Israel. For nearly thirty years Arafat's PLO had been the only show in town—there was no alternative Palestinian liberation movement. The rejectionist front of Damascus-based dinosaurs was good at rhetoric and the occasional spectacular act of violence, but nothing lasting would ever be achieved under the flag of the Popular Front, the Democratic Front, or Abu Nidal's Black June. Hamas had rewritten the rulebook; they presented a definitive and very real political challenge to the PLO's claim to be the one true voice of the Palestinian nation. Hamas was scoring victory after victory in university elections in Hebron, Bir Zeit, and Nablus, and their benevolent social infrastructure was winning the movement new converts on a daily basis. Peace with Israel was Arafat's last gasp as a player on the main stage of the Arab-Israeli conflict.

Getting the key players to the banks of the Potomac was no easy task. It took the chessboard maneuvering of numerous diplomats and statesmen to get the two men to stand beside each other in front of three thousand spectators and an international audience of several hundred million; several last minute snags threatened to cancel the historic proceedings even to the end. Arafat, master of the theater of the bizarre, had wanted to wear his gun to the ceremony and then, in a display of how the guerrilla had turned peacemaker, he had planned to unclasp the brown leather holster, produce the trusted Smith and Wesson he had carried for some thirty years, and then hand it to President Clinton. Clinton, Rabin, and the Secret Service immediately quashed the display. Rabin, too, had objections. He had opposed allowing Arafat to wear his khaki uniform to the ceremony, and had opposed even mentioning the PLO. Rabin was apprehensive about being in the same room with Arafat, let alone the faint thought of the two men locking hands in a handshake. The mood and the bizarre nature of the full-circle turnaround was a bit much for the old soldier. President Clinton, who had read from the Book of Joshua before dawn to gather inspiration, greatly respected Rabin's poise and composure.

The purpose of the ceremony was the signing of the Declaration of Principles, though the spectacle was as important as the diplomatically worded contract. It was a momentously memorable moment for Israelis and Palestinians alike, joining forces to forge a partnership for the next century. There were scores of problems facing the peace accords, legions of opposition, and the potential for violence to quickly eradicate the years of diplomatic efforts, sacrifice, and bloodshed that had led up to this unforgettable meeting. Nevertheless, when the speeches were complete and the posturing settled, as had been planned in a twenty-six-page script prepared by the White House and the State Department, Clinton shook Rabin's hand, then shook Arafat's, and then slowly slid away as the two men clasped hands in a gesture of difficult surrender and courageous beginning. History literally was sealed with a handshake.

In Tel Aviv, in Herzliya, and in other cities and towns throughout Israel there were those who welcomed the treaty signing with deep-felt emotion. Parents with small children embraced the prospects of peace and a "normal" coexistence with heart-racing enthusiasm as they envisioned a Middle East without the Arab-Israeli conflict hanging over their heads, dictating their futures. Similar sentiments were shared by residents of Ramallah, East Jerusalem, Nablus, and even Hebron. People yearned for an end to the turmoil and tragedy, and while years of occupation had taught them to be apprehensive toward any political developments, the signs of legitimacy were encouraging.

For many others, though, the price of peace was simply too high. There seemed to be great risk in moderation. How could generations of hatred and war be erased with the stroke of a fountain pen? Too much blood had been spilled. Rapprochement with the Jews was considered blasphemy by many Muslims, and right-wing Jews viewed surrendering land to the Palestinians as tantamount to going against the word of God. Both Rabin and Arafat, nervous enough about sharing the world stage—together—and having to embark on this dramatic new course, feared that violence would stain the agreement with the blood of the innocent.

Indeed, despite the unbelievable meeting on the White House lawn that sunny September morning, the world really had *not* changed before everyone's eyes. Yes, the reluctant, almost painful handshake between Arafat and Rabin may have seemed to indicate that swords might soon be beaten into ploughshares. True, in some homes, especially in Israel, the celebration ceremonies were mind-boggling. Ever since the arrival by plane of Egyptian President Anwar as-Sadat in March 1978, Israelis had looked forward to the day when Arab leaders would disembark at Ben-Gurion International Airport for state visits. But Arafat wasn't viewed as a Palestinian national leader. Rather, he was seen as a poster boy for hijackings and bombings. He possessed the face, the characteristics, and the murderous double-talk of a terrorist straight out of Hollywood casting. So, in many other dwellings there was little jubilation over the handshake, and Israelis did not venture into the streets waving Palestinian flags. Erasing the images of the massacres would not be accomplished with the joining of two hands in Washington. Peace required a national reevaluation of self. It required brutally honest introspection and it required vigilance.

In Gaza, where the sun had turned the late afternoon into an oven, the streets were empty as every TV set in the Strip was tuned to that remarkable event. Watching the ceremonies live via satellite was a squad of stone-faced soldiers from an elite undercover unit. They rubbed their eyes in disbelief and exhaustion. These nineteen- and twenty-year-olds had seen the peace process from a completely different field of vision. They had not been in Norway, sipping tea and discussing details of a diplomatic treaty, but they had played a part in the scenario that now found Arafat and Rabin standing together on the White House lawn. They had fought the brutal war, seizing suspects, shooting it out with Arafat's men and the holy warriors of al-Qassam. They had seen the struggle escalate from the Intifadah with kids throwing rocks and Molotov cocktails into a full-scale guerrilla war that made the troubles in Northern Ireland seem like a game of soccer. As the squad watched the newscast and listened to the "expert" opinion of pundits who believed they knew what they were talking about, the veterans of the Arab-Israeli gutter war got dressed for work. They affixed mustaches over pale lips with spirit gum, covered blond curls with kaffiyeh and shrouds, made sure their mini-Uzis had two thirty-round clips of ammunition ready, and checked that the laser aim-point device on their compact and lethal weapon was working. The soldiers didn't view the peace deal as a victory or as a defeat. They cared little for the trappings of title. To them, any handshake or agreement that pulled them out of Gaza was God's work.

In the Strip, as another night of work was about to commence, the men of the IDF's Samson unit donned Arab gowns and mini-Uzis as they entered the camps in search of the elusive ghosts of Izzedine al-Qassam. In Ramallah, men wearing red kaffiyehs walked nervously through side roads to drop off a cryptic message alongside a garbage can. In Kiryat Arba, men oiled their government-issue assault rifles and submachine guns and met in synagogues to discuss the sacrilege and possible recourse.

Darkness came early to the West Bank that fateful September night. The mood inside the Territories was one of disbelief and foreboding. As wrenching as the sight of Rabin shaking Arafat's hand was to most Israelis, so was the actuality of Arafat shaking Rabin's hand an abomination to many. Among the elderly, those who had hoped to one day regain the land that had been seized from them could not bring themselves to believe that the two hands clasping one another in Washington might one day reverse the wrongs they had endured for so long.

The middle-aged and the middle class knew that the situation in the Middle East was volatile. Political revolutions were usually carried out at the barrel end of a gun, or after there were no more throats to slit. Change was uncertain, and change got people killed. The younger generation, the foot soldiers of the Intifadah (which had actually seemed to achieve the potential for Palestinian independence by wearing down the mighty Israelis), were simply numbed by the images flashing on their television screens. They had been born under the Occupation and had expected to die under the yoke of the Israeli military. Yet they knew their street-fighting skills would still be required. No army simply abandons the quagmire without last licks and a final reckoning.

Life on the run had given Yehiya Ayyash time to hone his bomb-making skills with applications specially designed to meet the needs of the Izzedine al-Qassam Brigade. So far his track record was less than admirable. Although designed to kill hundreds by spraying a lethal shower of shrapnel some 360 degrees for more than two hundred feet, the car bomb in Ramat Efal destroyed nothing more than a yellow police robot and shattered some glass. The Mehula Junction car bomb, parked properly alongside a bus, could have torn a destructive path so wide that virtually all on board the targeted vehicle should have either been killed or seriously wounded. Each device, designed and built by Ayyash, required perfection, as did the tactics by which they were deployed.

Ayyash was always tinkering with explosive devices that could be produced fast, cheap, and with store-bought ingredients. After all, Israel was not Lebanon and brigade members did not enjoy a never ending supply of TNT or Semtex. Until Ayyash entered the scene, Palestinian terrorists had built improvised explosive devices by cramming a pipe with hundreds of match heads supported by specially treated cotton; the pipe was fitted to a 1.5-volt battery or larger, and the resulting electrical charge used to ignite and initiate the detonator and cause the match heads to explode in a fireball of destruction. The blasts these homemade devices produced were not large, but if you were unfortunate enough to be anywhere near the device when it exploded, chances were you would end up dead.

In the winter of 1993, Ayyash experimented with a formula of acetone and detergent that Israeli bomb-disposal officers found innovative. The moonshine TNT packed a powerful punch—similar to though less stable than industrial dynamite. The usefulness of such a device was clear: Not only would anyone with a twenty-shekel note in his hand be in a position to purchase all the necessary ingredients needed to make such a bomb, but the technology and tools were so commonplace that Ayyash could teach legions of Izzedine al-Qassam operatives to become "engineers."

In December 1993, Ayyash and his trusted deputy, Ali Osman Atssi, tested this new design on an IDF patrol in the village of Zawiya, only two miles north of Rafatt. The attack was a failure. The acetone mixture had failed to detonate once the electronic circuit was complete, and the timing device, meant to initiate the blast, had failed too. A few weeks later, however, in January 1994, Ayyash and Atssi tested a newer and more lethal homemade bomb. The device was planted on an IDF firing range near Rosh Ha'ayin, some five miles west of Rafatt. The two had snuck into the seemingly secured IDF facility at night and had planted the bomb, like a landmine, underneath a mat on which soldiers firing their weapons would lie in the prone position. By lying on the mat, the soldier unwittingly activated the detonation mechanism, removing the safety and priming it for action; the moment pressure was removed from the mechanism, the circuit was completed and the bomb went off. Two soldiers were critically wounded by Ayyash's invention, though IDF and Shin Bet investigators kept the incident hush-hush, fearing that disclosing the lax security at the base would undermine morale and, perhaps, invite other attacks against poorly defended military installations.

Booby-trapped devices and trip-wire landmines, the kind Ayyash tested in January 1994, were classic Hizballah tactics. The Lebanese Shiite guerrillas had killed scores of Israeli soldiers in insidious attacks with roadside devices. Yet before Ayyash could produce an assembly line of booby-trap bombs, a

storm of rage would engulf the Territories. The rules of engagement were about to change dramatically in the war waged by
Hamas against Israel.

It had been a cool winter by Middle Eastern standards, and rainfall had been plentiful. The hills around Hebron, usually barren
for eleven months of the year, had begun to blossom in a mi-
raculous explosion of green surrounded by oceans of white and
purple wildflowers. The promise of the Oslo Accords had provided many with the hope that spring would bring about an
end to the killing. Israeli forces were to begin withdrawing from
Jericho and Gaza shortly. For the first time in recent memory,
the Moslem holy month of Ramadan was a festive one.

Early on the morning of February 25, 1994, some seven hundred children and adults had gathered inside Hebron's Ibrahim
Mosque at the Cave of the Patriarchs. The sun had yet to rise
over the jagged peaks across the Jordan River to the east, and a
slight drizzle had begun. At 5:20 A.M. a man wearing olive-drab
fatigues and sporting captain bars on his epaulets and a purple
sports bag over his shoulder approached the northeast entrance
of the mosque. He calmly walked up to the guard on duty and
demanded to be let into the usually off-limits prayer area. He
had already passed through an Israeli Army checkpoint where
four soldiers, pulling the last hours of night duty, waved him
in. The Arab guard on duty knew the man was a resident of
Kiryat Arba. He had seen him before around the no-man's-land
that separated Muslim and Jewish worshippers at the shared
holy site. He knew the man was a fervent supporter of the militant Kach movement.

Mohammed Suleiman Abu Sarah made every attempt to keep
the officer out of the building, but there was little he could do.
"It is forbidden," Abu Sarah told the captain. But in a city run
by the IDF, there was little the unarmed Arab could do. As he
tried to resist the captain, a man wearing a yarmulke hit him

with the metal stock of his Galil assault rifle, knocking him to the ground. Abu Sarah was lucky. His life was spared.

That man from Kiryat Arba was Dr. Baruch Goldstein, a Brooklyn-born native and a physician who, one Friday morning during the month of Ramadan and the Jewish festival of Purim, simply snapped. Throughout history, men seeking spiritual salvation had traveled to the Holy Land only to succumb to passion and insanity. But Goldstein had crossed the invisible line of mental health armed with an assault rifle capable of firing 550 rounds per minute.

The mosque was packed to capacity. Cradling his weapon, Goldstein watched as the prayer services commenced. Worshippers knelt on plastic mats, eyes closed, as they offered their devotion to God, foreheads touching the ground in respect. Without warning, the physician peered through the sights of his IDF assault rifle, squinted his left eye to lock down on his targets, and, with the fire-selector switched to semiautomatic, he began to squeeze the trigger. Goldstein's barrage was not indiscriminate—he was taking aim for head shots. Blood sprayed on walls and on prayer carpets. Pandemonium ensued. Those attempting to flee stepped over the dead and the dying. Children screaming in anguish sought their fathers who, covered in blood and paralyzed by fear and disbelief, watched their sons killed before their eyes. According to survivors, it was impossible to tell who was hit and who wasn't because everyone was covered in blood.

Goldstein's murderous spree was methodical. When one thirty round magazine of ammunition was spent, he inserted a fresh clip into his assault rifle and continued firing in deliberate bursts. Goldstein took great care not to waste ammunition. He had brought seven magazines with him that fateful Friday morning—210 lethal 5.56 mm bullets—and in 10 minutes of incessant gunfire he managed to squeeze off 110 rounds. As Goldstein removed a spent clip from the red-hot barrel of the

Galil, a mob that had taken cover behind a wall rushed him in one desperate attempt to end the madness. Before he could insert a fresh magazine in his assault rifle, Dr. Baruch Goldstein was cornered by the mob and bludgeoned to death with a fire extinguisher. Goldstein's end was brutal. The angry mob ripped the Brooklyn-born physician's body to shreds.

Just as chaotic was the attempt to rush the wounded to local hospitals. The sound of gunfire and the screams of the victims alerted Israeli forces, who, faced with a human stampede of some seven hundred frantic souls, panicked; some of the soldiers posted at the Tomb, fearing that they were the targets, fired at the crowds. There was a mad scramble to ferry those suffering from horrendous gunshot wounds to the emergency room. Parking lots turned into triage centers. Dr. Goldstein's one-man crusade had been an efficient one. Some fifty Palestinians had been killed that Friday morning and more than seventy had been seriously wounded.

Throughout Israel, pagers and cell phones were ringing madly with news of the killings. Prime Minister Rabin, Foreign Minister Peres, Shin Bet director Ya'akov Perry, chief of staff Lieutenant General Ehud Barak, and O/C Central Command Major General Danny Yatom all began their final day of the work week living through their worst nightmare. Bad news travels fast, and reports from the Hebron massacre raced throughout Israel—and the Occupied Territories. By the time the news crews, journalists, U.N. officials, and even U.S. State Department consular officers had made their way from Tel Aviv and Jerusalem to the scene, a small army of Shin Bet investigators and military intelligence officers were attempting to piece together details of the insanity. Seasoned counterintelligence veterans, men who had thought they had seen it all, were shocked by the carnage. IDF chief of staff Barak, Israel's most decorated soldier and a special operations dynamo who had literally written the manual on missions behind enemy lines, was horrified by the bloody mess, calling it "thunder on a clear day."[1]

Immediately following the massacre there was inevitable talk of an Israeli conspiracy behind the killings. The question was raised about why the sentries at the Cave of the Patriarchs had fired at the crowd of fleeing Palestinians rather than at Goldstein; there were also unsubstantiated rumors that a second gunman had been party to the bloodbath. Inevitably, however, the Hebron massacre was a resonating defeat for the Shin Bet, whose national responsibilities included both Arab and Jewish terrorist groups. The Shin Bet should have known of Goldstein's intentions—as a fervent supporter of assassinated rabbi Meir Kahane's Kach movement, he was a known subversive with a violent streak. Days before the killing he is reported to have told a friend that he was "preparing for a massacre." Kiryat Arba, like Hebron, was teeming with informants and helpers who passed information to case officers and agents. News of Goldstein's intentions never reached the proper channels. Ominously, the man heading the Shin Bet's Non-Arab Anti-Subversive Division was Carmi Gillon, a noted Shin Bet expert on the radical Jewish underground movements.

Throughout the Territories, and even throughout Israel's Arab population, news of the killings sparked outrage and its inevitable byproduct: violence. In the West Bank and the Gaza Strip, some 250 Palestinians were injured in clashes with Israeli forces. In Nazareth and even in Jaffa, in the shadows of the Tel Aviv skyline, mobs of protesters battled police. Israel's Arabs had never resorted to violence en masse before.

In Kiryat Arba, however, news of the massacre was greeted with celebration. The annual Purim Parade, through the main thoroughfare of the city, carried on as if nothing had happened, even though the Israeli military presence around the hilltop community had increased tenfold. Some of the town's residents, pressed by reporters, considered Goldstein's murderous spree to be an act of tremendous self-sacrifice and giving to the Jewish people. "We should kill five hundred, not fifty," a settler screamed as he attempted to assault a Palestinian journalist.[2]

On February 27, the headline of the Israeli daily *Ma'ariv* summed up the national mood toward the massacre: "The Massacre, the Neglect, the Outrage." To many in Israel, Goldstein's massacre represented a minefield separating those who supported the peace process and those who were vehemently against it. For Hamas, the massacre represented opportunity.

Even though negotiations between the PLO and the Israelis started out tedious and sometimes even petty, the majority of Palestinians living in the West Bank and Gaza preferred slow peace talks to none at all. Meanwhile, the Hebron massacre became a lightning rod for Hamas. At a time when the movement was taking a backseat to Arafat and the Oslo Accords, Hebron was the fundamentalists' Pearl Harbor and Alamo wrapped up into one highly charged package. In response to Goldstein's murderous rampage, Hamas leaders vowed revenge—few in the Territories, or inside Shin Bet headquarters, doubted their sincerity or their abilities. In communiqués hand-delivered to wire service reporters throughout the Territories, the Izzedine al-Qassam Brigade called for five acts of vengeance that would commence at the culmination of the traditional forty days of Muslim mourning and prayer.

As a high-ranking battalion commander in the Izzedine al-Qassam Brigade, Yehiya Ayyash knew that some sort of military response to the Hebron massacre would be forthcoming. This was a crime that demanded swift and unforgiving punishment. But Ayyash was not allowed to commence an offensive on his own. He could select targets, pinpoint times and locations, and determine the means, but, according to a Jordanian intelligence official, "He was permanently at a traffic stop waiting for either the red or green light. When he had a red light, he did what all law-abiding citizens do. He stopped. When the green light was issued, though, it meant free reign and great liberty to inflict as much damage as humanly possible."[3]

The orders to mobilize Ayyash's cell came via fax, from either Teheran or Damascus, Shin Bet officials believe, disseminated through a third country with direct phone links to Israel and the Territories and then handed down to its final recipient via a long list of messengers. One would receive the message from a political director and leave it in a dead drop, somewhere public, where another operative would retrieve it and deliver it to a third dead drop, who would then pick up the note and deliver it personally to Ayyash. The last link in the chain was the most trusted member of the cell—usually the second in command, for he was, in reality, the only person who knew where Ayyash would be at any given time. It was a highly circuitous method for transmitting operational directives, but it was secure, and security was sacrosanct to Hamas.

To avenge the Hebron massacre Hamas would enact suicide bombings against the very lifeline of Israeli society: its ability to move from point A to point B. The attacks would be indiscriminate and unforgiving. When the order was received to avenge Hebron, Ayyash went into action. There were devices to design and construct, and martyrs to recruit who would bring the war directly to the enemy.

How does one convince a man that it is his obligation to sit inside a car packed to capacity with propane tanks, nails, other bits and pieces of shrapnel, and an explosive charge that will incinerate himself and possibly hundreds of people around him? Initially when Hamas adopted the suicide bomber strategy, it feared that finding recruits might be difficult. After all, dying in a hail of Ya'ma'm fire was a glorious way to achieve paradise; blowing yourself up amid a crowd of civilians was far less appealing to those seeking legend status in one last act of ballistic bravado. Following the Hebron massacre, Izzedine al-Qassam

operatives, known in the vernacular as "watchers," began combing the mosques and Islamic learning centers in search of men
who were dedicated to the principles of Islam as well as loners,
distant from cliques and groups of friends, individuals who had
minimum job prospects and even less chance of finding a suit-
able wife. Headhunters seek out the talented and the gifted. Izzedine al-Qassam targeted the hopeless.

Those selected for possible recruitment were screened by
Majd officers and examined for possible links to either Arafat's
Fatah or the Shin Bet. The "pitch," or recruitment strategy, was
a slow and methodical mind game. At first, known Hamas political officers embraced the potential bomber in public, inside a
mosque or prayer center, providing him with a sense of belonging and importance. Many of the young men on the Izzedine
al-Qassam shortlist for bomber hopefuls had never felt
important before. They had done poorly in school, were from
large, poor families where they were often lost in the shuffle,
and had suffered from years of anonymous mediocrity. Being
unimportant and unable to fight one's way out of the misery of
occupation and poverty was a recipe for producing the human
vehicle that would deliver twenty-five kilograms of explosives
into a crowd of people.

Once a potential bomber was hooked and his security check
came back clean, he was introduced into the ranks of an Izzedine
al-Qassam cell as a potential operative. The bomber-to-be was
told of his talents and virtues, and of the very special job that
the organization's commanders had envisioned for him. "There
is a very unique operation that only you can carry out," potential bombers were told. "It requires great courage and incredible
sacrifice." After being indoctrinated by prayer and shown endless videotapes of brigade operatives lurking throughout the Occupied Territories en route to engagements with Zionist forces,
the recruits are gradually made aware of the rewards awaiting
those who martyr themselves in the holy struggle against the

Jews. Among other things, they are promised that seventy-two virgins will greet them upon their arrival in paradise, and that they will drink from flowing rivers of honey. Dropouts from the suicide-bombing program have told Shin Bet and police investigators that the Mujahadeen are also promised places of honor in paradise, near Allah and his prophets.[4]

The delivery system for the Hamas revenge was nineteen-year-old Ra'id Zaqarna from the village of Qabatiya. Although known to the Shin Bet, which meant he had already undergone the unpleasantness of sitting inside an interrogation room, he was not one of the service's most wanted—there wasn't a price on his head and there weren't undercover squads or teams of special operators hot on his trail. Three family members, though, had earned the privilege of being wanted by the commandos and had ended up very dead after brief gun battles with the special forces. Zaqarna had no qualms about incinerating himself or a group of men, women, and children who just happened to be sitting alongside his vehicle at the point of detonation. His glory was not the seventy-two virgins or the rivers of honey. His coveted aim was revenge.

According to Ayyash's plan, Zaqarna and a comrade, Muhammed Ahmed Haj Salah Kamil, were to target a bus carrying soldiers as it traveled from Jenin toward the Beit Lid interchange, a junction on the road to the coastal town of Netanya that connected the sliver of land between the West Bank and the Mediterranean. The target selected by the Majd and other freelance Hamas intelligence operatives that sat by roadside bus stops and monitored traffic was scheduled to be attacked one week after Goldstein's carnage. But for some unknown reason it was decided by the political apparatus to wait out the forty-day mourning period. It was a cruel masterstroke at understanding the Israeli mentality as well as the nation's true vulnerabilities.

Working under a flickering sixty-watt lightbulb in a well-protected garage somewhere near Rafatt, Ayyash constructed the device that would spark his march toward notoriety. Inside the trunk of a stolen 1987 Sky Blue Opel Ascona, Ayyash strategically positioned the mechanics of his home-built killing device. The bomb consisted of seven gas cylinders hooked to an explosive charge of five antipersonnel hand grenades and a homemade brew surrounded by a rucksack containing carpenter's nails. A typical fragmentation grenade, the type used by soldiers in armies around the world, contained only sixty grams of explosives material but had a 360-degree destructive range that spread for ten feet.

Ayyash's car bomb had more than twenty kilograms of explosives packed into the compact metal package that was designed to shred the metal and fiberglass body of the car into minuscule fragments of shrapnel flying at some two thousand feet per second, cutting down anyone and anything in its path. The heat from the blast would envelop the car and much of the exterior of any vehicle in a thirty-foot radius. The fireball would produce a cloud of suffocating black smoke that would fill the lungs of anyone standing in its path. The bomb was indiscriminate and unforgiving.

When the sun rose on Wednesday, April 6, 1994, the mood was somber in the town of Afula, a middle-class town in the heart of the Jezreel Valley that connected much of Israel to the roadways leading to the Sea of Galilee. In less than twenty-four hours, Israel would be honoring the six million dead of the Holocaust with a special annual remembrance day set aside for the memories of those slaughtered in Auschwitz, Treblinka, and the other death and concentration camps of the Nazi final solution. Yom Ha'Shoah, Holocaust Remembrance Day, was the first of three national celebrations designed to pay tribute to sacrifice and celebrate Israel's creation. A week after Holocaust Remembrance Day is Israeli Memorial Day, when all those killed in

Israel's five major wars, countless wars of attrition, and terrorist attacks are honored. At midnight after Memorial Day, Israelis revel in Independence Day celebrations. Scheduling the annual celebrations so close to one another was by design: those who died in Europe and those who sacrificed themselves in battle had paved the path for the creation—and continued survival—of the Jewish state.

Holocaust Day is a national day of mourning. Survivors of Hitler's Europe are featured on television and radio broadcasts, the president and prime minister attend a memorial at the Yad Vashem memorial in Jerusalem, and schoolchildren throughout the country, from toddlers to high school seniors, study the Holocaust. At 11:00 A.M., air-raid sirens sound throughout the country as everyone everywhere stops whatever they are doing—from driving a bus to chairing an investor's meeting—and stands silently, head bowed, in a moment of prayer and honor. Israel literally stops in its tracks for the siren.

The men in Samaria did not want Ra'id Zaqarna driving around the roadways of Israel on Holocaust Day. The sight of an Arab man standing solemnly by a roadside and honoring the six million dead might have aroused suspicion. A policeman would have certainly taken notice, and motorists, made nervous by Hamas threats to avenge the Hebron massacre, would have jotted down the license plate of his Opel Ascona and phoned the local police headquarters. April 6 fell one day short of the Jewish day of mourning and one day after the Muslim season of sorrow. It was an ideal time to strike.

For much of the morning of April 6, Zaqarna drove along the roadways of the Jezreel Valley, through the plush green hills of some of the most beautiful countryside in the Jewish state, past majestic Mt. Tabor to the east along roadways bordered by flowering chrysanthemums. The warm air wafted across the valleys with the bouquet of wildflowers. It was spring in Israel, the most peaceful time of the year in a land known for heat and hatred. He drove slow and cautiously. He did not want to arouse suspicion.

At 12:15 A.M., Zaqarna pulled into the intersection of Afula's Ninth Division Street, close to where high school students, let out early because of the coming holiday, were passing through streets in search of snacks and a ride home. As a group of students boarded the No. 348 bus, carrying their schoolbooks and sipping cans of Coke, Zaqarna pulled his Opel in front of the bus and, in one final act, pressed a light switch positioned alongside the driver's side door. All it took was a flip of the switch. The Opel exploded in a blinding flash of yellow and orange light, spreading heat and death over a forty-meter killing zone. Those closest to ground zero were incinerated by the power, heat, and fury of the blast; others were hit with chunks of metal, bone fragments, and eleven hundred carpenter nails hurled by the energy of the blast in a piercing shower of death. A beautiful spring afternoon had been turned into a ghoulish and macabre scene. An engulfing cloud of black smoke rose to the heavens from the Opel and the targeted bus. The pavement was covered with a pool of blood and human tissue, and the stench of burned flesh permeated the air. The bus driver and several others sitting in the front of the bus sat frozen in time, their heads and torsos ripped to shreds by the force of the explosion. Teenagers who moments earlier had been chatting with one another about a soccer match or what they planned to do with their girlfriends now raced through the area on fire, like human torches. Emergency rescue workers and responding police and bomb disposal officers were aghast. Some had seen such things during military duty in Lebanon, but Afula was not Beirut. It was a sleepy town, a crossroad for both Arab and Jew. Mothers searching for their children amid the rescue efforts screamed in despair.

Shin Bet officials raced to the scene from as far away as Tel Aviv and Jerusalem headquarters. They were desperate for answers. Who was the bomber, who sent him, who built the bomb, how was the bomb built, and who else was out there directing this new wave of attacks? Shin Bet agents and special police investigators donned rubber gloves and meticulously searched the charred epicenter for any trace of the bomber's identity. The shredded remnants of an identity card were sought, as were any fragments of fingers that might belong to the driver.

Seizing those responsible for the Afula blast was a top priority. After all, there were political considerations. Immediately following the blast, dozens of right-wing demonstrators raced toward Ninth Division Street and, to the glee of news cameras, began chanting "Death to the Arabs!" and "Baruch Goldstein, King of Israel, will live forever!"[5] Right-wing members of Knesset called upon Prime Minister Rabin and Foreign Minister Peres to end the dialogue with Arafat. But the implementation of the Gaza-Jericho Plan was close at hand and Rabin was not about to allow a group of fanatics to derail the chance for Israel to buy itself a peaceful future.

Hours after the Afula blast, as special rabbinical crews scoured the nearby roadside for bits and pieces of victims for proper Jewish burial, Hamas issued a communiqué, a confession of sorts, taking responsibility for the bombing. The operation, the one-paragraph statement read, was the work of the Abdel el-Rahman Hamadan cell of the Izzedine al-Qassam Brigade. "You turned our Id al-Fitr [the end of Ramadan] into a black day," the communiqué warned, "so we vow to turn your independence day into hell."[6] Four more attacks were promised as revenge for the Hebron massacre.

The Shin Bet had never heard of that code name being used for one of the al-Qassam strike units in the area, though because the attack took place in Afula, just outside the northern tip of the Territories, investigators surmised that the perpetrators had come from Samaria. Upon further examination of what remained of nineteen-year-old Ra'id Zaqarna and his portable artillery shell, the device was the handiwork of one of Samaria's most notorious residents. Shin Bet officials did not publicly credit Ayyash with the blast, but they knew the design and the simplicity to be his own. The Engineer from Rafatt had joined the big leagues. Nine had died in the Afula blast and fifty-five had been seriously wounded.

Afula had been the opening of what promised to be a season of bloody revenge. Hadera would be the second act.

On the morning of April 13, the line of passengers hoping to board the 9:30 bus to Tel Aviv was longer than usual inside Hadera's small and sleepy central bus station. Hadera itself was small and usually sleepy. A quiet working-class Israeli town some thirty minutes north of Tel Aviv, it existed on its own relaxed frequency. Very little ever happened in Hadera; for excitement people traveled to Tel Aviv, or to closer Netanya. Hadera was busy for a change, busy for Memorial Day, with travelers heading to and from ceremonies, cemeteries, and business appointments, making it one of the most traveled days of the year.

Bus drivers had received a memo from the corporate headquarters and the police to be on the lookout for explosive devices, though a preliminary check of the 9:30 bus revealed no packages left behind, and no devices hidden under seats or in overhead luggage racks. As the soldiers, students, old men and women, and tourists boarded the bus, they were joined by a man with a dark complexion and a black duffel bag. He was Amar Salah Diab Amarna, twenty-one, from the village of Yabed, who had been recruited in the mosque for just this very assignment.

As the bus pulled out of its berth at 9:40, packed to standing room only, Amarna lowered his bag, looked around at those he was about to incinerate, and flipped the light switch on two kilograms of homemade Grade A Ayyash explosives. The device cost less than a hand grenade or a land mine to make, yet it produced a blast, combined with the confined spaces of the crowded bus, that sparked a muffled fireball that shredded flesh and metal. Some were killed by the concussion of the blast, others burned black by the intense heat of the acetone-based explosive. By placing the bomb on the floor, where shrapnel could rip through vital arteries located in the groin area, Amarna achieved a high body count. Those not wounded critically by the blast scampered out of the bus over the bodies and body parts of the dead and the dying. Six men, women, and children died that spring morning, and an additional thirty were seriously hurt.

Israeli bomb squad crews raced to the scene to make sure that Amarna's device had been completely neutralized by the blast. As they poked and prodded their way through the blood-covered floor of the bus, a second device exploded nearby. A pipe bomb had apparently been timed to coincide with the arrival of rescue crews and emergency personnel. The insidious terrorist strategy took many Israeli security officials by surprise, even those weathered to the point of numbness by the wars against the PLO and Hizballah.

At 11:00 A.M., Shin Bet officials and police bomb technicians joined the ranks of their fellow countrymen throughout Israel to stand in a silent salute at the wail of the air-raid siren marking the commencement of Memorial Day ceremonies. Those on the scene whose clothes and gloves were covered in blood could only imagine how many would die at the hands of the Hamas bombers until Memorial Day 1995.

Yehiya Ayyash was no longer just the misguided electronics wizard who went to work for Hamas, and his name was no longer spoken of solely at briefings in Shin Bet conference rooms. The Engineer now became page-one news and the stuff of pulp fiction. He was the master technician, the brains behind the detonator, the man who, at least according to the media's search for a face on which to pin the evil of Hamas, was waging a one-man war against the Jewish state. He had become one of the most wanted men in all of Israel—and he was wanted dead or alive.

Ayyash played the cat-and-mouse game with the Shin Bet with incredible guile and skill. He never slept in the same safe house or cave more than once; his movements were known only by a handful of dedicated operatives who would never betray him; and his fame, usually the death knell for any self-preserving terrorist seeking anonymity, became his saving grace. Residents of the West Bank, and not necessarily card-carrying members of Hamas, volunteered to risk their lives and their homes in order to protect "The Engineer," or bring him food or clothing or even photographs of his children. Wigmakers and tailors donated hairpieces and costumes so Ayyash could masquerade as an old man, a Jewish settler, or even a widowed young woman; farmers, butchers, and merchants offered food and other staples; and, of course, the Izzedine al-Qassam network provided its share of cash and forged identity cards.

But Ayyash must have realized that he could not run forever. Sooner or later the security forces would catch up with him. The Shin Bet was tenacious and unforgiving. Its agents, spending long days of backbreaking and mind-numbing work in the field, would guarantee the eventual arrest of a wanted terrorist. Their zeal only intensified if it meant seizing or killing a terrorist with blood on his hands.

Indeed, the Shin Bet had come close to uncovering Ayyash and his cell on several occasions. The most harrowing call for Ayyash's operation was in January 1994, when three terrorists were cornered by Israeli military forces and killed in a fierce firefight near Hebron University. After the Afula and Hadera bombings, Israel's efforts against Hamas intensified, not only against low-level cell members who killed collaborators but also against high-ranking terrorist commanders.

On February 13, 1994, an Izzedine al-Qassam strike team executed what, even by Shin Bet standards, was considered a classic ambush. The target of the operation was one Noam Cohen, the officer-in-charge of the Ramallah field office whose network of informants and observation posts had compromised many a Hamas cell and operation. Cohen, a native of Jerusalem, had been a Shin Bet agent since 1990. He was young, energetic, and dedicated—known to work twenty-hour days, sometimes seven days a week. Soft-spoken and charismatic, Cohen was responsible for reducing the number of terrorist incidents in the Ramallah area and its reaches into the northernmost tier of Jerusalem.

That day Cohen and two partners were driving their unmarked Mercedes in the village of Bituniya, on the outskirts of Ramallah, en route to meeting with an informant who would lead them to Abdel Muna'am Muhammed Yusuf Naji, one of the Shin Bet's most wanted, hunted by Cohen and his agents for some two years. Abdel Muna'am was known in the business as a "player"—someone who played both sides to the middle until he was either killed or ordered to kill. Abdel Muna'am was one of Noam Cohen's regular *sayanim*, or helpers. He had provided moderately useful intelligence to his handler, though his real objective was to gather intelligence on Shin Bet operations in the Ramallah area. As a counterintelligence agent in al-Qassam, Abdel Muna'am knew that there was a fine line in both pitching and catching. Shin Bet agents, especially Cohen, were sharp, and the time would come when the spy game would be compromised and Muna'am would either find himself inside a Shin Bet interrogation room or suffer a Hamas punishment reserved for ineffective agents: being lynched in an olive tree with your testicles sliced off and pinned to your chest. Abdel Muna'am realized that the only way to save his life was to end Cohen's.

Early that day, as Cohen's driver pulled the Mercedes west onto Jaffa Street into a side street where the meet had been planned, they were met by a hail of gunfire. The scene looked like a Hollywood shoot-out as the masked men peppered the Mercedes with bursts of AK-47 and Uzi fire. Cohen, the apparent target of the ambush, suffered thirty bullet wounds, most to the head and chest. His two partners managed to return fire, though they were seriously wounded and rushed to Jerusalem's Hadassah-University Hospital at Ein Kerem.

Cohen was the second Shin Bet agent killed in the line of duty in thirteen months. It had taken Noam Cohen some two years to get close to Abdel Muna'am. Now, with a dead Shin Bet agent to his credit, investigators were certain that the wily Hamas gunman would slip deeper into the abyss of the Territories, or perhaps Gaza and then Egypt, perhaps forever out of the reach of Israeli counterintelligence. Yet Shin Bet commanders and psychologists, the men who studied the mindset of the Izzedine al-Qassam Brigade soldiers, knew it was unlikely that Abdel Muna'am was going anywhere. "Hamasniks are creatures of their own terrain," claims a Shin Bet agent in Ramallah. "Take them out of their natural environment and they feel trapped and insecure. Their families are here, their friends are here, and the hiding spots they used to play in as kids are here for them to use as adults. The men we want aren't going anywhere. It's just incumbent upon us to go out and find the sons of bitches."[7]

Secret service agents, counterterrorist police officers, and other tactical professionals need to be able to separate the personal aspects of hunting a wanted killer from the emotional desire to avenge one of their own. "Agents cannot become involved in personal emotions while hunting terrorists," says Ya'akov Perry, "it is unprofessional and counterproductive."[8] Nevertheless, even after the Afula and Hadera bombings, the Shin Bet focus remained on the liquidation of the cell responsible for Cohen's murder. The war of the "spooks" was supposed to be void of emotion and feelings. In reality, it was the most personal form of warfare one could find.

*   *   *

Until April 6, 1994, Muna'am was the most wanted man in all of Israel. The Shin Bet had come close to the elusive operative once before, on February 25, when a Izzedine al-Qassam safe house in Abu Dis, east of Jerusalem, was surrounded by Israeli special operations personnel. One of Muna'am's men surrendered; the other member of the Cohen hit team, Abdel el-Rahman Hamadan, opted to die in a hail of automatic weapons and antitank missile fire.

The force on call to deal with Muna'am was the Ya'ma'm—the counterterrorist commandos of the National Police. Although bureaucratically under the direct command of the Border Guards, the Ya'ma'm had quickly developed into the tactical arm of the Shin Bet. Unlike the IDF's special forces units that performed the ultradangerous work of hunting fugitives in the Territories, the Ya'ma'm was a professional force whose ranks were filled by older and more experienced individuals. The Ya'ma'm, according to Shin Bet agents, was far more reliable operationally than the conscripts of the IDF special operations unit. The Ya'ma'm practiced a professional work ethic based on skill, bravado, and courage that left little room for Murphy's Law. The Ya'ma'm worked well with the Shin Bet—agents enjoyed the sullen seriousness of the Ya'ma'm operators. They were always on call, attached to a myriad of beepers, cellular phones, and Motorola radios wherever they went. The sense of alert increased after the Afula and Hadera bombings; Ya'ma'm home base in central Israel was at a fever pitch. The boiling point came on Tuesday, May 31, 1994.

The Shin Bet had been cultivating a source, connected to another source, who would be meeting Muna'am on Monday, May 30, in a village near Ramallah. The intelligence was considered absolutely reliable, and the Shin Bet summoned the Ya'ma'm to provide tactical backup. Meeting in the Ramallah military headquarters, the Ya'ma'm operators sat attentively as several Shin

Bet case agents briefed them on the village, on Muna'am, and on their contacts in the field who were not to be harmed. It might be a common criminal who has agreed to help the Shin Bet in order to avoid prosecution and maintain his criminal empire, or it might be a despicable traitor and completely untrustworthy, but as long as his information was useful, he was to be protected *at all costs*. In this case the helper had been particularly useful and his handler was adamant about safety.

In the field, the Ya'ma'm had prepared for a long night. Operators sat inside beat-up vehicles or behind buildings, ready to attack. Peering through a pair of camouflaged field glasses, the Ya'ma'm commander and his Shin Bet counterpart scoured the area in search of three men who would be walking to the predetermined spot for the meet. Tensions were high. Just before sunset, three figures were seen walking through the village square. One of the Shin Bet handlers positively identified the figure wearing the red-and-white kaffiyeh as Muna'am. The Ya'ma'm snipers raised their weapons and began the slow and methodical breathing pattern needed to take a smooth shot. The arrest party coiled their thigh and calf muscles, ready to pounce into action.

The final authorization to attack was never issued by the Shin Bet supervisor, who had a gut feeling that a tactical solution at this point in time would jeopardize the safety of his helper, who was standing next to Muna'am. With a long list of high-level Hamas operatives still on the run, his helper was important. The Ya'ma'm commander was incensed by the Shin Bet's apprehension. "The plan was perfect, all the players were in place, and we had him in our sights. Why the fuck did you abort?" The Ya'ma'm commander called his superior, he called his superior's superior, and he was even tempted to call the Shin Bet superior officer. But in the end, the Shin Bet were the absolute masters in the field and their word was law.

The following day another opportunity arose to take out Cohen's killer. Muna'am once again tempted fate as he was about to meet an operative in the village of Aram, halfway along the highway from Jerusalem to Ramallah. At just after 4:00 a blue-and-white commuter bus, ferrying laborers back to their homes near Ramallah, was about to complete its late-afternoon run. The bus was crowded and the main street in the village was bustling with activity. At the northern edge of the town, amid several parked cars, the bus driver pulled into a secluded spot to unload his last two passengers. One was thin and gaunt and carried a Coke bottle in a blue plastic bag while clutching his left hip with a nervous grasp. The second man was calm and collected as he smoked his filtered cigarette. Muna'am and his Majd bodyguard acted as if they were certain that the special forces would never attempt a grab amid civilians or on a bus. But laying in wait that sunny May afternoon inside a Ford draped in the Palestinian flag was a squad of the best tactical operators inside Israel. They wore jeans and T-shirts and kaffiyehs that concealed communications devices and headphones.

As the Ya'ma'm operators pulled black balaclavas over their faces and cocked their mini-Uzi submachine guns, the commander of the Ya'ma'm task force, masquerading as a Palestinian, grabbed Muna'am by the shoulder and said, "Marchaba!" Hello! "Are you Abdel Muna'am Najer?" By the time Muna'am could reach for the 9 mm Beretta he carried tucked into his left waistband, it was too late. Muna'am was killed by a two-round greeting to the head and chest. Dozens of men in olive fatigues and black masks flooded the area, blocking off streets and ordering residents and storekeepers inside. Border Guard units and IDF patrols rushed in. Some of the agents headed back to their unmarked cars and cell phones to call Jerusalem and Tel Aviv. Others could not rip themselves from staring at the body of Muna'am with part of his brain blown out.

*　　*　　*

Settling the score with Noam Cohen's killer was a sobering bit of reality for Ayyash. He knew that time was running out for him as long as he remained on the run. The Shin Bet and their tactical backup were taking no prisoners. Unlike Muna'am, Ayyash was not a street fighter. He rarely posed with an AK-47 for covert snapshots to be distributed among the mosques and Hamas learning centers. He was not the type to pull the trigger behind the left ear of an enemy soldier. He was an analytical thinker, not a warrior.

More unsettling to Ayyash still was the death of his close confident and his cell's executive officer, Ali Osman Mohammed Atssi. The Shin Bet had been on Attsi's trail for more than a year. He had moved throughout the Territories playing the identical game of cat-and-mouse as Ayyash, but as a lower-level commander he was far more mobile and had to take greater risks. Atssi also lacked Ayyash's charisma and iconlike appeal. The Shin Bet remained close on his trail following the Rosh Ha'ayin incident and the Afula and Hadera bombings. Agents working out of the Nablus military headquarters interviewed dozens of witnesses, sources, and other helpers. On July 11, 1994, the field work paid valuable dividends.

Acting on information viewed by the Shin Bet as *Zahav Tahor* (Hebrew for "pure gold"), a combined Shin Bet and IDF undercover unit task force cornered Attsi and his Majd bodyguard, Basher Amuddi, inside a Nablus safe house tucked away behind the main market in the city's sprawling casbah. The undercover operatives, nineteen- and twenty-year-old soldiers from the famed Cherry squad, had been prowling the street for hours. Although the majority of the soldiers were blond kibbutzniks, young and lean kids from the country's agricultural cooperatives, they were all in costume that evening in a colorful assortment of disguises. Some were dressed as aging laborers returning from a day's work in the nearby fields, others in the tight-fitting polyester fashion designs popular among the city's unemployed who spent their days and nights hanging out on streetcorners. Some were even dressed as old women. They became an indistinguishable part of the Nablus landscape that evening—looking, dressing, and smelling like the locals with all but one important exception. Underneath their galabia gowns, black dresses, and sport coats, the men carried mini-Uzi 9 mm submachine guns, some equipped with silencers. They carried miniature Motorola receivers, all connected to a central dispatch with a communications officer controlling the operation from inside a battered old van acting as a forward HQ.

The Shin Bet case officer had hoped to also snare Ayyash that evening, although he would have been more than happy to just find out information about Ayyash's or Atssi's whereabouts. Many of the Shin Bet officers nervously peering through night-vision goggles from an observation post were itching for an opportunity to interrogate Ayyash's trusted deputy. They had hoped to grab him at the entrance to the two-story stone house, but Atssi had sensed an ambush. With his back to the wall, Atssi barricaded the small three-room flat and readied his AK-47 for the showdown.

The undercover unit commander cordoned off a three-block area, and on a winding staircase he pleaded with Atssi to surrender. The Shin Bet case agents, too, were hoping for the chance to get Atssi inside the soundproof walls of an interrogation cell. Atssi was a rarity in Izzedine al-Qassam circles—he knew the whereabouts of many of the brigade's most wanted men, including Yehiya Ayyash.

Atssi, however, seemed determined to exit the earth in a hail of gunfire. The gunfight was brief and one-sided. Israeli forces called to the barricaded home launched a furious barrage of antitank missiles at the location, reducing the stone frame to shattered chunks of rock and metal. Inside the rubble, the undercover squad commander tossed a fragmentation grenade into the collapsed room where Atssi and Amuddi were hiding.

After the blast and the cascading fallout of incandescent metal, the commandos raced in with their machine guns and automatic rifles at the ready. Shin Bet investigators waved away the smoke billowing from the smoldering frame of the doorway to officially identify the two dead terrorists.

Atssi's bullet-riddled demise came as a personal blow to Yehiya Ayyash. The thirty-year-old Atssi was a friend and a confidant, one of the only individuals throughout the Territories who knew where Ayyash was twenty-four hours a day. Ayyash viewed Atssi as a protector, a triggerman who would back him up for that final showdown with the Israelis. According to Israeli sources, Atssi was the number two man on a long list of wanted Hamas terrorists that was growing shorter by the week.[9] Ayyash remained at the top of the list.

Notes

[1]Peter Hirschberg, "Murder in the Air," *The Jerusalem Report*, September 28, 1998, p. 22.

[2]George J. Church, "When Fury Rules," *Time Magazine*, March 7, 1994, Volume 143, No. 10, p. 55.

[3]Interview, Amman, with Major B., July 29, 1997.

[4]Khaled Abu Toameh, "When Fury Rules," *The Jerusalem Report*, September 4, 1997, p. 35.

[5]Christopher Walker, "Nine Die in Suicide Attack On School Bus; Israel," *The Independent*, April 8, 1994, p. 12.

[6]Sarah Helm, "Israelis Die in Second Hebron Revenge Attack," *The Independent*, April 8, 1994, p. 12.

[7]Interview, Ramallah May 4, 1992.

[8]Interview, August 15, 1998.

[9]Roni Shaked, *"Mispar 2 Hoosal; Nimshach HaMatzod Aharei Mispar Ehad,"* *Yediot Aharonot*, July 12, 1994, p. 2.

Chapter 4

The Autumn of
Hope and Fire

In a part of the world known for miracles, Tel Aviv is truly Israel's miracle on the sea. A vibrant city of one million souls, it is surrounded by dozens of smaller towns, known as Greater Tel Aviv, that encompass more than one-third of the Israeli population. Jerusalem might be the spiritual capital of the country and its alleged seat of power, but Tel Aviv is where everything happens. With the exception of one or two South American countries, all foreign nations have their embassies in the Tel Aviv region. Banks, industry, and high-tech corporations are located in the Greater Tel Aviv area. The Israel Defense Forces headquarters, the Israeli Defense Ministry, is situated right in the center of downtown Tel Aviv, and it is the worst-kept secret in Israel that all three of Israel's intelligence services are based "somewhere" in the Greater Tel Aviv area. It isn't that the Sabras of modern Israel have forsaken Jerusalem or abandoned the beauty of Haifa or the desert oasis of Beersheba. Tel Aviv is simply the heart and soul of the country.

Many have compared Tel Aviv to Beirut in its golden years,

although the only obvious trait the two cities share is Mediterranean beachfront. Beirut in the magical years of Lebanese tranquility before the civil war had opulence, decadence, and beauty. Beyond the squalor and misery of the Palestinian refugee camps, Beirut had history, cash, casinos, sex, and, to the east, snow-capped peaks and majestic mountain vistas brushed with the towering green beauty of cedar trees. Tel Aviv, for the most part, is an ugly city—crumbling asphalt buildings darkened by pollution and neglect, narrow overcrowded streets, and buses that mar the most placid of byways with ear-splitting gear-shifting. With all these negatives, the true miracle of Tel Aviv is its promenade along the Mediterranean. The sea is a sanctuary from from the rigors of life in Israel, and from life in the region.

Like the Tel Aviv seafront, the state of Israel was slowly yielding to the notion that it could escape from the fifty-year yoke of bloodshed and war now an integral part of their society. The summer of 1994 offered incredible promise to the Jewish state and the entire Middle East. The region had reached a milestone. Israel's miracle on the sea was gearing itself to become not only the epicenter of Israeli life, but a capital of the Middle East as well.

The refreshing and relieving winds of change first picked up in the filth and misery of the Gaza Strip on May 11, 1994, when, in a low-key ceremony, Israeli troops relinquished a small military outpost to Palestinian policemen who had been undergoing training in Jordan and Egypt. According to the Declaration of Principles signed on the White House lawn on September 13, 1993, Israel should have started folding its tents and removing the photographs of Prime Minister Rabin from its installations in Gaza and Jericho by April 13. But the political fallout from the Goldstein massacre in Hebron and the two bombings in Afula and Hadera had stalled the peacemakers.

On May 13, in a predawn evacuation that was not unlike a

tenant leaving his apartment hours before eviction, the residents of Jericho awoke to find the Star of David no longer flying in the town square and the city's main streets patrolled by men wearing camouflage fatigues, not yarmulkes, who carried AK-47 assault rifles and spoke a very familiar accented Arabic. For the first time in twenty-five years, Israel had traded land for the promise of peace. Jericho, however, was considered a gesture. The town had more tourist value than strategic importance, and the only "hostile activity" reported in the salient was a souvenir vendor getting a little too pushy with a group of Hadassah women from Long Island. Jericho was a freebie and a test. Gaza was the first prize on the Palestinian agenda.

Although there were a few Jewish settlements inconveniently dotting the periphery of Gaza's borders, there was no serious argument against evacuating Gaza—in fact, many Israeli military and intelligence officials couldn't believe that anyone would want it in the first place. Even by the kindest of descriptions, the Gaza Strip was a hellhole in tragic straits. On a good day, when the winds swoop off the Mediterranean surf into the narrows and caverns of the flat territory, the Strip smells of sewage. There are one million men, women, and children crammed into 360 square miles of the Gaza Strip, making it one of the most crowded places on the planet. Gaza is impossible to police, a breeding ground for militancy of every stripe, and Israel surrendered it with the smile of a used car salesman unloading his biggest lemon on a grateful customer. "Even if all we get out of the Oslo Accords was the painless surgical removal of Gaza from our systems," claimed a retired Israeli brigadier general who had served more time in the Strip than he cared to remember, "then this gamble is one of history's greatest victories!"

Israel had fought many battles in the Strip since independence in 1948 and had lost hundreds of lives in the process. The IDF and the Shin Bet had battled Egyptian intelligence agents, Fatah, the PFLP, the PFLP-GC, the DFLP, the Abu Nidal Faction, and lastly, Hamas in the alleyways, refugee camps, and beaches of Gaza. Now it was Arafat's turn.

At precisely 3:15 A.M. on July 1, 1994, Yasir Arafat ended more than a quarter century of Israeli occupation when he crossed the Egyptian border at Rafath in a motorcade of bulletproof Mercedes limousines and Land Rovers to reclaim the first foothold of what Oslo earmarked as the Palestinian Authority, which everyone understood as the initial brick in a future Palestinian state. It was the first time that Arafat had been to Gaza in more than thirty years, and his return was remarkable. Zigzagging through the narrow and poorly paved roadways of the Strip, Arafat's motorcade passed through the filth and crowded misery of the refugee camps in view of several Israeli settlements allowed to remain in place by the Oslo Accords; outside Kfar Darom, across the No 4. Highway from the Dir el-Balach refugee camp, armed settlers declared themselves ready to kill Arafat.[1] Lining the route were hundreds of Palestinian security personnel—their backs facing the motorcade, their eyes glancing suspiciously at any potential threat to their returning hero.

In Gaza City, a crowd of ten thousand greeted Abu Ammar. A sea of green berets blended with the throngs of Strip residents who could not believe that Arafat had come home. Yet Arafat was smart enough to realize his support in Gaza City was shared by devotion to Hamas. In a sign of respect and political savvy, Arafat saluted the jailed Sheikh Yassin in his address and promised fundamentalists that, "In the name of Allah we are bringing victory to the believers."[2] Hamas wasn't just a movement that threatened Israel. It was a political rival seeking exclusivity over the soul of the Palestinian nation. Arafat realized that Hamas had worn the Israelis down, and the men of the Izzedine al-Qassam Brigade were as responsible for his new power in Gaza as were the hair-splitting negotiating sessions with the Israelis. Hamas was a force to be reckoned with in

Palestinian politics, and Arafat had assembled a small security army to do his bidding.

For the political leadership of Hamas, Arafat's return was seen as a mixed blessing. Publicly they vowed to intensify the military struggle against Israel as well as attempt to torpedo the peace process; they viewed the willingness to live side by side with the Jewish state as sacrilege. But privately they realized that there was a new sheriff in town and that the rules of engagement had changed. Compared to Arafat's henchmen, the Shin Bet were boy scouts. There were no less than twelve police agencies in the new Palestinian Authority—each determined, no matter what the cost or body count, to ensure Arafat's political and physical future.

Many in the Palestinian police agencies were former Fatah operatives who had survived the internal battles of the camps in southern Lebanon and the Fatah civil war in 1983. They had fought the Israelis, the Jordanians, the Syrians, the Lebanese, the Druze, and the Phalangists. They had been raised by the barrel of the gun and were unlikely to allow serious political opposition to *el-Ra'is*, the Leader, their affectionate name for Arafat.

There were twelve Palestinian law enforcement and secret police agencies, consisting of some forty thousand men under arms, meant to replace the vacuum created by the departing Shin Bet. They included the National Security Apparatus (*al-'amn al-watani*); the Civil Police (*al-shurta*), the main law-enforcement body, headed by Ghazi Jebali in Gaza; Public Security (*al-'amn al-'ammi*), the general security service similar in mandate to the Israeli Shin Bet; the Palestinian Preventive Security Service (*al-'amn al-wiqa'i*), the principal body involved in coordinating with Israeli security services; the Criminal Investigation Department (*al-bahth al-jina'i*); the Intelligence Department, (*mukhabarat*), charged with arresting and dealing with the political opposition and dissidents; Military Intelligence (*istikhbarat*), tasked with spying on the Israeli security services as well as acting as a forceful internal affairs to some of the other

Palestinian services; Force 17 (*quwa sab'a 'asher*), Arafat's prae-
torian guard formed in Lebanon as a special operations commando force, also responsible for guarding Arafat; Coast Guard
(*bahriyya*), an odd agency known for corruption and its particularly brutal treatment of political prisoners; Special Forces (*al-
quwat al-khassa*), to oversee the operations of other security force
branches; and the Civil Defense Corps (*al-difa' al-madani*), responsible for emergency services. So security-minded and paranoid was Arafat's ruling circle that they even proposed a secret
police force for colleges and universities, to be known as the
University Security System (*jihaz 'amn al-jami'a*). The intelligence
service had been designed to monitor the political atmosphere
on campus and arrest students who oppose the Palestinian Authority; it was never implemented.

The Shin Bet viewed the withdrawal from Gaza with mixed
emotions. The agents from the Arab Desk had no sentimental
attachments to the Gaza Strip—no landmarks of beauty, and few
fond memories. There wasn't an agent in the Shin Bet who
would miss the suffocating humidity, or the dangers. There was
nothing romantic about arresting a suspect and then waving
one's Browning Hi-Power in the face of a mother pleading for
her son's release, or searching a one-bedroom hovel in a refugee
camp as the ten men, women, and children who lived in the
sardinelike conditions cursed under their breath, fearful that a
Palestinian flag or any other paraphernalia might earn them a
year inside a detention center.

Gaza was the place that many a young agent first handled an
informant and an operative. It was in Gaza, in day-long stakeouts of coffeehouses and brothels, that agents were able to learn
the intricate, often nauseating reality of counterintelligence and
counterterrorism. Gaza was a cauldron of hate that had little
economic value but, like any covert battlefield, was an intelligence goldmine. Here was the pulse of the armed resistance and

the spiritual center of Hamas. When the Shin Bet packed its filing cabinets and removed the microphones and video cameras from behind the two-way mirror inside the main IDF HQ, it also abandoned relationships, contacts, and an infrastructure of espionage and counterespionage that took nearly thirty years to build.

There was no price that could be put on the Shin Bet's investment in Gaza for the countless hours put into building networks and closing cases. Many agents had lost their lives in midnight gun battles in the casbah; many others saw their marriages disintegrate because of the endless hours dedicated to fighting the Palestinians instead of being at home with their families. Yet according to agreements with the new Palestinian Authority, Israel would not be relinquishing its Gaza intelligence assets; it would simply have to receive the data through a funnel of Palestinian services that would liaison with the Shin Bet, as well as the Mossad and A'man, on a regular basis.

The departure from Gaza in May, and Arafat's return in July, had made the Shin Bet's task of monitoring Hamas far more difficult. It was forced to rely on data analysis rather than the spoken word of agents for its intelligence gathering, and it could no longer deploy a heavy hand on human assets left behind in the Palestinian Authority: the Shin Bet could no longer threaten a suspect or a helper with detention, torture, or economic blackmail. "They went from pythons to aging tigers with bleeding gums and false teeth," a member of the Preventive Security Service told an American intelligence official in Gaza following Arafat's return. "I doubt their effectiveness will ever be the same."[3]

If the Shin Bet needed a suspect followed or pertinent information from inside the Strip, they now needed to call upon their former adversaries for help. Arafat's services, as per arrangements worked out in the framework of the Oslo Accords, did supply the Shin Bet with the occasional tidbit and morsel, but it was always a day late and a dollar short. Israel's intelligence apparatus in Gaza had all but disappeared. If Israel were to wage its war against Hamas, it would need to dedicate its resources to the west bank of the Jordan River.

Jordan's King Hussein had watched the implementation of the peace accords between Israel and the Palestinian Authority with great interest. Indeed, it paved the way for him to formalize a relationship and peace treaty with Israel. For both sides, peace with Jordan was a win-win situation for the Israelis—a nation that had never experienced a win-win scenario in its nearly fifty years of independence. After all, peace with Jordan was something of a given. The frontier with the Hashemite Kingdom— the elongated snake path that followed the edge of the Golan Heights south along the dwindling sweet water of the Jordan River, which reached the entrance to the Red Sea at the Gulf of Aqaba—had been relatively quiet since the early 1970s. There were occasional incidents of terrorists crossing the Jordan and attacking targets on the Israeli side of the river, but they were few in number and never carried out with the knowledge of the Jordanian authorities; in fact, Jordanian forces along the frontier were just as concerned about Palestinian elements crossing west as they were about Israeli forces crossing east.

Behind the façade of Pan Arab conferences and foreign ministry communiqués, Jordan maintained a de facto strategic understanding with the Jewish state. There were even covert contacts at the highest levels of government between Amman and Jerusalem. King Hussein is reported to have personally forewarned Israeli Prime Minister Golda Meir of the impending Egyptian and Syrian war plans—a warning the Israelis chose to ignore. The heads of the Mossad, the Shin Bet, and A'man were reportedly in routine contact with their Jordanian counterparts. Jordan placed no territorial claims on the state of Israel; the West Bank was deemed a chunk of territory lost to the Palestinian cause. Even during the Gulf War, when a Jordan strangled by

Iraqi pressure and Palestinian internal difficulties sided with Baghdad in a game of cat and mouse, Israeli defense strategists drawing up contingency plans for an Israeli invasion of Iraq did not view the Jordanian military as a foe.

The Jordanians, for their part, realized the unkind hand it had been dealt in the geographic poker game of Middle Eastern politics. Surrounded by Iraq, Saudi Arabia, Israel, the West Bank, and Syria, the Hashemite Kingdom of Jordan was sandwiched by threatening neighbors, each with its own designs and agenda concerning Jordanian policies, sovereignty, and territory. In many ways, Israel was the most benign of the neighbors, hoping for a political, military, and Palestinian status quo. King Hussein was a master of political survival in this minefield and like anyone fighting for survival, he played for time until opportunity provided him with a chance to leap above the fray.

The Israeli-Palestinian peace accords were King Hussein's opportunity. If the Palestinians and Israelis had come to terms on how to come to terms, then Hussein no longer faced any barriers preventing him from establishing an overt relationship with his neighbors to the east. According to legend, and legends run deep through the pulsating arteries of everyday existence in the Middle East, King Hussein of Jordan, on one his covert trips to Israel, had donned a disguising toupee as he sat inside the limousine of Prime Minister Yitzhak Rabin and marveled at the sites, sounds, and smells of Tel Aviv. The two, according to reports, had met half a dozen times afterward—in secret. The personal relationship between King Hussein and Israeli Prime Minister Rabin was an enormous catalyst in moving the peace accords along. Both men genuinely cared for one another, and they trusted one another. In fact, the peace accords being worked on between Jordan and Israel were not considered merely a formal end to hostilities, but as the formal beginning of a full-fledged strategic alliance.

Therefore, on July 25, 1994, when President Clinton witnessed

Israeli Prime Minister Rabin and Jordan's King Hussein shake hands on the White House lawn and sign the Washington Declaration (ending the official but never consummated state of war between the two belligerents), it lacked the awe and dramatic reverberations of the Rabin-Arafat embrace. Yet the handshake, a public declaration of friendship and goodwill, was nothing short of epic. Formal relations between Israel and Jordan were viewed by many in the Labor government, especially Foreign Minister Shimon Peres, as a golden opportunity for Israel to establish overt ties to many of the nonbelligerent Arab states in the Middle East—from Morocco, with which Israel already maintained close relations, and Tunisia in North Africa, to Oman, Bahrain, Qatar, and the United Arab Emirates in the Persian Gulf. The potential for a Middle East of moderation, energized by Israeli high-tech and fueled by Arab petrodollars, foretold of a future of unlimited promise for the next generations of Arabs and Israelis.

The inauguration of this new region was to be the signing of the Israeli-Jordanian Peace Treaty, scheduled to take place in a high-octane and highly emotional ceremony in the Arava Desert. President Clinton was scheduled to attend the ceremony, as were dignitaries from the four corners of the globe. To many Israelis, peace with Jordan seemed the beginning of the end to a fifty-year history of blood and warfare. To Shin Bet director Ya'akov Perry, the peace treaty signing was seen as a golden opportunity for Hamas to make its presence felt once again. There would be blood before peace could blossom. But where?

The West Bank was quiet that fateful and historic summer. Hamas regrouped, planned, plotted, and waited. Cells of the Izzedine al-Qassam Brigade laid low and out of reach of the Shin Bet, the Israeli Border Guards, and the Israel Defense Forces. Disengagement was a tactic—an inexpensive means to buy time, cache weapons, and gather intelligence. The leaders of Hamas, as well as the masters who pulled their strings in Teheran, Damascus, and the United States, would not allow the fostering of a new era to the region without a spectacular act of violence designed to fragment support for the peace process inside Israel while putting Arab leaders on notice that shaking Rabin's hand on the White House lawn came with inherited risk and violence.

In Gaza, Palestinian secret service agents, investigating an Islamic Jihad cell, came across a series of faxes sent from Teheran: "Intensify Acts of Terrorism."[4] Faxes from Teheran were rarely ignored. They were commands meant to be obeyed.

Yehiya Ayyash spent the summer of 1994 in anonymity. He moved around primarily after dusk, at night, going from safe house to safe house. Because of the Shin Bet effort to locate him, his reputation had spread like wildfire throughout the towns and villages of Samaria. In Shin Bet interrogation rooms and in predawn raids on the homes of suspected Hamas operatives and Izzedine al-Qassam foot soldiers, the name Ha'Mehandes, or Engineer, was bandied about more than Ayyash. In Palestinian circles he had developed something of a pop-star status. Usually, in the mindset of Middle Eastern idol-worship, terrorists were elevated to hero status because of a vicious gun battle in which they died, or because of a spectacular attack they perpetrated against an Israeli target. Ayyash was the mind behind the trigger—not a pair of bare-fisted knuckles. And, some Israeli security officials contest, it was exactly because of this cerebral approach to his bomb building that he became a hero in the minds of many Palestinians, even those who were not necessarily Hamas supporters. At last the Palestinians possessed a player who was as smart as the men who hunted him and as untouchable as anyone had ever been in the torrid history of the terrorist war. Few could have realized just how much Ayyash's stock would rise in the weeks to come. Soon, Hamas would be an organization feared around the world and Ayyash's name would become common knowledge in capitals throughout the region and throughout the world.

October 9, 1994. It was a cool and crisp Sunday night in Jerusalem. The city had been hit by the dry and frosty air even before the sun descended westward over the lowlands toward the coastal plains and the Mediterranean Sea. The mood in Jerusalem was festive. The lucrative tourist season had come and gone but Israel was less than three weeks from signing a peace treaty with Jordan. Additional security forces patrolled key intersection and tourist sites, but it was hoped the month would pass with nothing but celebrations and relief.

Just before midnight, two Hamas terrorists armed with automatic rifles sprayed the congested Nahalat Shiva'a shopping promenade with a barrage of bullets and antipersonnel fragmentation grenades. The two, veteran Izzedine al-Qassam street fighters Hassan Mahmud Abbas and Isma Mahna Isma'il Juabay, had been dropped off by a driver in a sedan bearing yellow Israeli plates. They managed to kill two civilians and wound thirteen before they were shot and killed by armed citizens. As police officers responded to the midnight chill in their battledress jackets, Jericho 9 mm pistols at the ready, a crowd of angry protesters had surrounded the two dead terrorists as well as several innocent Arab passersby. There was hatred in the indiscriminate barrage, and it was being repaid with interest.

The crackling of gunfire and the screams of those scampering for cover were heard several hundred meters away in the lobby of the nearby King David Hotel, where U.S. Secretary of State Warren Christopher was staying. Gunfire and explosions were not common in the City of David, and it prompted special agents from the State Department's diplomatic security Service to grab their SIG-Sauers from their leather holsters and leap into action. Christopher was in the region to finalize details of the Israeli-Jordanian peace treaty, as well as to attempt to jump-start stalled negotiations between the Palestinian Authority and the Israeli negotiating team. Christopher's involvement would be crucial in light of the Jerusalem killings.

A crowd of demonstrators had gathered around the gruesome crime scene and began to chant "Rabin is a traitor." The handwriting was on the wall—but the Nahalat Shiva'a murders were only the beginning.

Hamas had opted on a three-pronged strategy of selective engagement to subvert the peace initiatives. At the same time that Abbas and Juabay were spraying the pedestrian mall with indiscriminate bursts of automatic-weapons fire, a young nineteen-year-old corporal in the elite 1st Golani Infantry Brigade was involved in a gut-wrenching, knuckle-scraping fight for his life at a dark and deserted stretch of roadway near Jerusalem. He was trying to get from a military course in northern Israel to his girlfriend's house in Ramle, just southeast of Tel Aviv. A friend from the army dropped off the young corporal at the Bnei Atarot Junction, near Ben-Gurion International Airport, where the soldier was likely to find a ride for the fifteen-minute drive to Ramle. It was all so typically Israeli. All so ordinary. After all, the three men in the car who picked him up appeared to be Orthodox Jews.

Yet when the slim and wide-eyed soldier with an infectious smile didn't show at his girlfriend's house or phone his parents in Jerusalem, worry set in. A search party was organized, the Israeli military was notified, and photographs of the soldier were posted at police stations throughout Israel. Soldiers had disappeared before, gone AWOL. But this soldier was happy and proud and looked after his younger brothers and sisters. The third son of a family of seven children, he was an Orthodox Jew whose mother had emigrated from New York in 1969. This was no simple disappearance. There was evil in the vanishing, and by Monday morning when news of the disappearance was read by Shin Bet director Ya'akov Perry and Prime Minister Rabin, the apprehension was palpable. Men whose instincts were forged in battle often feared the worst. Their hunches would be right.

The soldier's name was Nachshon Mordechai Waxman, and his tragic week-long ordeal would forever sear the name of Hamas into the collective memory of Israel's security forces.

On Tuesday, October 11, 1994, a man whose face was concealed by a red-and-white kaffiyeh walked calmly into the Associated Press office in East Jerusalem and dropped off a note. The receptionist was too busy to get the man's name or try and see his face. But the piece of paper, written on Hamas letterhead, had an ominous sense of urgency.

> The Izzedine al-Qassam Brigade hereby proclaims its responsibility for the abduction of the Israeli soldier Nachshon Mordechai, I.D. No. 03228629. He is alive and we are treating him as a prisoner of war under the Islamic guidelines.
>
> We demand from the Israeli government the following:
>
> The immediate release of Hamas founder Sheikh Ahmed Yassin, as well as Sheikh Abdel Karim Obeid and Sheikh Mustafa Dirani.*
>
> Second, we demand the release of all Izzedine al-Qassam prisoners.
>
> Thirdly, we demand the release of fifty Hamas operatives given harsh prison sentences; twenty-five prisoners from the Islamic Jihad; fifty Fatah prisoners; twenty prisoners from Dr. George Habash's Popular Front for the Liberation of Palestine; ten prisoners from the Democratic Front for the Liberation of Palestine; twenty Hizballah prisoners; fifteen prisoners from the Popular Front for

*Both Sheikh Obeid and Sheikh Dirani, high-ranking Hizballah commanders, were abducted by Israeli special forces in southern Lebanon in order to exact the release of Captain Ron Arad, an Israeli navigator shot down over Lebanon in 1986, and believed to be held in Iran.

the Liberation of Palestine General Command; and the release of all female prisoners and detainees.

To our brothers behind bars and their families, this is the price we pay for your release.

We bless the operation, and honor the memory of our martyrs Hassan Mahmud Abbas and Isma Mahna Isma'il Juabay.

If the Israeli government will not obey our demands, the death of the soldier will be your responsibility and we will also negotiate over the release of his remains.

The deadline for acquiescing to our demands is Friday night, October 14, 1994, at 9:00 P.M.

Later that day Hamas released an eerie videotape designed to bring the matter to the hearts and minds, as well as living rooms, of every Israeli family. In a blurry and low-lit room, a Hamas terrorist, his face concealed by a kaffiyeh, was seen clutching an M-16 assault rifle and Nachshon Waxman's identity booklet. Then, another operative was seen hovering over the sullen-looking corporal, his face appearing dazed and exhausted in an expression seemingly resigned to a cruel and horrible fate. "I am Nachshon Waxman. The members of Hamas kidnapped me and want their prisoners to be released. If not, they will kill me. I ask that you do what you can so that I'll get out of this alive." As if the videotaped plea for his life wasn't demeaning enough, the masked Hamas gunman hovering behind, his hand on Nachshon's shoulder, asked, "What do you ask of your mother?" "Is my family watching me?" the confused soldier asked, "Do I look all right? I hope to return to you if Rabin decides to release the prisoners."

Indeed, Esther Waxman was watching. She wept openly as she realized her son's desperation.

Hundreds of thousands of Israelis watched the tape on the nightly news. Everyone had been a soldier at one time, and everyone knew of someone in the military, whether a son or daughter, husband or brother in the reserves. The cornerstone of Israel's ironclad counterterrorist strategy had always been absolute: no negotiations and no surrender. But Waxman's tragic predicament was different. "It was like, 'There but for the grace of God go I'," claimed a retired Israeli special operations officer. "There was a feeling that we should just give in and get on with it and do whatever the bastards wanted to save the poor guy."

The intelligence effort launched by the Shin Bet and A'man to locate Waxman was massive—unlike anything the State of Israel had seen before and even beyond the scope of the dragnet cast over the Territories following Nissim Toledano's abduction. In the twisted currency of the Byzantine hostage-market, nothing captivated the heart like sons and daughters. The eyes of the nation turned to Rabin and his chief of staff, Lieutenant General Ehud Barak. Rabin turned toward Yasir Arafat. Many inside the Israeli intelligence community believed that Waxman was being held in Gaza.

The kidnapping of Nachshon Waxman was seen as a litmus test of the Israeli-Palestinian peace process. Already, Arafat was in hot water. The AK-47 assault rifle used in the Jerusalem shooting earlier in the week had been traced to the Palestinian police in Gaza. There were also reports that Hamas and Islamic Jihad activists were being openly recruited by the Palestinian police and intelligence services. If Waxman was in Gaza, the Israelis wanted Arafat to locate him—nothing else. Military commanders shook in their boots at the thought of Palestinian commandos storming an Izzedine al-Qassam safe house with a hostage's life on the line. Israel would handle the tactical resolution to the incident, though Prime Minister Rabin made it perfectly clear, in both public statements and messages sent through Secretary of State Christopher and Egyptian President Hosni Mubarak, that Arafat was personally responsible for Waxman's life.[5] Christopher in particular had been personally disgusted by the kidnapping, and all the pressure the State Department could summon was placed squarely on Arafat's fledgling Palestinian Authority. Arafat despised diplomatic hardball, and he hated ultimatums. More important, he hated the thought of his legitimacy tied to the fate of an Israeli soldier and the fundamentalist fanatics. He was also slated, along with Rabin, to receive the Nobel Peace Prize. Arafat knew it would be impossible for him to shake the image of terrorist if he accepted the prize covered in Nachshon Waxman's blood.

Few slept in Gaza that week. Palestinian policemen kicked their way through doors and homes of hundreds of suspected Hamas activists. The scene was reminiscent of the bad old days when Israel was the sheriff in town, though the procedure quite different. Suspected Hamas operatives were beaten openly in front of their homes; some reportedly had the barrels of pistols placed inside their mouths. In Gaza's Oranim Heights, in the Jebalya refugee camp, some two thousand Palestinian policemen had rousted the residents out of their beds for a thorough and brutal search of every home and every shack. Roadblocks were established at every intersection; policemen were issued strict orders to shoot anyone who offered even the slightest resistance.

Oranim Heights was home to the hard-core leadership of Iz-zedine al-Qassam. It was in Oranim where fax machines rang off the hook with political instructions from the United States and Great Britain, intelligence-related instructions from Teheran, and military orders from Damascus. It was in Oranim that Arafat had hoped that his myriad of intelligence services would locate the abducted Israeli corporal.

In Israel, the stoic Waxman family maintained an anguished vigil in their home in the Ramot neighborhood of the Israeli capital. Esther and Yehuda Waxman made a televised appeal to the kidnappers, pleading for the safe return of their son, for the "sake of God and all of us." As the clock slowly ticked toward

Friday, the mood in Israel turned somber and grim. Hamas had executed those it kidnapped in the past, and few doubted the organization would be moved by the pleas of a nation or the efforts of Arafat, a man they viewed as a traitor. On Thursday evening, as the sun abandoned the Judean Hills for its march toward the coast, fifty thousand worshippers assembled at the Wailing Wall to pray for Waxman's release.

Prime Minister Rabin realized he couldn't rely upon divine intervention. His faith lay with his trusted Shin Bet chief and confident, Ya'akov Perry, and indeed the Shin Bet came through. An informant tipped them off that Waxman was being held very close to home in the village of Bir Naballah, only two miles north of Jerusalem. Spotter teams of agents had already placed the two-story house under surveillance and teams of reinforcing agents had been dispatched to the town in deep cover and disguise. The revelation came as time was running out. The deadline for the release of Sheikh Yassin and the two hundred prisoners was set for 9:00 P.M.

Israeli security sources were not surprised that Waxman was being held in Bir Naballah. The village of six thousand inhabitants was known in Shin Bet computers as a Hamas stronghold. It was located as close to an upper-class Arab suburb as could be found around Jerusalem. There was a lot of money in the village, and strong links to the Palestinian diaspora in Europe and the United States; in fact, half of the villagers were American citizens who resided most of the year in the United States. The Hamas safe house where Corporal Waxman was being held, interestingly enough, had been built and was owned by a Palestinian-American living in Virginia.[6] It had been rented four months prior to the kidnapping.

Rabin faced a gut-wrenching dilemma as the deadline approached: negotiate a settlement for the life of the kidnapped corporal, or attempt a rescue. Either course carried with it tremendous political and emotional risk. Setting a precedent by negotiating with kidnappers and murderers was like walking through a minefield, especially as Rabin straddled a razor-wire fence in his attempt to fend off right-wing opposition to the peace accords with the Palestinians. A military solution was equally risky. Hostage rescue was not an exact science. It carried tremendous danger and the potential for disaster. Although a negotiations channel with Hamas had been established to lay the framework for a negotiated settlement, Rabin remembered when he faced an equally difficult decision as prime minister: in 1976, when 103 Jewish and Israeli hostages were held at Entebbe, Uganda. He was a military man who believed that risk sometimes outweighs inaction. Rabin, also the serving Defense Minister, ordered the security forces to rescue the kidnapped soldier before the Hamas deadline.

The Israeli National Police Border Guard hostage-rescue unit, the Ya'ma'm, prepared for a raid, as did Sayeret Mat'kal, the General Staff Reconnaissance Unit, the IDF's elite commando team tasked with both intelligence gathering and counterterrorism. Both units presented detailed rescue plans, but the commander of the Ya'ma'm, David Tzur, was abroad, and with the Israeli chief of staff and most of the generals on the General Staff former Mat'kal operators, the General Staff Reconnaissance Unit was ultimately selected to execute the mission.

Sayeret Mat'kal is the type of military unit that cannot be judged by conventional standards. One of the mottoes of the unit, a poorly paraphrased quote by Jewish historian Josephus Flavius, is "No great victories without great risks!" Sayeret Mat'kal is the closest thing Israel's military has to a mission impossible task force. The unit is so important to Israel's security that it is rumored the chief of staff of the Israel Defense Forces has a list of the unit's members in his desk, and that he, and those on the general staff, knows each of them personally. One of the unit's published nicknames is the Chief of Staff's Boys.

Sayeret Mat'kal was created in 1957, the result of some very serious shortcomings in Israel's ability to spy on its Arab neighbors. The brainchild of Major Avraham Arnan, a legendary intelligence officer who ran *shtinkerim*, or informers, in Jordanian-held East Jerusalem, Sayeret Mat'kal was to be an ultrasecretive intelligence-gathering force conducting deniable forays deep behind enemy lines throughout the Middle East and beyond. Until Arnan battled the narrow-minded bureaucracy of the IDF General Staff for the sanction to form his unit, the army relied on outside elements, mainly agents and "sympathetic friends" to obtain its intelligence data; but often the material was tainted and late. The IDF desperately needed an *internal* and *reliable* source of information. This would be no easy task, and so this force would have to be made up of the toughest, most intelligent and innovative conscript sons of the state.

Arnan first recruited veterans from the infamous Unit 101, the retaliatory commando force that a young and upstart major named "Arik" Sharon formed in 1953. Then he turned to urban kids, especially those young Israelis whose parents had come from the Arabic diaspora. Although discriminated against in the European-dominated Labor Party, which led Israel in the late 1950s and early 1960s, and usually excluded by the air force and the other elite reconnaissance commando units, these kids understood the Arab mentality, knew Arabic, and, most importantly, had a chip on their shoulder that translated into a competitive edge that the other Sabras (native Israelis) would have to emulate.

Arnan set out to "Arabize" his men. European Jews, or Ashkenazim, were sent to the desert for instruction by Bedouin tribal chiefs. Finally, Arnan ventured to the country's kibbutzim—Israel's nationwide well for pilots, commandos, and combat officers. The kibbutzim are a special-forces talent pool that the British Army's elite 22 Special Air Service Regiment (SAS) and the U.S. Army's Delta Force and the U.S. Navy SEALs all envy. Kibbutzniks tend to be healthy, physically fit, and used to living in a society with a firm bureaucracy (like the military); this trait also ensures that they know how to bend the rules when required, something that would definitely be needed in a unit like Sayeret Mat'kal.

Perhaps most important, *kibbutznikim* are subjected to peer pressure unlike that of any other civilization on earth. Status in the kibbutz depends on one's status in the military. The better and more selective the unit, the higher the status. Upon conscription into the IDF, a typical eighteen-year-old kibbutznik wants to become a pilot; in a worst-case scenario, should he be ousted from the flight training, he will settle for a paratroop or reconnaissance unit. Sayeret Mat'kal, however, is the unit that every kibbutznik dreams of entering. According to a former reconnaissance commando and born-and-bred kibbutznik, "There were many times during the torturous trial period before being accepted into the unit that I wanted to quit, but the fear of returning to the farm as a washout terrified me and propelled me to continue even though my physical will had already ended."

In 1959, Avraham Arnan found one such competitive and capable kibbutznik—a soldier around whom he would shape his unit. That soldier was a young conscript named Ehud Barak. The man who would come to embody the Sayeret Mat'kal persona, Barak was a stocky and brash soldier possessing untapped courage and charisma. His innovative style, bravery behind enemy lines, and zealous attention to the mission at hand convinced many that, if he wasn't killed or captured on some secret mission, he would one day become chief of staff or even prime minister.

Arnan modeled Sayeret Mat'kal along the lines of the British SAS, Captain David Stirling's legendary band of rogue warriors of the Second World War; in fact, a plaque with the SAS motto WHO DARES WINS hangs above the main table at the Sayeret Mat'kal mess at their base somewhere in central Israel. As a rogue force, Sayeret Mat'kal was separate from the regular IDF, and in many ways those serving in the unit were released from regular active service. They were the best of the best and had to earn that reputation behind enemy lines.

Sayeret Mat'kal operates in small bands called a *Tzevet* (team) trained in virtually every facet of ground combat, expert in every weapon to be found in the Middle East and capable of acting independently of the larger formation. "One of the truly remarkable aspects about Sayeret Mat'kal," according to a former naval commando officer who worked with the unit, frequently many miles behind enemy lines, "was how they prepared for an operation. It didn't matter how big their target was or how small, they studied it exhaustively. Each soldier knew his task, as well as that of the others on the mission. Every contingency was thought of and responses prepared—if a million things could go wrong with an operation, they would plan and be prepared for a million and one things to go wrong." Sayeret Mat'kal's absolute professionalism in the field and behind enemy lines brought results, but they remain classified to this day. "If you *don't* hear about their exploits in the headlines," confides an officer in the IDF field security division, "it means that it's business as usual with the unit."

Virtually all of Sayeret Mat'kal's intelligence-gathering operations remain state secrets of the highest order, although reports have hinted that the unit "routinely" reconnoiters enemy lands—from Syria to Libya to Iraq. Yet it is counterterrorism, and more specifically hostage rescue, that put the unit on the international map. Long before GSG-9, long before Delta Force, there was Sayeret Mat'kal. Among the unit's known operations are Operation Gift, the audacious December 28, 1968, raid against Beirut International Airport where thirteen Lebanese airliners were destroyed in retaliation for Lebanon's assistance to Palestinian terrorist attacks against El Al aircraft in Europe. Another was Operation Isotope 1, the May 9, 1972, rescue of nearly a hundred passengers on board a hijacked Sabena Belgian Airlines Boeing 707 at Lod Airport. The Mat'kal commandos dressed in white coveralls to masquerade as airline mechanics; one of those wounded in this groundbreaking mission was a young lieutenant named Benjamin "Bibi" Netanyahu; Netanyahu's unit commander was Ehud Barak.

The two operations that best personify Sayeret Mat'kal are Operation Spring of Youth, the April 9-10, 1973, raid against Black September in Beirut, and, of course, Operation Thunderball, the July 3-4, 1976, rescue operation at Entebbe. Operation Spring of Youth was the culmination of Israel's covert war of elimination and revenge against the Black September group for perpetrating the Munich Olympic massacre where, according to reports, Mat'kal operators were part of the infamous Mossad hit teams that roamed Europe.

Operation Thunderball is, of course, the most famous commando raid in history—the substance of legend, mystique, and endless Hollywood treatment. On June 27, 1976, an Air France flight from Tel Aviv to Paris via Athens was hijacked to Entebbe, Uganda, by a mixed lot of German and Palestinian terrorists acting with the full collusion of Ugandan strongman Idi Amin and his military. When the terrorists performed their symbolic *selektion*, separating the 103 Jewish and Israeli hostages from those that were eventually released, Israel had no choice; the action brought back images of the Holocaust, and Israel had to act decisively before Jews were once again readied for the slaughter. In a courageous decision, the Israeli government despatched Sayeret Mat'kal, along with several other commando units, to Africa. Following a brutal eight-hour flight inside the bellies of an armada of Hercules transport aircraft, the Israelis landed undetected at Entebbe. The Mat'kal commandos, masquerading as Idi Amin's bodyguards, black Mercedes and all, managed to eliminate the terrorists and rescue the hostages. Typifying the "follow me" ethic of command that was perfected by Sayeret Mat'kal and similar units, Mat'kal commander Lieutenant Colonel Jonathan "Yoni" Netanyahu, Benjamin Netanyahu's brother, was killed leading the task force. He was the sole Israeli combat fatality.

Prime Minister Rabin monitored developments around Bir Naballah as the setting sun ushered in the Sabbath and the final hours before Waxman's deadline. He hoped that Sayeret Mat'kal could pull off yet another Entebbe, and yet he knew the risks involved. Sometimes, all the phases of the operation gel in such a way that the mission, from beginning to end, is executed perfectly, with the terrorists being either killed or captured and the hostages freed; casualties, if kept to an absolute minimum, can still consititute a victory. At Entebbe the most meticulous of preparation, innovation, and actual execution allowed for the rescue for over one hundred hostages but also resulted in hostage casualties. Even operations characterized by the best of intentions and the most remarkable displays of heroism are thwarted by fate and bad luck.

At 14:00 hours, the Mat'kal force that would attempt to rescue Waxman, led by Captain Nir Poraz, arrived at an anonymous military base in Jerusalem for a briefing by Chief of Staff Barak and his intelligence staff, who were monitoring events outside the safe house in Bir Naballah. A Shin Bet observation team in the village had provided an incredibly accurate layout of the targeted house, including all openings (windows and doors), potential assault routes, and even blueprints of the building's interior. The Mat'kal team, having won the chance to carry out the mission in a competition of plans with the Ya'ma'm, now refined its assault strategy and prepared the two-team attack plan.

Yet as the rescue force was en route to the village, Mat'kal observers, crawling unnoticed toward the house, informed the operation commanders that a black Mercedes, driven by known

Hamas terrorists, had pulled up to the house. Was the Mercedes driver there to warn the kidnappers about a rescue or was he delivering the order to execute the hostage? The unknown ripped at the commander's gut and caused anxiety in the minds of the men on the ground, grinding their bodies in silence toward a target. The need to execute the mission intensified.

By 17:15 the Mat'kal operators were in place. At a CP setup in the base in northern Jerusalem, Chief of Staff Barak, his deputy Major General Amnon Lipkin-Shchak, Military Intelligence commander Major General Uri Saguy, the head of Central Command Major General Ilan Biran, West Bank commander Major General Shaul Mofaz, Manpower Branch commander Major General Yoram Yair, Shin Bet director Ya'akov Perry, and Police Superintendent Alik Ron all monitored the transpiring events on a series of radios; all the officers, except Major General Yair, were undercover, wearing civilian clothes. In the event of an emergency, two IAF transport choppers were on immediate standby alert status moments from the action.

At 19:15 hours, as the sun began to set over the coastal plains, the Mat'kal operators started toward the safe house, moving silently and quickly inside the village, which was still bustling with worshipers returning from the mosque's evening prayers. Becoming invisible was a Mat'kal trademark, though tonight the eerie blue or purple haze covering the village caught and held compromising shadows. Remarkably, the Mat'kal operators managed to reach the walls of the house without being detected and without sparking an alarm from the al-Qassam sentry. One force of operators climbed the building's outer walls to the roof, where they waited in ambush, thinking the terrorists would likely race upstairs at the opening burst of the Israeli assault. They also served as an auxiliary entry team, just in case the main force, led by Captain Poraz, encountered difficulties.

Once the roof was secured, the primary assault element led by Captain Poraz moved in through the main and western entrances of the house. Captain Poraz ordered his sappers into action. Silently and methodically, explosive charges were placed on three doors where the Mat'kal were to attempt entry: two doors on the ground floor in the northern approach, including the main entrance, and an entrance on the western side of the house leading into the kitchen, a porch, and the living room. This first phase of the operation had gone better than expected. It was now time for the explosive flurry of courage and fire.

At 19:47 hours the Mat'kal sappers detonated the three explosive charges on the main entry points to the house—only one exploded properly; additional charges had to be brought up and quickly detonated. From the main northern doorway a dozen Mat'kal operators quickly raced into the house, up a flight of stairs, and into the living room. A terrorist, perched on the sofa in the prone firing position, was immediately decimated by a burst of gunfire. The operators moved through the sparingly furnished flat in well-rehearsed choreography in search of targets, but Nachshon Waxman, bound and gagged, was held in a small room inside the flat by two abductors, the room barricaded and fortified. The only door into the small room was reinforced by a heavy steel plate bolstered by steel bolts.

The operators attempted to breech the doorway with explosives, but the charges mangled the steel into a twisted barrier even more formidable than the locked door. The terrorists then began firing their weapons through the walls at the oncoming commandos. "Surrender," Captain Poraz shouted in Arabic, but the terrorists responded with a chilling reply of their own in Hebrew: "We'll kill Nachshon and then die!" Realizing the ordeal was over, one of the terrorists fired seven rounds from his AK-47 into Corporal Waxman's neck, chest, and stomach, killing the hostage after brutally torturing him for nearly a week. (According to reports, Waxman's body was badly bruised and was missing fingernails and toenails. He was also reported to have been savagely bitten by one of his kidnappers.) The kidnappers then began hurling grenades and explosive charges at the Israelis, as well as firing in all directions. In the charge to enter the room, Captain Poraz, the first in, was hit in the head by a 7.62 mm round and killed instantly. Twelve more operators were also seriously wounded in the ferocious close-quarter melee. It had been a bloody night in the hills north of Jerusalem.

The battle for the house in Bir Naballah lasted an incredible fifteen minutes. When the smoke cleared and the stench of blood and cordite dissipated into the air, three kidnappers lay dead next to Waxman. They were later identified as Abdel Karim Badr, Taysir el-Natsheh, and Tsalah Hassan Jedala, better known in Hamas circles as the Jerusalem Gang. All had been wanted by the Israeli authorities for several years for the murders of nearly a dozen Israelis in Jerusalem and the surrounding West Bank communities. Shin Bet officials had known they had a propensity for violence yet had never given them credit for such sophistication and daring. The kidnapping of Waxman was a highly sophisticated operation. The trio had masqueraded as Orthodox Jews and had maintained communications silence with their cell commanders in the West Bank and Gaza, not even using cellular phones or walkie-talkies. In fact, they had received coded radio instructions via the Al-Quds radio station broadcasting from Damascus.[7]

What had begun with hope for salvation had ended in a bloodbath. Major General Yair broke the news to Nachshon's parents, while Prime Minister Rabin and Chief of Staff Barak addressed a stunned and heartbroken Israeli public. "This sort of operation is very complicated and involved, and the unit carrying it out acted in a very determined way under difficult conditions, facing serious opposition during the implementation," stated Barak. "It was the right thing to do." In the Waxman home, the bereaved family prepared for a funeral. In East Jerusalem, the parents of Abdel Karim Badr handed out sweet candies in honor of their son, who had just entered paradise.

The raid had ended in disaster. Israelis, including high-ranking police officers, told wire service reporters that the delays in breaching the door left the raid with little chance for success. One senior official was quoted as saying, "Rescuing a hostage is a matter of seconds. It took fifteen minutes because the commandos weren't prepared." Former Israeli police commissioner Assaf Hefetz, the founding father of the Ya'ma'm, went so far as to say that "Sayeret Mat'kal's operation to rescue Nachshon Waxman was a terrible screw-up!"[8] There were reports that A'man and Shin Bet commanders had bickered openly about which team to use for the rescue, as well as which tactics should have been employed. The death of Corporal Nachshon Morde-chai Waxman tugged at the Israeli soul, as did the subsequent Israeli infighting, a no-holds-barred national pastime. Waxman's murder had caused the country to forget about the peace with the Palestinians and peace with the Jordanians, and it caused Israelis to forget about Yehiya Ayyash. Kidnappings and murders, after all, were not the sole specialty of Izzedine al-Qassam.

Dizengoff Street in Tel Aviv has been described as Fifth Avenue, Oxford Street, and the Champs-d'Elysses all wrapped up into a Middle East boulevard. It certainly provides the pulse of Israel's largest city. Dizengoff Street is where, many years ago, the art-ists and powerbrokers assembled in outdoor cafés to ponder the thought of the day or to escape the frequent madness of Middle East life, and it was there where the young and the beautiful came to shop and be seen. People felt hip on Dizengoff; they felt secure walking the dimly lit tree-lined street while they held hands with lovers or pushed a baby stroller. Dizengoff Street is certainly the main artery that fuels the lifeblood of the city.

The means to travel that artery is primarily the No. 5 bus from

The family of the Engineer—the parents of Yehiya Ayyash with his son.

The home of Yehiya Ayyash in Rafat.

The coffin of Yehiya Ayyash is carried to the mosque as thousands of Palestinian admirers rush to touch it.

Photo © Samuel M. Katz

An Israeli army jeep drives slowly through a village east of Rafat in search of Yehiya Ayyash.

Photo IDF Spokesman

Israeli soldiers, equipped with night vision goggles, arrest a wanted Hamas activist during a midnight search of a Nablus refugee camp.

Photo © Samuel M. Katz

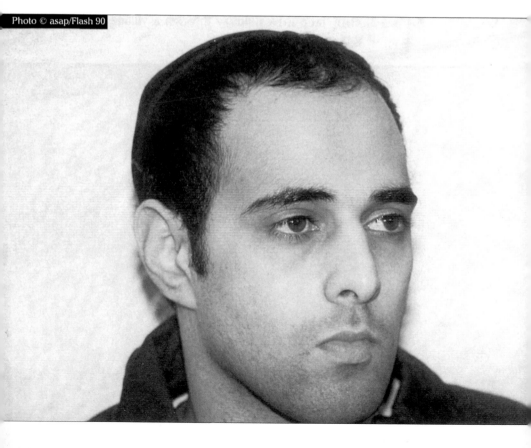

Yehiya Ayyash, "The Engineer."

Carmi Gillon resigned as head of Shin Bet on January 8, 1996, three days after Yehiya Ayyash had been killed, amid attacks for security blunders at Prime Minister Rabin's assassination.

Photo © asap/Flash 90

Rear Admiral (Res.) Ami Ayalon, a highly decorated commando and combat officer, became Gillon's successor as head of Shin Bet.

Photo © asap/Flash 90

A bomb set off on the No. 5 bus on Tel Aviv's Dizengoff Square on October 19, 1994 produced a blast so powerful that it lifted the vehicle off its chassis. Twenty-one people were killed, some fifty seriously injured.

Photo © asap/Flash 90

Among the five victims who died in Jerusalem on August 21, 1995 when a suicide bomber blew up a bus at Ramat Eshkol was an American teacher from Connecticut. More than 100 were seriously hurt.

Photo © asap/Flash 90

An early-morning explosion of a bus near Jerusalem's central bus station on February 26, 1996 killed twenty-five, including 2 Americans.

the Dan Transportation Company. The No. 5 is a straightforward route around Dizengoff, commencing from the market-
minded madness of the Central Bus Station along to Allenby
Street and then Rothschild Boulevard, past the national theater,
to Dizengoff Street, where it carries students, soldiers, shoppers,
housewives, and seniors. The route ends at Pinkas Street, in the
north tier of the city known for its liberal politics, high living
standards, and snobbish demeanor. The *Tzfonim*, as those from
North Tel Aviv are known, were an elitist bunch and the No. 5
was *their* bus.

The No. 5 bus is a shuttle. It is always crowded with busy
people hurrying from point A to point B. It was an ideal target
for Yehiya Ayyash.

Ayyash's last foray into bus bombings had been something of
a disappointment. In the mind of a terrorist with a very limited
operational lifetime, the body count in Hadera was admirable
but far from spectacular. The bombing had warranted aboveboard attention by the Shin Bet, but the smoldering skeleton of
a bus that served as a grave for six victims did not achieve great
notoriety. The device, after all, had been small. It was lethal and
fairly compact, but its range and destructive bang-for-the-buck
was limited. Yehiya Ayyash was interested in destroying a bus
and everyone on board. To achieve this objective, Ayyash would
have to switch from his trusted acetone concoction to a device
with far more conventional strength. His Samaria Battalion had
cached explosives purchased from organized crime gangs in Israel, as well as material smuggled through the porous frontiers
of Gaza. In some ten kilograms of industrial-strength military
TNT, Yehiya Ayyash had the tools needed to destroy his bus.
In one Saleh Abdel Rahim al-Souwi, he had the delivery system.

In the world of Hamas martyrs, Saleh Abdel Rahim al-Souwi
was another character straight out of central casting. Fair-
skinned, intelligent, and cool-tempered, he was a native of
Qilqilya, a town on the southwestern most fringe of the West

Bank that bordered the affluent Israeli suburb of Kfar Saba. With a slim frame and a round cherubic face, al-Souwi looked harmless; but behind his placid manner lay rage and a thirst for revenge that had gone unnoticed by the Izzedine al-Qassam talent scouts. His brother, Hasin, had been killed in a shoot-out with Israeli forces in 1989, and the elder al-Souwi had vowed revenge. In fact, according to intelligence reports, al-Souwi joined Hamas specifically to avenge his brother's death.

The Shin Bet knew all about Saleh Abdel Rahim al-Souwi. An agent from the Arab Desk had wanted to "interview" him, but he never showed up for his appointment at the sprawling IDF HQ in Qilqilya. Although he was a fugitive, he wasn't one of Israel's most wanted. There were no IDF dragnets for his arrest, and the Ya'ma'm wasn't on call to surround his hideout.

On the run, al-Souwi entered the world of the Hamas operative—traveling from mosque to mosque, studying, learning, preparing, and being prepared. According to testimony given to Shin Bet investigators seeking a connection between Hamas commanders in the United States and cells in the West Bank, al-Souwi was a close friend of Ayyash. The two had been seen together frequently, and al-Souwi was considered a reliable and highly capable officer in Ayyash's battalion. Ayyash had realized that the Tel Aviv operation would become epic and when the orders to execute a "unique" mission inside the enemy heartland was received, via coded transmission from Damascus, he would need a reliable messenger.

Izzedine al-Qassam intelligence operatives were no strangers to the hustle of Tel Aviv. In the good old days, before closures and curfews, many had worked inside the sprawling city as laborers, dishwashers, sewage attendants, and at just about every filthy job imaginable—jobs Israelis refused to do. Hamas spies had carefully monitored Tel Aviv's sprawling interneighborhood web of buses and had watched which routes were most crowded and which ones passed through Dizengoff Square, a city center marked by benches and an Agam sculpture and water fountain. Many of the operatives had traveled the city's bus routes themselves, looking for any opportunity that could be used operationally. Were the passengers suspicious of the Arab riders? Were riders aware of men with heavy bags or backpacks? Did the drivers carry side arms? The preoperational intelligence effort that Hamas invested into each of its attacks was impressive and increasing in scope and sophistication each and every time.

A day before the operation, al-Souwi made a living testament to the virtues of martyrdom. Clutching an Israeli-made, IDF-issue, Glilon 5.56 mm assault rifle, the calm and emotionless al-Souwi spoke about the operation and his role. "It is good to die as a martyr for Allah," he said. "Sages end up in paradise."[9]

Most suicide bombers, for security reasons, did not learn about explosives or their mission until twenty-four hours before their mission. An intimate knowledge of the destructive power of explosives might, after all, give them second thoughts. Saleh Abdel Rahim al-Souwi was no stranger to explosives or operational tradecraft. Yet a mind driven by vengeance can overcome any fear or trepidation. Days before his mission, al-Souwi spent hours inside mosques chanting and praying passages of the Koran designed to set body and mind at ease. According to reports, a favorite passage of his states, "Think not of those who are slain in Allah's way as dead. No. They live on and find their sustenance in the presence of their Lord."[10]

Abdel Rahim al-Souwi's date with paradise was just before 9:00 on the morning of October 19. He was driven from the West Bank to one of the first stops along the No. 5 route by Muatab Mukadi, a messenger and arms procurer in Ayyash's cell. Al-Souwi boarded the crowded bus on the northbound run from the Central Bus Station to the northern end of Tel Aviv. After paying his fare, al-Souwi calmly walked into the spacious cabin and took a seat on the left hand-side of the bus, choosing the aisle seat rather than a window seat. The bus was crowded but not packed. Most of the passengers were busy in conversation or reading the morning papers, discussing the final draft of the peace treaty to be signed next week with Jordan.

At 8:55 A.M., driver Salah Ovadia, a father of six, guided the bus past the bustling Dizengoff Center Shopping Mall on the corner of King George Street and raced through a green light underneath Dizengoff Square toward a stop at the corner of Queen Esther Street. Pedestrian traffic on Dizengoff was bustling. Tourists and shoppers strolled the street, and workers were just opening up the Middle East food stands and restaurants catering to tourists. The sun was creeping up through a high autumn sky. A humid breeze rolled in from the west and the beach five blocks over.

At 8:56, Abdel Rahim al-Souwi calmly stood up as Ovadia maneuvered the bus toward its stop. The brown bag by his feet was attached, courtesy of a wire riding through a slot in his trousers, to an electrical switch in his jacket pocket. The bag contained the shell of an Egyptian land mine, crammed with twenty kilograms of military TNT packed beneath a generous supply of nails and screws. The device was stable and reliable and one of the best ever built by Ayyash. Without a word, and without emotion, al-Souwi simply flipped the switch and turned the rectangular bus into a fireball. "At first there was a brilliant flash of light, and then a deafening roar," an eyewitness told police.

The force of the explosion was so powerful that it lifted the vehicle off its chassis like a toy and then bounced it back to earth with the angry hand of God. The heat of the blast was hellish—it melted most of the fiberglass frame of the bus, leaving behind only a metallic skeleton. The force of the explosion was without mercy. A controlled explosion inside an enclosed space produced a devilish wave of energy, heat, and shrapnel. Bodies were torn to shreds and thrown through melted windows onto the street below and rooftops nearby. Limbs were projected like missile into the seating area of nearby restaurants. A cloud of black smoke billowed above the chinaberry trees that lined the street. Leaves were covered in blood. Salah Ovadia lay motionless in his seat, dead.

Chaos followed al-Souwi's deed. There is no calm and orderly manner to respond to a man who incinerates himself on a bus, taking scores of women and children with him. Women, blown to their knees as far as a block away, screamed in an uncontrolled cadence as they viewed the smoking remnants of the bus and the dead and the wounded torn apart on the paved street. Reportedly, the crime scene was so horrific that beat cops responding to the scene vomited at the sight of the torn bodies and the stench of blood and charred flesh.

Police units raced to the scene, as did emergency medical crews, firemen, and bomb squad technicians. There wasn't a sapper on the job that Wednesday morning who didn't remember reading the post-incident reports of the Hadera bombing and the second device left behind to deal with the rescuers. Sappers wearing Kevlar body armor waded through the blood and body fluids to search for a second device, or perhaps a booby-trapped calling card attached to the bomber. By 9:15, the first ambulances reached Ichilov Hospital, some ten blocks away. The emergency room was awash in blood. The hospital, used to handling cardiac cases and the occasional car wreck, looked like a battlefield triage center.

Amid the blood and smoke, crowds of demonstrators gathered and began chanting "Mavet La'Aravim," or "Death to the Arabs," in a frenzy of anguish. Tel Aviv police arrested scores of Arab suspects in and around the blast area, though most were detained to save them from crowds eager to exact Middle Eastern payback—mob-style.

Along Dizengoff Street, black-coated rabbis and Orthodox

men from the Hevra Kadisha burial society grabbed plastic bags and tweezers as they searched for body parts; no matter how big or small, they were to be recovered and afforded the proper Jewish burial. The search for body fragments carried the rabbinical crews up trees and to nearby rooftops for fingers, arms, and shards of scalp tissue. The search for clues was carried out by men wearing blue slacks and button-down shirts on Dizengoff. The deafening clap of al-Souwi's bomb was heard through the thick glass at Shin Bet headquarters. The agents and desk officers raced to the scene, only to stand silently and stoically in stone-faced disbelief. Many of them lived in Tel Aviv. More important, their wives and children walked those streets and rode the city's network of buses. Tel Aviv was supposed to be a safe haven removed from the madness. Counterterrorism was supposed to be waged in alleyways in West Bank cities and inside refugee camps. Suddenly, the Shin Bet felt very helpless.

The blast was so powerful that the U.S. embassy, located some five blocks from ground zero at Dizengoff, shook from the afterblast. The embassy was packed that morning with agents from the U.S. Secret Service and the State Department's Diplomatic Security Service, in country working the advance detail for the arrival of President Clinton and Secretary of State Christopher for the following week's peace treaty ceremony in the Arava Desert. The advance teams working dignitary protection did not like the sound of police and emergency vehicles racing toward the melted remnants of city buses. Explosions were bad for business. The special agents from Washington, D.C. did have good reason to be concerned.

Prime Minister Rabin, on a state visit to Great Britain, raced home to Israel following news of the blast. It had been a rough month for the beleaguered Rabin in an October that should have been filled with nothing but celebration and eager anticipation for the future. Instead of thinking of the seven days until he'd be sitting under the desert sun, flanked by King Hussein and President Clinton, he now had to produce sound bites and statements to the press designed to appease a nation demanding an end to the violence. Rabin would be visiting the crime scene and would act to console families torn to shreds by al-Souwi's moment of martyrdom.

Twenty-one people were killed in the blast and some fifty seriously wounded. It was the deadliest terrorist bombing in Israeli history.

The bombing of the No. 5 bus in Tel Aviv was seen by many in Israel, Jordan, and even the Palestinian Authority as the embodiment of true evil. Now, on front pages, evil had a face. In newspapers around the world the next day, the name Yehiya Ayyash, and his photo, were published for the first time. In the pages of London's prestigious *Independent* to the tabloid headline-grabbing bold type of the *New York Post*, the name Ayyash was now synonymous with indiscriminate wholesale slaughter. The Engineer became synonymous with others in terrorism's notorious hall of fame, along with the Red Prince and the Jackal. Stories about his exploits became full-length features, as were falsehoods about Ayyash's exploits and training. Some reports claimed that Ayyash had built some half-dozen carbombs and had personally killed countless collaborators and Israelis. Other reports claimed he was trained in Iran during a top-secret visit to the Islamic Republic.

The Shin Bet and the Israeli police, who leaked the name "Engineer" to the press in the first case, were initially pleased by the coverage Ayyash was receiving. At last the indiscriminate violence had a name, a face, a mother, a wife, and a son. There was now an enemy to focus on, to hate, to kill. Promoting Ayyash as public enemy number one would justify extraordinary measures that Rabin would soon entrust to his security services. Centralizing the hate and the thirst for revenge into the image of one man whose face appeared in newspapers and magazines throughout Israel deflected a growing mistrust of the peace process.

To the Palestinians, however, the personalizing of the war of the bombers created a hero—and the Palestinians had been void of a hero for some time. Ayyash was elusive, cunning, invisible, and deadly—everything the Palestinians hadn't been in the nearly fifty years of conflict with the Jewish state. Moderate Palestinians, even after Dizengoff, spoke of him with reverence. T-shirts bearing Ayyash's face soon became the best-selling fashion statement of kids and teenagers throughout Gaza and the West Bank. Ayyash was a rock star on a stage of fire and every day that he managed to elude the Shin Bet and the IDF, he earned scores of new fans and admirers.

A day after the blast, A'man chief Major General Uri Saguy met his counterpart in Jordanian intelligence, General Tachsin Shordam, for lengthy discussions in Aqaba. A tall man with a granite chest and the beguiling smile of a spymaster, General Shordam was a veteran of the counterterrorist campaigns his country had often fought in the shadows, far from the headlines of tabloid papers and far removed from CNN coverage. Ostensibly the meeting was an introductory session to set the stage for interdepartmental liaisons once Prime Minister Rabin and King Hussein signed the peace treaty, as well as a briefing on security measures that would be provided to President Clinton.[11] The meeting was more than handshakes and the wording of a memorandum to forward to the U.S. Secret Service. The exchange lasted well over three hours and Hamas was the primary topic of conversation. Publicly, General Shordam condemned the Waxman kidnapping and murder and the Bus No. 5 bombing; privately he is said to have pledged the full support of the Jordanian intelligence and special operations community in the war against Hamas. Israel was preparing its soon-to-be official regional ally that the gloves were coming off in the war against Hamas. The Jewish state would need all the help it could get.

In an emergency meeting of the Israeli cabinet on October 24, 1994, Prime Minister Rabin instructed the heads of the Mossad and the Shin Bet, along with A'man chief Major General Uri Saguy and senior operational and special forces planners, to seek out and terminate the heads of Hamas; hundreds of low-level Hamas supporters were rounded up and questioned by the Shin Bet, and troops in the West Bank were issued with "shoot-to-kill" directives when dealing with Hamas suspects. A list of the leaders was distributed and the orders given.[12] Yehiya Ayyash topped the long list of men deemed too dangerous to be allowed to walk the back alleys of the Middle East any longer. Rabin's directives reminded many of the legendary Israel hit teams that selectively and successfully terminated the top commanders of Black September in the wake of the 1972 Munich Olympic massacre. The hit teams fought in Beirut, the Mediterranean, and Europe in a campaign designed to remove the brains from an organization that had proven to be cunning, relentless, and brutal in its determination and execution. Mossad veterans, who made names for themselves in those dark days after Munich, realized that this war would be different and bloodier. Hamas was similar to Black September, but far more lethal.

News of Rabin's edict was the worst kept secret in Israel. On the morning of October 23, 1994, Israelis picked up their morning papers to read the following headlines blasted on the front page of the *Yediot Aharonot*: "Rabin Has Instructed the Mossad and the Shin Bet to Eliminate the Heads of Hamas—One of Rabin's Aides Told the Observer: 'Yehiya Ayyash, the Mastermind Behind the Murderous Attack on Dizengoff, Is Considered a Dead Man. It's Only a Matter of Time Before We Get Our Hands on Him'."

At 7:00 on the morning of October 26, 1994, in the heart of

the sun-filled desert shared by Israel and Jordan, a delighted President Clinton took center stage and acted as ceremonial witness to the signing of the peace accords ending fifty years of war between Israel and Jordan. A regal King Hussein, looking proud and cheerful, watched as thousands of balloons were released into the autumn sky as a celebration of the historic signing. Rabin, weary and preoccupied, appeared anxious. The assembled crowd of five thousand dignitaries appeared oblivious to Rabin's concerns, however. Soldiers from both nations, wearing colorful medals and berets, mingled in an atmosphere of goodwill in anticipation of the new Middle East they would forge as allies.

Yet even the soldiers who were so relieved to bury their swords after so many wars and battles could not remain oblivious to the massive security net safeguarding the ceremony. Hamas, Israeli intelligence had learned, had been planning an attack to disrupt the presidential visit. The nature of the attack was never verified, though after the Waxman kidnapping and the No. 5 bus bombing, few were willing to take any chances. Some twenty thousand police officers and troops were deployed nationwide in preparation of Clinton's visit; in Jerusalem alone, six thousand police officers safeguarded the Clinton itinerary— some five hundred alone stationed outside the King David Hotel. More than a hundred Secret Service agents, supported by twelve Shin Bet bodyguards ringed the presidential party. Special explosives detection equipment was flown in from the United States, as were two specially equipped Blackhawk helicopters flown from the United States. It was the largest security operation in Israeli history—until even this effort would be overshadowed one year later under very different circumstances.

The signing of the peace treaty with Jordan should have captivated the attention of all of Tel Aviv's residents that sunny morning, but the thoughts of over a million people were elsewhere. On the corner of Dizengoff and Esther Ha'Malkah Streets, Jewish mourning candles dotted the scene where the innocence of a city, along with its sense of security, had been obliterated in the flash of a fireball. Passersby stared at the twenty-one glimmering candles and rabbis chanting the Kaddish, the Jewish prayer of the dead. "All the Arabs must die," a kiosk owner whose storefront was sprayed with the debris of bus and bodies yelled to a woman buying sunflower seeds, "Baruch Goldstein was right!" The blinding cycle of biblical hatred was repeating itself on Dizengoff Street.

Ayyash had proven in the fall of 1994 that Hamas was capable of mounting a clear and present danger to the very fabric of Israeli security with little more than a man willing to die and some explosives strapped to his chest. And, in the kidnapping of Corporal Nachshon Waxman, Hamas had proven to the Israeli political hierarchy that it knew of several ways to claw at the Israeli psyche and rip it to shreds. Most important, however, the deadly October of 1994 had marked a new twist in Israel's war against the Islamic Resistance Movement. It was no longer a nation versus a movement. It had become more personal. Ayyash was now the most wanted—and hated—man in the history of Israeli law enforcement.

Two weeks after the Dizengoff bombing, as body fragments were still being discovered by horrified residents of the neighborhood in a two-block radius around ground zero, men wearing Arab garb and sporting mini-Uzi submachine guns under their frocks walked the hills of Samaria in search of what had now become the most talked-about face in Israel. The men, soldiers in the Israeli Army's elite "Cherry" undercover squad, were hoping to snare Ayyash as he attempted to visit his family in Rafatt. The operators were all highly trained professional gunmen, many still in their teens. They knew the nation was relying on them to rid Israel of the gravest threat to its hopes for peace.

Inside the secure offices at Shin Bet headquarters, and at

A'man computer stations, nineteen-year-old women soldiers with top-security clearances manipulated high-resolution graphic images of Yehiya Ayyash to configure his appearance with a beard, as an Orthodox Jew, even as a young Arab woman. Israel's spies knew him to be a master of disguises, and the hunt was on. The order from Prime Minister Rabin was clear: Kill Ayyash!

Notes

[1]Sarah Helm, "PLO Chief Returns to a Subdued Welcome," *The Independent*, July 2, 1994, p. 8.

[2]Ibid., p. 8.

[3]Interview, Tel Aviv, August 1, 1997.

[4]David Regev, "*Be'A'za Nitfasu Faxim Me'Iran: Higbiru Ha'Terror*," *Yediot Aharonot*, September 9, 1994, p. 1A.

[5]David Regev, "*Hichziru Li At Bni Hai*," *Yediot Aharonot*, October 12, 1994, p. 8.

[6]Roni Shaked, "*Mivtzar Ha'Hamas*," *Yediot Aharonot*, October 16, 1994, p. 8.

[7]David Horovitz and Ehud Ya'ari, "Can Hamas Blow Up the Peace Process?" *The Jerusalem Report*, November 17, 1994, p. 21.

[8]Ya'akov Galanti, "*Ha'Mivtza Shel Sayeret Mat'kal Le'Hilutz Nachshon Waxman Haya Fashla Nora'it*," *Ma'ariv Weekend Supplement*, December 26, 1997, p. 7.

[9]Clyde Haberman, "Living Martyr Leaves Taped Statement," *The New York Times*, October 20, 1994, p. 2A.

[10]Harvey W. Kushner, "Suicide Bombers: What Makes Them Tick," *Counter-Terrorism and Security International*, May 1996.

[11]Smadar Perry, "*Lo Ne'afsher Le'Hamas Li'Fo'l Mi'Shetach Yarden Neged Yisrael*," *Yediot Aharonot*, October 21, 1994, p. 4.

[12]"*Rabin Hore Le'Mossad U'Le'Sha'Ba'K: Chisloo et Bechirei Ha'Hamas*," *Yediot Aharonot*, October 28, 1994, p. 3.

Chapter 5

The Ticking Bombs

Qilqilya was a festive town the morning after the Dizengoff bombing. The family of al-Souwi made it a point, once his identity was confirmed by an Israeli police lab using DNA technology, to do what all families of the martyred did in the war Hamas was waging—and winning—against the Jewish State: it threw a party. Poor families in Qilqilya had little extra cash to buy pickles, dates, olives, and gigantic sacks of pita bread, let alone extra shekels for the slaughter of a lamb and cartons full of soft drinks and candy. The tab would be picked up by the mosque and the men no one talked about in public but who had become the new sheriffs in town. To the counterintelligence agents watching from across the way, the celebration must have seemed like a bar mitzvah of sorts—similar to the outdoor celebrations they themselves had received back when the world seemed a lot simpler. Men sang and danced, women prepared food and gossiped, and small children played around a photo of the shaheed, already encased behind the glass of a gold metal frame reserved for those killed in battle. Much of the neighborhood assembled outside the al-Souwi family home.

The celebration, known to sometimes last as long as a week, was short-lived. On the afternoon of October 20, 1994, Shin Bet agents, along with civil administration personnel and some two hundred troops wearing body armor and carrying assault rifles and light machine guns, surrounded the al-Souwi home. "You have one hour to take your possessions and get out of the house before we raze it," an army officer told al-Souwi's mother. Sappers were already setting the blocks of TNT.

Destroying the house of a terrorist was a punitive measure that dated back to the British Mandate. It was cruel and after the fact, but it was meant to convince fathers to convince their sons that carrying out a terrorist attack, no matter how justified in the the grander struggle, meant enormous hardship for the family. Yet the threat of collective suffering had not been a factor in al-Souwi's decision to detonate himself on board a bus in Tel Aviv. As much of the southern Qilqilya watched, the al-Souwi family residence was reduced in a flash to a cloud of spreading gray smoke and debris. Most of the young soldiers assembled for the daylong affair were old hands at house demolitions and most found the work stressful and disturbing. Yet many were from Tel Aviv. They had ridden the No. 5 bus. They knew families who celebrated differently than the clans in Qilqilya. The explosion seemed like fitting retribution.

On November 3, 1994, Hani Abed, a thirty-five-year-old up and coming star of the Islamic Jihad in Gaza and a man known to have been behind the killings of several Israeli soldiers, left his office in an Islamic college in Khan Yunis to drive to the Jebalya refugee camp and a covert meeting with senior Hamas operatives. The meeting was to discuss the new crackdown by the Palestinian police as well as the threats of Israeli Prime Minister

Rabin to unleash the Mossad and Shin Bet to hunt down and kill senior Hamas leaders anywhere in the world. The Islamic Jihad had always taken a backseat to the more flamboyant and headline-grabbing Hamas, but the Waxman kidnapping and Dizengoff bombing changed the rules of engagement as far as both the Israelis and the Palestinians were concerned. It galvanized opponents against a common enemy. After all, if both the Palestinians and the Israelis could act as an allied entity in the search for Waxman's kidnappers, then so too could Hamas and the Islamic Jihad.

As Abed put some documents in the trunk of his battered white Peugeot 504 sedan, a safety device was neutralized and triggered a powerful explosive device. The blast was deafening and produced a huge orange-and-black fireball. Most of Abed's body disintegrated in the explosion; his car was destroyed and windows as far as seven block away were shattered. No group claimed responsibility for the assassination. Abed was known to have had his ideological disputes with Hamas, yet one of the Jihad's leaders, Sheikh Abdullah Shami, said, "Only Israel could do such an expert job in rigging the car bomb that killed Abed." Surrounded by masked gunmen cradling Israeli-produced Glilon assault rifles taken from murdered Israeli soldiers, Sheikh Shami vowed that vengeance would be exacted in Tel Aviv. Hundreds of supporters chanted "Death to Israel, death to America!"

Hani Abed was considered an up-and-comer in the Islamic terrorist underworld. Smart, brave, and ruthless, he was also a charismatic personality. People followed him and learned from him. Abed had taken classes in electronic circuitry and bomb building from Yehiya Ayyash. The Islamic Jihad was about to turn a corner in its until then limited campaign against Israel. Yehiya Ayyash had sparked fire in the hearts and minds of the Jihad. Hamas had, in one week, proven how Israel's sense of security could be shattered like a pane of glass pounded with a sledgehammer. For the Jihad, the time to strike at Israel was now.

The Islamic Jihad in Palestine traces its roots to a small group of university students from the Gaza Strip who were educated in Egyptian universities and who were deeply influenced by the preaching of Muslim Brotherhood leaders and imams in Cairo. The Muslim Brotherhood in Egypt had been integral to the Egyptian political and religious infrastructure since independence, especially among Egypt's poor under the regimes of King Farouk and presidents Nasser and Sadat. The explosive Iranian revolution in 1979, in which religious fundamentalism had been fueled by a charismatic exiled leader, helped create a phenomenon that ousted the regime of the most powerful pro-Western leader in the Near East and attracted new followers to militant Islam in Egypt and among the Palestinian students in universities in Cairo, Alexandria, and the Nile Delta.

Two of the most prominent Palestinian disciples of this militant Islamic renaissance were Dr. Fathi Shiqaqi, a physician from the town of Rafath in the Gaza Strip, and Sheikh Abdel Aziz Odeh, a religious preacher from the Jebalya refugee camp, also in the Gaza Strip. Shiqaqi, a native of the Fehra refugee camp, upon graduation from Bir Zeit University in the West Bank, where he received a bachelor of science degree, studied medicine in Sykarzik University in Egypt, known as one of the main centers of Islamic radical thought in the country. Deeply influenced by the Iranian revolution, Shiqaqi published *Khomeini: The Islamic Solution and Alternative* in 1979 to express his enthusiastic support for the Iranian Islamic revolution. He praised it as "a singularly effective working model in humanities revolution." The Iranian example became a cornerstone of the Islamic Jihad's political and military orientation. Following his studies in Egypt, Shiqaqi returned to Israel, where he practiced medicine in the

Al-Mutla Hospital in East Jerusalem; later he moved back to Gaza and opened a small private practice.

Shiqaqi's fundamentalist beliefs propelled him to seek out and recruit other Gazans who, like himself, had either studied in Egypt or had been deported from Egypt as a result of subversive activity. One such man was Sheikh Abdel Aziz Odeh, a Muslim cleric who, years earlier, had earned academic distinction in Arabic and Islamic studies, both from the Dar al Alim in Cairo, as well as an Islamic Law education from Sykarzik University. Immersed in his Islamic studies, Odeh became a fiery supporter of the Egyptian Muslim Brotherhood, the Gimat al Islamiya, known for his zealous oratory. In 1975 he was deported from Egypt for his involvement with the Muslim Brotherhood, and he moved to the United Arab Emirates, eventually returning to Israel in 1981, where he served as the imam and preacher at the Sheikh Izzedine al-Qassam mosque in the Beit Lahiya section of the Gaza Strip. His fiery sermons in the mosque were public service announcements for the Ayatollah Khomeini and the Iranian revolution, including directing the struggle not only against non-Muslims but primarily against the Arab regimes that have "deviated" from Islam or persecuted the Moslem Brotherhood.

At first, Shiqaqi and Odeh's concerns were with the organization's cultural propaganda, recruitment, and political conversions through sermons conducted in mosques and at other religious meetings, as well as through pamphlets, flyers, and other publications. A small cadre of operatives known as the Islamic Pioneers began to seek out a working relationship with the other resistance factions of the Palestinian liberation movements. This relationship strengthened its militant stance to many of the fundamentalists, as well as provided access to weaponry, terrorist tradecraft, and operational experience. Many of the operatives from Fatah and the Popular Front were trained by KGB and East Bloc instructors and these "experts" quickly taught their allies in the Jihad many of the do's and don'ts of terrorist operations. The first Islamic Jihad strike came in August 1983, with the murder of Aharon Garus, a Yeshiva student from Hebron. The attack, a drive-by shooting, was an unsophisticated entry into the Arab-Israeli conflict; Islamic Jihad commanders, including Sheikh Odeh, were quickly arrested and imprisoned. In 1988, Dr. Fathi Shiqaqi was expelled from the Gaza Strip—banished to exile in Lebanon.

Inside Lebanon, and later on in Syria, where Assad's intelligence services found promise in the doctor from Gaza, the Islamic Jihad regrouped and restructured. With Syrian support—and weaponry and cash—Fathi Shiqaqi consolidated his hold as the unquestioned military and political commander of the Islamic Jihad; his deputy, Dr. Ramadan Abdullah Shallah, an aspiring preacher with zealous conviction and religious piety, became one of the organization's true ideologues. Using his skills and devotion he recruited new members and established networks throughout the territories. Shallah founded the Islamic Fund to collect and disseminate contributions to finance the relief and social welfare projects with which Islamic Jihad served converts and the faithful.

The Islamic Jihad's military campaign had never amounted to anything more than indiscriminate attacks of spontaneous violence. In July 1989 a terrorist on board the No. 405 intercity bus heading to Jerusalem from Tel Aviv grabbed the steering wheel and veered the packed motor coach into a steep ravine; sixteen passengers were killed in the crash and some twenty-five seriously wounded. With the exception of an ambush in Egypt in February 1990, in which a bus full of Israeli tourists was hit in a murderous crossfire, the Islamic Jihad had shied away from the use of firearms or explosives. They had specialized in cutting throats, stabbing, and other hands-on attacks favoring the use of axes, daggers, and picks to kill and maim. They were, according to an Israeli law enforcement official, "cold-blooded animals fond of cold-metal killing instruments." Yet the Islamic

Jihad could not escape the events unfolding before their eyes, or the means by which Hamas had single-handedly usurped the momentum of the peace accords signed by Prime Minister Rabin and PLO chairman Arafat. The Islamic Jihad wanted "in" on the conflict, and joining forces with Hamas was a marriage of convenience for Shiqaqi and his lieutenants.

Hani Abed was the link to that marriage; something of a matchmaker, bride, and groom all in one. Abed was involved in the world of Palestinian terrorism—the kind of man who drew up operational plans, coordinated and manipulated cells of operatives, and who sent men to their deaths. He was also the Islamic Jihad's liaison to Hamas and its prized bomb builder Yehiya Ayyash. Abed generated a great deal of interest from the Israeli intelligence community.

Israel never confirmed or denied its role in Hani Abed's death—Israeli policy in covert assassinations is to never take official credit for a hit. Nevertheless, few inside Shin Bet headquarters were surprised when news of Abed's explosive termination was broadcast. At last, a link between the two organizations had been severed. But by the time Abed was killed, he had already cemented an operational alliance with Hamas and had seen to it that Yehiya Ayyash had trained several Jihad operatives in the art of improvising store-bought explosives. In fact, Ayyash even supplied several devices to the men of the Jihad as a bonus. The three bombs were powerful—like the one al-Souwi attached before boarding the No. 5 bus on October 19, the bombs Ayyash provided to the Jihad were built from military-grade TNT. Mechanically sound and powerful, they were small enough to fit inside a kit bag or knapsack.

The Islamic Jihad wanted to select a target that would, like the Hamas bombing of the No. 5 bus, shatter a fragile psychological security. Israelis were becoming jittery. They no longer engaged their neighbors in fiery discussions or routine social encounters. Instead, they searched the eyes of those standing next to them on line at cash machines or on board city buses. People who looked Arab or in some way seemed suspicious were reported to police. Security units patrolling the streets of major Israeli cities began spot-checking the identity cards of those who looked even slightly Palestinian.

The Jihad's planners wanted to select a target that would pay homage to Hamas and Yehiya Ayyash, the man who had helped them elevate the struggle to the next level. At a junction some thirty minutes north of Tel Aviv, operators found a weak spot—where an attack could inflict a horrific death toll as well as serve as poignant reminder to the Israelis that there wasn't a place in the country they could not strike.

The Beit Lid Junction is hardly a landmark in modern Israel. Tourists rarely venture to the crossroads off the old main highway connecting Tel Aviv and Haifa, just one mile away from the coastal resort and diamond center of Netanya. There are no ancient ruins in Beit Lid, no historical reminders linking the junction to the Babylonians, Herod, the Romans, or Jesus. Yet Beit Lid is a point of considerable significance to many in Israel. As a crossroads separating the state of Israel from the northern tier of the West Bank, most roads to Tulkarem, Jenin, and even Nablus lead through Beit Lid. On Sunday mornings Beit Lid was swamped with thousands of young soldiers and aging reservists heading back to West Bank duty from weekend leaves. A kiosk at the junction, one amply stocked with snacks, soft drinks, and, most important, smokes, serviced the soldiers leaving the confines of Israel proper for treacherous one- and two-week stints of occupation duty. And perched on the southwest corner of the crossroads: the maximum-security Ashmoret Prison. Ashmoret, with its endless rows of shiny razor wire and electronic sensors, was a no-nonsense facility where sentries from the Israeli Prison Service stood guard armed with assault rifles and precision weapons. There was one famous inmate in Ashmoret. His name: Sheikh Ahmed Yassin.

At 9:30 on the morning of January 22, the crowd outside Bella Zioni's kiosk was bustling. Soldiers gulped down cans of Coke and fried-egg sandwiches before a few week's worth of military cooking. Conscripts lined up at a pay phone to tell their girlfriends one final good-bye, and reservists, some with their own cell phones, argued with wives, yelled at employees, and scolded kids as they struggled to juggle knapsacks and assault rifles for their annual stints of reserve duty.

That morning, the drizzle and the cold did not dampen the spirits of the soldiers heading to the northern tier of the West Bank. The Shin Bet had learned that terrorists were planning an operation targeting Israeli soldiers, but the intelligence wasn't specific enough to warrant nationwide security precautions. Specially trained squads of soldiers had been assigned to patrol bus stops and hitchhiking stations where soldiers routinely gathered, and teams of these guards were on duty that morning at Beit Lid, though they didn't pay particular notice to the two quiet soldiers at opposite ends of the open area walking quietly in their olive fatigues carrying packed-to-capacity kit bags. The uniforms they wore were IDF issue. Innocuously, the two mingled amid the sea of olive, waiting for the moment to strike.

The first of the two soldiers, Anwar Soukar, walked slowly toward the pay phones near the kiosk. The twenty-three-year-old Gaza native clutched his stomach and buckled to his knees, making the sounds of a man about to heave his intestines onto the pavement. As concerned soldiers gathered around him, he opened his kit bag and flipped a light switch fastened to a foot-long slice of eight-inch-wide plumber's pipe and a wrapping of nails. The circuit triggered a detonator which in turn ignited the five kilograms of TNT crammed inside. The explosion was massive. Soldiers near ground zero were ripped to shreds by the force of the blast and the razor-sharp shrapnel hurled in a 360-degree spray of destruction. Some soldiers were decapitated by the explosion; others were forced to die a slow and painful death as their throats and lungs burned with the toxic heat of the bomb's blast. Drivers passing by were splattered by the blood and body parts of the dead and wounded. It was, according to a police inspector responding to the carnage, "a nightmare beyond the scope of human comprehension."

The deafening thud of the explosive device, and the cries of the maimed and dying, sparked a full-security lockdown across the street in Ashmoret Prison. Corrections officers feared that the blast was a diversion to a possible full-fledged assault on the prison meant to liberate Sheikh Yassin. Prison Service officers drew their weapons and donned flak vests as they rushed the confused Yassin back to his cell.

Meanwhile, emergency crews by the droves descended upon the kiosk and bus stop at Beit Lid Junction. To many, the smoke, heat, and stench of bodies ripped open was becoming all too familiar. Ambulances skidded in pools of blood as medics raced to tend to the wounded. As the rescuers picked through the corpses for those still breathing, a soldier who appeared at ease with the bloody chaos approached ground zero. He was dark-skinned and seemed some five years older than most of the other soldiers. Racing into the crowd of rescuers, he reached the center of the original blast and without a word of warning flipped a switch nestled in his upper torso, detonating an even larger device. The fireball, muffled by the thick cloud of smoke and the sea of olive uniforms, rose a hundred feet into the air. Those not killed by the first blast were now cut to pieces by the second explosion.

Beit Lid was no longer a traffic stop en route to the West Bank. It was a crime scene where twenty-one soldiers were killed and more than sixty were critically wounded.

*　　*　　*

Prime Minister Rabin learned of the bombing as he was reading through the final draft of a speech he was to give at the Yad Vashem Holocaust Memorial to commemorate the fiftieth anniversary of the liberation of the Auschwitz death camp. He had hoped to end the day with somber reminders of that painful episode of history when, before the establishment of the state of Israel, Jews could be systematically slaughtered. Yet instead of addressing an international crowd at the Holocaust memorial, Rabin found himself at Beit Lid Junction on a macabre tour of what was becoming a national nightmare. Police and Shin Bet personnel attempted to clean up the area before the prime minister's arrival, though blood and gore were everywhere. Rabin appeared shocked by the destruction; the red berets on the ground, some floating in deep pools of blood, brought the tragedy home. Rabin's grandson Yonatan was serving in the elite 35th Paratroop Brigade at the time. Was he among the dead or the wounded?

Yet as Rabin surveyed the crime scene, covering his mouth as he carefully walked through the ruins of what should have been a normal Sunday morning in central Israel, a third and even larger bomb lay hidden inside a kit bag only a few yards from the entourage. The device had been left in an IDF-issue kit bag by the second bomber in order to be picked up after the first two explosions by a third martyr. But Shahdi Abed al-Rahim Kahlout never made it to the junction because of transportation problems. The third device, meant to be carried near the Shin Bet team that surrounded Prime Minister Rabin, would have raised the stakes in the Middle East to brinkmanship levels. Instead, as soldiers and policemen cleared the debris from the roadside area, the bag was discovered by officers who at first thought it belonged to one of the dead or wounded. Police bomb squad experts examined the device along with Shin Bet investigators. Finding it in working order was a stroke of luck. It could be retained for physical evidence.

The architecture of the device was familiar. The EOD specialists and Shin Bet agents had seen it before, in a postblast recon-
struction following the Afula, Hadera, and Dizengoff bombings.
The Beit Lid massacre bore the signature of Yehiya Ayyash. His
fingerprints were all over the dead and wounded. "I want to
see the bastard dead," a Shin Bet agent told one of the bomb-
disposal officers. "I don't care what the scenario is or how it
happens, I want to see this mother-fucker dead!"[1]

The Beit Lid bombing was a brilliant terrorist operation—a gesture of destruction designed to slice through a national artery
and bleed dry the country's sense of security. The Oslo Accords
were already in a critical state, and every terrorist bombing after
the No. 5 bus massacre would spark internal Israeli debate as to
the merits of peace with the Palestinians. The targeting of young
soldiers, the icon of Israel's veil of security, was greatly disturbing. After all, if bombers could decimate so many soldiers, the
very men and women tasked with defending Israel's citizens,
then who would—or could—stop indiscriminate Hamas horror?
As noted Israeli political commentator Hemi Shalev wrote in the
daily *Ma'ariv* immediately following the blast, "No peace, not
reconciliation, not brotherhood, not life together, but separation."[2]

The martyrdom of Anwar Soukar and Salah Shaaker, the two
Jihad bombers who made it to Beit Lid, was an additional torpedo launched at a sinking peace process. With each terrorist
strike, the Israeli public was losing its patience with the carnage
and the inability to once-and-for-all stop the bombings. Closures
meant nothing, as the Territories were porous frontiers of mountains, hills, and fields that were impossible to seal.

"I know that many are asking, have you brought us peace, or
terror?" Rabin lamented in a public address following the blast.
"The road to peace is not easy." The political crisis caused by
the bombing was serious; a no-confidence vote barely survived

the Knesset floor the following day. In fact, the existence of the third device was kept secret for months after the massacre. Israeli security officials did not want the public panicking, thinking that their leaders were targeted as well.

Rabin had great reason to fear for his personal safety, though he realized that the threat was not truly directed from Gaza or the West Bank. As the pale and visibly disturbed Rabin toured the bomb site, right-wing protesters had gathered amid the wreckage to provide an eardrum-blasting vigil: they saw Yitzhak Rabin leading Israel down a dark and suicidal path. Many of the agents in Rabin's Shin Bet's protective security detail, young men in their twenties straight out of the ranks of the IDF's elite units, seemed overwhelmed by the chants and the cries of the protesters shouting "Rabin is a traitor!" As the disapproval intensified, and residents from nearby towns and agricultural settlements raced to add their voice to the mix, dozens of rabbis from the Hevra Kadisha burial society grabbed paint scrapers and small plastic bags to collect body fragments for proper Jewish burial. The sight of the rabbis, placing heads and limbs into bags, did not quiet the mob. As Rabin was whisked away in his bulletproof limousine, the crowd became violent and clashed with police. They began screaming "Death to Rabin!"[3] One man, wiping blood off the soles of his shoes, cried, "How much more of this madness are we expected to take?"

In Gaza, in Damascus, and in Teheran, the Islamic Jihad claimed responsibility for the attack as vengeance for the assassination of Hani Abed. Jihad leader Abdullah Shami proudly accepted responsibility for the attack and was quickly detained by Palestinian security forces; Arafat, in an attempt to placate a jittery Israeli electorate, called Prime Minister Rabin to privately offer his condolences.

Shin Bet field commanders who had rushed to Beit Lid realized that a triple bombing was more than mere Middle Eastern tit for tat. The existence of the third device indicated to many in the Shin Bet hierarchy that the Hamas and Islamic Jihad alliance possessed a degree of military sophistication in the terrorist arena that hadn't been seen on the Arab-Israeli battlefield since 1972 during Black September's assault on the Israeli Olympic compound in Munich. The mysterious men from Gaza, Ramallah, and Hebron were skilled players in the terrorist sweepstakes. They were smart professionals and completely dedicated. Frustrated Shin Bet officials could do nothing more than sanction massive sweeps of the Territories in the hope of finding a human needle in a haystack.

The Beit Lid bombing came at a point of great transition in the halls of Shin Bet headquarters. Israel's venerable covert counterintelligence and counterterrorist guardians were undergoing a period of great change and tremendous uncertainty. The evacuation from Gaza had sparked a change in the agency's approach to intelligence gathering and counterterrorism, from a hands-on operation involved in late-night meetings and ambushes to one forced to rely on a former adversary and to modify its tactics to sophisticated technical means.

The "mythical period," as many veterans of the service fondly recall those uncomplicated days, for the Shin Bet in the Territories began after Israel's lightning victory. For an agency that had spent the first nineteen years of its existence hunting down Arab and Soviet spies and infiltrating Arab villages inside Israel—sometimes even marrying Arab women as a cover—field work in the territories was new, it was sexy, and it was fun and dangerous. The Occupied Territories were the greatest school in the world for the Shin Bet, and Gaza was its Hell's Kitchen and Harvard University rolled into one bloody package. Young operatives became heroes in the Territories, seasoned agents turned into legends. Fieldwork, as a result, became a way of life inside the Shin Bet. There were agents who didn't know what an office looked like or how to type three lines on an interrogation statement. Yet a generation of agents had learned how to become invisible at dusk, how to appear more Palestinian than a twelfth-generation Hebron native, and they knew every nook and cranny of the Territories—better than they knew their own homes. These agents had developed supersensitive instincts and senses during their endless battles in the trenches. They could look into a man's eyes and know, right there and then, if he was telling the truth or lying; legend has it that they could smell the nicotine on the fingers of a suspect and know what brand of West Bank cigarette he had been smoking. They were proud and capable warriors, though their field of dreams had been taken from them.

The two Beit Lid bombers were Gazans, and in order to assemble material on the incident, the Shin Bet agents were forced to rely on the tidbits of data that Jibril Rajoub's Preventive Security Service was willing to provide. The relationship was one-sided and strained; many times Shin Bet agents were able to learn more from watching CNN or one of the European superstations on cable than from their meetings with the Palestinians. The Shin Bet, man to man, was out of its league in the art of interservice liaisoning with both the Palestinian services and the Central Intelligence Agency moderators out of the Tel Aviv station who, like gunmen in a Sicilian cash transaction, were meant to guarantee security and the flow of information. "Shin Bet agents were masters in the field," claimed an American federal law enforcement official who labored in bridging a working relationship between the Israeli and Palestinian services, "but when this operative was forced to sit down in a wood-paneled office, sip sweet tea, and munch sugar cookies as he and a counterpart started talking turkey, the inherent shortcomings in people skills in the Shin Bet repertoire became painfully apparent."[4] Men who were the first through a door on a dark summer's night made poor diplomats and resentful paper pushers.

Exacerbating the state of transition and uncertainty, Ya'akov

Perry formally ended a seven-year reign as the director of the Shin Bet. Perry had been in the organization for twenty-eight years, and he had served as the service's director for an unprecedented seven years. A close confident to Prime Minister Rabin, Perry was a legend in the Israeli intelligence community. His career began by accident—a musician by heart, Perry had joined the Shin Bet as a way to show his father that he could actually hold down a real job. Yet once inside the secretive world of the Shin Bet, Perry excelled as an agent, a field case officer, a supervisor, and one of the select few who made it to the upper echelons of command. During his career as a field agent and boss, Perry had battled KGB spies, Palestinian terrorists, and Lebanese guerrillas.

Perry was appointed director following two particularly painful chapters in the service's shadowy history: the arrest and wrongful conviction, thanks to Shin Bet overzealousness and physical abuse, of a Circassian officer in the IDF accused of being a PLO agent; and, the cold-blooded killing of two terrorists taken off a hijacked bus in the spring of 1984. In the ensuing investigation, cover-up, and internal political scandal that rocked the core of the Israeli secret service, the Shin Bet falsified evidence, tainted documentation, and subverted witnesses. When the truth came out after a Watergate-like frenzy in the Israeli media, Shin Bet director Avraham Shalom and several of his top deputies were forced to resign. In the wake of the bizarre scandal, a government commission was established to investigate the Shin Bet's relatively free hand at usurping judicial practices. The commission, chaired by former Chief Justice Moshe Landau, emphasized the desperate need to root out the endemic false reporting that was common practice in Shin Bet investigations—and cover-ups—as well as to establish a concrete guideline by which agents would conduct interrogations. It was a mighty tall order for an agency that was so top secret—most

Israelis hadn't a clue as to what it actually did, or what its legal powers were all about.

Perry was the man who had brought the Shin Bet out of that abyss. An organizational dynamo whose charismatic flair and renaissancelike manner was just the medication the ailing service needed, had brought the Shin Bet from the dark days of the Intifadah to a security alliance with both the Palestinian and Jordanian counter-intelligence services. Perry had seen the service turn full-circle and, at the age of fifty-one, and a lucrative career in the private sector before him, Perry had decided to call it quits in his papers. He had tried to resign on several occasions previously, but Prime Minister Rabin would have none of it. Much of the behind-closed-door work revolving around the Oslo Accords were achieved by Perry and his subordinates who secretly met in Rome and other European capitals with their counterparts in Arafat's security apparatus. Rabin trusted his spymaster, and he relied on his unique read on the changing Middle East in implementing the details of the peace accord with the Palestinians. Perry was smart, cunning, reliable, and relentless. But now, the chase had become frustrating. The hunt for the Hamas field commanders, especially Yehiya Ayyash, had largely been unsuccessful. The war had grown brutal and unforgiving. Arrests, interrogations, and closures were pointless if young soldiers or women heading to market would be blown to bits in sophisticated suicide operations. Perry's career had been a remarkable one, but one final trophy eluded him, and one face haunted him as he departed the halls of Shin Bet HQ one very last time.

Perry's handpicked successor was forty-four-year-old Carmi Gillon, the resident Shin Bet expert on the Jewish right wing. Gillon's appointment shocked many inside the service, and several high-ranking department chiefs resigned as a result, including deputy director Gideon Ezra. Gillon was Perry's protégé, though the two had markedly different personalities. Gillon, a Jerusalem native and son of a fifth-generation of lawyers and judges to a noted Rehavia family, wasn't a classic Shin Bet agent. He hadn't come off of a successful tour as an officer in a reconnaissance-commando unit in the IDF only to be bored by the civil sector. He wasn't a Rambo and he wasn't a James Bond. In fact, Gillon began his career in the Shin Bet as a security officer assigned to protecting Israeli embassies and installations overseas; most of his work was, incidentally and ironically, in protection. Slowly and methodically, Gillon rose up the Shin Bet ladder of command to assume key posts. Low-key, Gillon was more of an analyst than a field man. According to Peleg Radai, one of the Shin Bet agents forced to resign after the 1984 bus incident, "Gillon was basic, trustworthy, and serious."[5] His master's thesis for Haifa University warned of the threat posed by the Jewish right wing to the very fabric of the Israeli democracy, and his work in infiltrating and crushing the "Spark," the Jewish underground that embarked on a campaign of terror against moderate Palestinians in the early 1980s, cemented his rise through the ranks at Shin Bet headquarters. Many insiders viewed the choice of Gillon as head of the Shin Bet as nothing short of remarkable.

Prime Minister Rabin viewed Gillon's straightforward approach to the day-to-day running of the Shin Bet as prudent. The departure from Gaza, and the realignment of Israel's immediate enemies and newfound alliances, was a traumatic change for the service. Gillon, both Perry and Rabin felt, would be able to successfully strike the delicate balance between the Shin Bet's two contradictory objectives: fighting a lethal wave of terrorism while, for the first time in Israeli history, forced to be accountable for their methods and results to the democratically elected legislators in the Knesset. Indeed, legislation was being drafted to outline the exact limits of Shin Bet authority and operational methods. Yet for a man whose expertise was the Jewish right wing, both Perry and Rabin, according to reports, were impressed enough with Gillon when he filled in for Perry during a leave of absence in late 1994 that they viewed him more than capable to lead the Shin Bet at the zenith of its brutal war against Hamas.[6] On March 1, 1995, Gillon became top man at Shin Bet headquarters.

From his first day in the director's chair at Shin Bet HQ, Gillon realized that his most pressing concern was the destruction of the Hamas and Islamic Jihad blitzkrieg that was killing Israelis in droves and quickly eroding the last fibers of support for the Oslo Accords. Combating Hamas meant finding—and either arresting or killing—Yehiya Ayyash.

Shin Bet agents who had been hunting Ayyash since the Ramat Efal incident had, by the summer of 1995, realized two very sobering tenets about their hunt for the Engineer: Ayyash was much smarter than any of the other Hamas gunmen they had sought—and either seized or killed—previously; and that Ayyash was unlikely to be compromised by poor security, a traitor in his ranks, or any of the other mistakes that usually culminated with the Ya'ma'm or some other elite squad of trained triggers surrounding a safe house. The Shin Bet would have to be resourceful in snaring Ayyash. It would require cunning and guile and the same outmaneuver artistry that the service had previously displayed in the hunt for the very best that the KGB or the East German Stasi had sent to Israel. Hunting down Ayyash would require tenacity tethered by brilliance, and the delicate art of using brute force. Most of all, the hunters would need a generous dose of luck.

Yehiya Ayyash had managed to insulate himself from the inner workings of Izzedine al-Qassam operations, commanders, and cell leaders. Only a handful of men whose dedication and loyalty were unyielding—even inside the bunker of a Shin Bet holding cell—knew where he was at any one given time. Hamas operators lucky enough to receive a one-day seminar in the art of explosives from Ayyash had no idea, up until the start of class, who they'd be meeting or what they'd be studying. Since no one willing to talk knew his whereabouts, he was impossible to pinpoint or trap. And since he had become a master of disguises in what was closing in on his third year on the run, fewer still knew what he looked like. His narrow face, spectacles, and intelligent grin had by the spring of 1995 become front-page imagery in newspapers throughout Israel and the Middle East, though he could have been any one of the million or so people milling about in the West Bank at any given time. He had mastered camouflaging himself as an old man and even an old Arab woman. His small library of Majd-supplied identity papers, passports, drivers licenses and even gun permits was dazzling. Indeed, according to legend and intelligence reports, Ayyash's favorite disguise was that of an Orthodox Jewish settler or even an Israeli Army reservist. At least dressed as one of the enemy he'd be allowed to carry a weapon and, if everything looked alright at first glance, be permitted to drive through checkpoints unhindered and armed to the teeth.

Following the Beit Lid bombing, Ayyash's legendary stature throughout the Territories grew by leaps and bounds; many Palestinians understood the necessary evil of bombing civilians, though killing soldiers, the dreaded tools of the Intifadah, was cherished, even by those not toeing the Hamas line, as holy work. Shin Bet agents pursuing leads to Ayyash's whereabouts were stymied by the legend. According to one popular story that had become folklore in the Territories, Ayyash was cornered in a safe house near Rafatt by the Shin Bet and the undercover squads. After holding off the advancing Israeli teams for hours in pitched battles, angels descended from heaven to pluck Ayyash to safety as bewildered Israeli commandos and agents looked on. Children in village elementary schools swore that they saw Ayyash personally kill Shin Bet agents with his trusted assault rifle. According to one law enforcement official working in the American embassy in Tel Aviv, "To the Palestinians in the territories, Ayyash was like Babe Ruth, Jackie Robinson, Audie Murphy, and Santa Claus wrapped up into one terrifying package!"[7]

The legend of the Engineer grew each day he wasn't killed or caught. "I see him with Israeli soldiers surrounding him," Muyasser Ayyash, Yehiya's sister-in-law, told reporters. "They are about to kill him but he turns invisible and walks right by them."[8] The more Shin Bet agents pressed the family members in Rafatt about his whereabouts; the more anonymous tips turned out to be dead ends; the more men and women who ended up in Shin Bet interrogation rooms; the grander the legend became. When Shin Bet agents drove through certain West Bank towns and villages en route to a meet, or to simply reconnoiter the terrain, they were met with verbal fusillades, some tossed by kids, promising that no one will ever be able to find the Engineer because he is a ghost and a hero. But what angered many in the Shin Bet, and indeed the Israeli special operations community was the fact that by having such little success in the pursuit they had helped contribute to the Engineer becoming a cult figure.

Yehiya Ayyash wasn't just a fugitive, he was a national hero. Folk songs were written about him, parents began naming their first-borns Yehiya, and women embroidered tablecloths with his image. Yehiya Ayyash had become the Palestinian version of a rock star, a sports hero, and a national leader. He was seen as an elusive enigma that was larger than life and more powerful than the region's most acclaimed intelligence service. Worse, the myth of one man humbling the vaunted Shin Bet and Mossad was a word-of-mouth recruiting poster for those wanting to martyr themselves.

The soldiers, spies, and policemen who hunted Yehiya Ayyash were angered by the legend and the taunts they received from the locals but not humbled. They were battling the clock. "We all knew that if we get him, perhaps even as he was building a device, it would mean one less massacre," claimed a former Ya'ma'm team leader. "We knew that each day that went by that we didn't get the SOB, the odds that a bus would blow up or a group of shoppers would be incinerated by a blast became more likely." Many of the soldiers and spies on the trail of Ayyash were on the verge of burnout, an operational hazard rarely talked about in Shin Bet circles. Following pointless leads took its toll on men who were nurtured by determination and caffeine. Agents, especially seasoned veterans of the hunt, were frustrated beyond words by their complete lack of success in getting to Ayyash. Many began to take the hunt personally. "Anger could never become a part of the equation, nor could vengeance," according to Ya'akov Perry. "The agents in the service need to remain focused on being professional, otherwise their effectiveness is compromised."[9]

Many agents believed that Ayyash had long since fled the West Bank and had found safe haven in Gaza, where getting to the wily bomb maker would be difficult but not impossible.

The spring sun had crested over Gaza with a warming and refreshing glow on the afternoon of April 2—the Strip was still at least a month away from the unforgiving heat of the Sinai summer. The smell of fried foods and uncollected trash lingered in the Sheikh Radwan neighborhood like a heavy blanket around the sounds of children screaming without a care in the world as they kicked a discarded can of 7-Up, imagining themselves to be World Cup soccer champions scoring goals for Palestine. Melodic rhythms from Toshiba boom-boxes spreading folk tunes throughout the blocks of three-story low-income flats echoed in an endless chorus of songs and sounds. Inside a nondescript apartment, on the second-floor of a faceless building on the block, a dozen men wearing tank tops and trousers worked in a flat-turned-factory, laboring at a slow and deliberate pace on their product. April, they hoped, was going to be a busy month.

The second-story factory wasn't a sweatshop, and it wasn't mass-producing bootleg blue jeans or sneakers, like many businesses in the Strip. Instead, the factory churned out top-grade explosive devices, compact reliable bits of pipe and nail bearing the trademark of one Yehiya Ayyash.

Sheikh Radwan was the kind of neighborhood where everyone knew everyone else and, depending on the circumstances, nobody knew anyone. It was Gaza, after all, land of mystery and violence where popularity and anonymity were coinciding assets that sometimes came in handy. People made it their business to know everything and at the same time know nothing. Everyone in Sheikh Radwan knew that the second-floor apartment was a stronghold for the resistance, but it was never advertised. Men came and went at all hours—some carrying laundry bags, others carrying guns. One visitor in particular had sparked the curiosity of several local residents. He was tall and lanky, with a narrow pale face and sullen eyes. The face seemed very familiar.

Because they were in Gaza, the men in the flat felt safe from the long arm of the dreaded *Shabak*. Men who survived on their wits and by never taking chances suddenly felt at ease and confident. Their guard was, even for a brief instant, cheerfully lowered. Because they were in Gaza, the knock at the door seemed so ordinary. A child carrying a package, claiming the man around the corner had asked that it be delivered. Deliveries were often made to the apartment; children, for the promise of a ten-shekel note, were only too happy to take on freelance messenger work.

In the flash of a blinding burst of yellow light and the ear-splitting roar of a massive explosion, just another spring day in the Sheikh Radwan district evaporated in a cloud of dust and the sweet and sickening smell of blood. The powerful explosion tossed the building down like a house of cards swatted flat by the hand of an angry child. The blinding cloud of dust and debris made initial rescue efforts difficult. Palestinian Authority fire crews and emergency medical technicians raced to the scene in the frantic effort to pull the dead and the dying from the smoldering rubble; rescuing bombing victims, after all, was something new to the Palestinian Authority. Nine people were killed in the afternoon explosion, including two small children. Thirty men, women, and children were seriously wounded. Among the dead were Kamal Kahil, Yehiya Ayyash's deputy operations officer, and Hatim Hassan, another Izzedine al-Qassam lieutenant, who battled one another for a spot on Israel's most wanted list, ran the facility and were killed in the explosion, as were several of their Majd bodyguards. Yehiya Ayyash had been in the apartment only moments before.[10]

Palestinian security responding to the bomb blast uncovered an enormous cache of weapons and explosives, including 150 antipersonnel hand grenades, thousands of rounds of ammunition, several pistols, machine guns, assault rifles, and, most ominous, industrial-sized vats of potassium and sodium hydroxide powder; in fact, the combination of leaking water pipes and exposed chemical agents initiated a toxic cloud that forced two-dozen people to emergency rooms. At a press conference following the explosion, a somewhat relieved Brigadier General Ghazi Jabali, the police commander of Gaza, stated, "Had the chemicals blown up, the entire Sheikh Radwan district would have disappeared."

At night, as floodlights were brought in to help locate victims of the afternoon explosion, several men sporting full beards and knapsacks assuming the shape of Carl Gustav submachine guns joined in the search. The men weren't looking for dead or wounded but rather any bits of evidence that might compromise anyone's location or identity. The men were from the Majd, and they wanted to make sure any communiqués, faxes, forged identity cards, or other sensitive bits of Hamas paraphernalia did not end up in the hands of the wrong people.

Was the bombing of the Sheikh Radwan apartment a planned strike meant to remove two men on Israel's most wanted list? Was it something more? Was it a simple work accident—a mistake of two wires crossing one another when they shouldn't have? After all, according to intelligence reports, Yehiya Ayyash had been in the apartment to supervise the construction of a complete inventory of knapsack bombs he had perfected in his weeks on the run. The devices were, in the world of Hamas, state of the art. New sport knapsacks, the kind every Israeli school kid carries, laden with a few kilograms of explosives scraped together from the center of old Egyptian land mines that had been scavenged in Gaza. The battery, shrapnel, and detonator were all neatly packaged inside the backpack—the detonator switch, cleverly concealed as a button alongside a strap, would be small enough to not spark the curious notice of anyone on a street corner or on board a bus. Kamal Kahil and Hatim Hassan were working on several of these backpack bombs when their factory was destroyed. Palestinian police found several of the prototypes on their premises.[11]

Palestinian Authority officials, as well, were wary about publicly pointing a finger at the Israelis, especially since several key Palestinian intelligence chiefs were working on active intelligence that the cache was to be used by Hamas to target Chairman Arafat as punishment for his cooperation with Israel. The state of Israel *never* took credit for the bombing in Sheikh Radwan—nor would it, as is standard operating procedure for the Shin Bet, A'man, and the Mossad. The blast remains one of those Middle Eastern mysteries that, in the span of some fifty years, is usually solved or forgotten. Yet Hamas pointed its finger at Jerusalem for the assassination of the two Izzedine al-Qassam commanders, and its leaders in Gaza, as well as in Damascus and Teheran, vowed revenge. It came seven days later.

At just before noon on April 9, Khaled Mohammed Khatib, a twenty-four-year-old construction worker from the Nuseirat refugee camp in Gaza sat behind the steering wheel of his commercial van on the main highway leading from Ashqelon to the string of settlements still in the Strip. Trucks, minivans, and even Israeli military vehicles passed along the narrow highway to and from the settlements that dotted the Strip. At 11:45, Khatib found what he was looking for: a crowded bus traveling to the isolated Israeli settlement of Kfar Darom. The bus was his target—his path to paradise. Ramming the bus at full speed, Khatib flipped the trigger switch that had been built into the steering column, igniting a massive explosive device filled with ball bearings and nails that was crammed in the rear of his van. The force of the blast was massive. The midsection of the bus melted amid roaring flames; shrapnel was projected in a 360-degree shower of death and destruction. Nine soldiers and civilians were killed in the bombing, including Alisa M. Flatow, of West Orange, New Jersey, a Brandeis University junior on leave. Twenty others were seriously injured.

Two hours later, just up the road from the Kfar Darom bombing, Imad Abu Amouna from the Shati refugee camp in Gaza used an Ayyash-designed car bomb to incinerate himself and part of a convoy of Israeli military vehicles near Netzarim. Amouna's kamikaze act of martyrdom wounded nearly thirty soldiers and civilians, though none was killed.

It had been a bloody day in Gaza.

The charred skeleton of the bus was still smoldering when Prime Minister Rabin's military chopper touched down in the late afternoon. The dead had been removed from the area, and the wounded had been rushed to trauma centers where doctors, now experts in treating bomb victims, repaired lacerated extremities and scorched vital organs. Rabin's Shin Bet protective detail, recalling the third device meant to explode at Beit Lid, were understandably anxious over their principal touring a terrorist attack site so close to the Gaza tinderbox. As Rabin toured the scene and spoke to reporters, police bomb-disposal experts were blowing up suspicious packages nearby. Shin Bet investigators picking through the debris, including what remained of Khatib's blue van, were outraged. The bombing bore the signature of Yehiya Ayyash.

When Israel handed over control of the Gaza Strip to the Palestinian Authority, it was confident that the massive barbed-wire barrier, reinforced by minefields and electronic sensors, would be able to keep the Palestinians inside their newly autonomous enclave. All human and vehicular traffic between Israel and the Palestinian Authority's domain was supposed to be scrutinized through the Erez Crossing, a Checkpoint Charlie of sorts that served as a funnel between Israel and the Strip. In reality, however, the fortified frontier was porous and nearly impossible to patrol. There were holes in the glistening concertina wire that surrounded the Strip, and many of the electronic sensors designed to act as trip wires were not even connected to master circuits. The IDF patrolled the frontiers, with its fleet of command cars and Bedouin trackers, along specially built sand roads adjacent to fences that were designed to display footprints and other physical signs that the fence had been breached. Hamas commanders could simply dispatch operatives across the fence to the Territories to disseminate instructions or deliver explosives and weapons. And, when Izzedine al-Qassam cell commanders warranted too much attention from Shin Bet teams and undercover squads, they could come out of the cold and find refuge in Gaza.

Ayyash's late-night ventures to and from Gaza had become routine—in fact, almost too routine. Evading the Shin Bet and the undercover squads should not have been so effortless, and it is believed that senior Hamas officials pleaded with the Engineer to stop tempting fate. Some even tried to convince him

to flee to the Sudan or to Iran, where they were certain the Israelis would be unable to touch him. He had taught a generation
of bomb makers the art of improvised explosives construction,
and he had trained intelligence operatives in the art of target
selection and acquisition. He had, in a bloody year of unrivaled
success, been complicit in the indiscriminate murders of seventy
men, women, and children. He had earned the distinction of
being the most notorious "freedom fighter" in the history of the
Palestinian liberation movement. A year of bombings and two
and a half years on the run had earned him the right to retire
and find seclusion and security in a Majd training facility near
Khartoum, or the Hamas embassy in Teheran. Ayyash would
have none of it. His heart—and his work—was in the West
Bank.

On a warm spring morning in the West Bank, an old man re-
quiring the assistance of a bamboo cane slowly trudged his way
along the dirt road of a small and nondescript village. A plain
white kaffiyeh adorned the elder's head, and a long gray beard
brushed against a charcoal-colored gown. As he walked in front
of a one-story house, the old man stopped, wiped a stream of
sweat from his forehead, and waited for what appeared to be a
sign from Allah to continue on his journey. The sign, in fact,
would come from his commander in the form of three short
blasts on the horn of a beat-up Fiat Uno parked down the road.
In a swift and fluid move, the old man threw off his gown,
removed a mini-Uzi submachine gun from a holster tucked
neatly underneath his arm, and raced to the front door of a one-
story house. He was soon joined by several men carrying M-16
assault rifles, dressed in a variety of masquerades ranging from
teenagers sporting Sheikh Yassin T-shirts to old widows dressed
in black mourning gowns. The target, a Ford Sierra with two
men inside, was quickly surrounded; the driver, foolish enough
to resist, was cut down in a 5.56 mm fusillade while the pas-

senger, frozen by fear, was whisked into the trunk of an Opel Rekord that had pulled up in a screeching cloud of dust. The take-down took all of eleven seconds.

The training exercise, carried out by operators from the Israeli National Police Border Guards' elite undercover unit known as the Ya'mas, had become a daily routine following the No. 5 bombing in October 1994 and the Beit Lid bombing in January. The commander of the Border Guards unit, a thirty-seven-year-old veteran of the bitter counterterrorist wars, was confident in the ability of his force to capture or kill Ayyash; after all, in the four years they'd been around they had captured seventy Hamas terrorists and killed fifty. Although made famous, or infamous as some claim, as a result of their infiltration and counterterrorist operations during in the Intifadah, Israelis have been disguising themselves as Arabs for nearly a hundred years in the unstoppable cycle of violence of the Arab-Israeli conflict.

Jewish Mista'arvim date back to 1909 and the "Shomer," an organization designed to provide security to the first Jewish settlements in Palestine. Shomer guards rode Arabian horses, dressed in traditional Arab garments, and learned to speak fluent Arabic to not only gain the respect of their neighbors but also find out what they were up to.

The Haganah, the military arm of the Jewish settlements in preindependence Israel, created its own Arabist intelligence unit during the bloody Arab revolt of 1936–39, when agents in Arab garb were dispatched to infiltrate local Arab villages. During the Second World War a Haganah Arabist platoon called the Syrian Company was set up with British support to carry out sabotage missions deep behind Vichy lines in Syria and Lebanon. Most of the volunteers to this small though unique unit were of Oriental descent—men whose families had come from the Arab diaspora and who were fluent in Arabic and Arab customs. Commanded by Captain N. N. Hammond, an eccentric British intelligence officer and professor of Greek history at Cambridge, the Syrian Company received extensive small arms, sharp-shooting, demolition, communications, and hand-to-hand combat training, as well intensive Arab language, customs, and culture instructions. Another "Arabist" unit was Shachar (dawn), more a force of intelligence plants than commandos, who penetrated large worksites to gather information and recruit double agents; they also opened small cover businesses and peddler stands at Arab markets to camouflage their activities. Many of these agents transferred to the Shin Bet and the Mossad to carry out intelligence and special operations.

The Ya'mas wasn't the only special operations unit honing its skills for a showdown with Ayyash. Similar exercises were carried out throughout Israel, at the training base of Duvdevan, the IDF's undercover squad, as well as, according to the *Jerusalem Post*, Sayeret Mat'kal. At the Mat'kal training base, a top-secret location somewhere in central Israel, the operators were dedicating additional time to practicing precision firing. Targets with Ayyash's face were persistently peppered with dead-on bursts of M-16 and AK-47 fire, kicking up a cloud of dust from sandbag bullet traps. The unit, as cocky and confident as any in the Israeli order of battle, was not taking chances in its mission to find Ayyash. Even Flotilla 13, the IDF/Navy's elite special operations force, was involved in the search for Ayyash—diverting from its usual ground-assault training time to conduct operations in the West Bank.[12]

The special operations forces had come close to snaring Ayyash on more than one occasion. They had lain in wait in muddy fields at the gates of Rafatt, hoping to kick in the front door of his parent's house as he made an incognito visit to his wife and child. "There had been nights," recalled a former Ya'ma'm officer, "when the unit would be involved in the routine work of maintenance and training when a call would come from the Shin Bet requesting our immediate services for an ambush on a vehicle, a restaurant, a safe house, or even his home in Rafatt. Whenever an informant or a suspect, humbled by the humiliation, pressure, and endless questioning of an interrogation, would provide even the slightest clues as to his whereabouts, we would race toward the suspected location ready for action."[13] There were times when the Ya'ma'm or any of the other half-dozen tactical teams on call would blow through a wall or kick down a door to find nothing—an empty room, a van full of startled commuters, or restaurants packed with terrified patrons. Sometimes the commando raids had missed Ayyash by only a few minutes. "On more than one occasion," recalled the Ya'ma'm officer, "we had burst through a front door only to find the mattress on the floor soaking with sweat." An agent on one such missed opportunity likened the elusive prey to a cat with nine lives.[14] Others, remembering these missed opportunities, could feel Ayyash lurking over their shoulders, giggling at their misfortune. They swore they were so close to Ayyash that they could even smell him.

For a man who had stymied one of the world's most successful and experienced counterterrorist and counterespionage agencies for so long, mainly as a result of the clever and cunning manner in which he controlled and directed his cells of operatives, Yehiya Ayyash had become reckless when it came to matters that tugged at his heart. He took enormous risks in communicating with his family, and exposed himself to the business end of a Ya'ma'm thirty-round termination each time he ventured close to Rafatt to see his wife and son. All roads in the Israeli manhunt led through Rafatt, and at times there were so many operators milling about undercover, in deep cover, or concealed by the surrounding hills that the town resembled a commando convention center.

Shin Bet teams involved in the hunt for the Engineer knew that ultimately the only way to get to Yehiya would be through his family, though surveillance of the Ayyash clan had produced few concrete clues. Shin Bet teams who covered Ayyash's wife and parents had failed to pick him up on several clandestine rendezvous and reunions Yehiya managed to enjoy with his family either in Rafatt or in safe houses elsewhere in the West Bank. In the almost weekly raids on his Rafatt home, Shin Bet agents would discover notes from Yehiya to his family and even photographs of a bearded Ayyash clutching his son with one hand, an assault rifle with the other. Shin Bet investigators uncovered one additional and irrefutable piece of evidence bound to escalate his rock star image further and proving that Ayyash had not allowed something as trivial as the IDF, the police, and the Shin Bet to stop him from seeing his family. In June, it became known that Heyam was pregnant. She would be expecting her second child in January 1996.

The Shin Bet, and A'man, had requested assistance from Arafat's multitude of security services in snaring Ayyash during one of his many cross-frontier journeys to and from Gaza, but the Palestinian Authority was busy with a Hamas war of its own. On March 12, 1995, two intricate forty-kilogram bombs were found hidden along a roadway used by Arafat's motorcade; on May 20, a powerful explosive device was discovered inside Arafat's Gaza headquarters and neutralized by bomb disposal officers trained by the FBI. Arafat, and his inner circle of competing and plotting intelligence services, had, through years of conditioning, developed a paranoid and outwardly brutal siege mentality toward assassins. All of the Palestinian Authority's intelligence and police assets would be dedicated to uncovering the would-be assassins and crushing them without mercy—all other matters would have to wait.

On the hot and muggy morning of July 24, 1995, the No. 20 bus was making its way south on Jabotinsky Street, past the Ramat Gan Diamond Exchange, to the entrance of the Tel Aviv city limits. The Monday morning rush hour was typical Tel Aviv—

a slow crawl through choke points jam-packed with vehicles. Passengers on board the bus contemplated yet another day when they'd be late for work. Bus driver Moshe Ilan, a fifty-five-year-old veteran of the frustrating reality of Israeli gridlock, carefully maneuvered the rectangular box of a bus through the narrow lanes and packed thoroughfares.

The passengers that morning had little time to notice a young man with a dark complexion attentively gazing out the window as he readjusted his yarmulke over his close-cropped spikes of black hair. He carried a knapsack and a blank and vacant stare. At precisely 8:40 A.M., he pressed a small button affixed to the strap of his pack. A blinding flash of light was followed by the complete blackness of heat, smoke, and death. Seats melted in the fiery gush, windows were blown fifty feet, and anyone in the path of the shrapnel and fire was killed instantly. Hands and legs, blown from their bodies, were strewn about the bus and on the street below. Motorists and pedestrians around the bus hit the pavement for cover and then raced to the bus to pull victims out of the wreckage. Five people died that morning, and an additional thirty were seriously wounded.

Just after 9:00 A.M. a call came in to the Associated Press office in East Jerusalem claiming responsibility for the attack, boasting that "Youth from Hamas from the Yehiya Ayyash group from the West Bank carried out the attack." Yehiya Ayyash had been silent for nearly three months. His cells had managed to remain hidden and secretive, and his pipeline of students, explosives, and instructions traveling to and from Gaza and the West Bank had proven impervious to Israeli intelligence. The Shin Bet had targeted Rafatt, but it was now Ayyash himself who would bring the war close to home. Moshe Ilan's bus had exploded in the shadows of the Tel Aviv skyline. The junction, now scorched an eerie black and dark red from the fire and blood, was just behind Tel Aviv's largest rail station, within walking distance of the Kirya, the sprawling patch of real estate in the heart of

Tel Aviv that was home to IDF headquarters, the Israeli Defense Ministry, and a number of intelligence organizations. Israeli generals and spymasters who heard the bomb from their offices realized that there was a message in the explosive terror.

Unlike previous bombings, Prime Minister Rabin did not tour the carnage on Jabotinsky Street. Instead, Police Minister Moshe Shahal and IDF chief of staff Lieutenant General Amnon Shahak obliged the cameras for the mandatory walk-through of the smoldering ruins. Protesters had raced to ground zero the moment news of the bombing was broadcast over Israeli radio, and they jostled the police minister and the chief of staff in a shoving match and verbal barrage designed to illicit a heavy-handed police response. As Rabin's surrogates surveyed the Ramat Gan crime scene barely able to bottle up their rage and disgust, a small but highly vocal crowd of right-wing supporters had assembled and commenced their boisterous chant. In a unified tone, the crowd began to shout "Rabin Rotze'ach, Rabin Boged" ("Rabin's a murderer, Rabin's a traitor") in a melodic assault that sounded like cries for support during a British soccer match. News teams dispatched to the bombing soon began to focus their Betacams on the zealous demonstration, and the men in beards and knitted skullcaps screaming about the bloody toll of the peace process became somber headline news.

The sight of a physically sickened Rabin wading through the blood and body parts was not a postcard of support for the virtues of the deal with the Palestinian Authority. It was the lead story—and image—on the Israeli nightly news, as well as on CNN, the American networks, and all of the major European broadcast services. The Hamas bombing campaign was no longer a tool of vengeance. Baruch Goldstein's murderous interpretation of his Jewish obligations had long since been avenged—casket for casket. Hamas was now involved in something much more diabolical and long-term. It was attempting to become a voice in Israeli politics, and it was succeeding.

The suicide devices had become a highly effective political tool, swaying public opinion against the Oslo Accords and against any rapprochement with the Palestinians. Unlike the ambulance-chasing diehard right-wingers who carried placards in their cars awaiting the chance to demonstrate in front of carnage, the protesters on Jabotinsky Street were average citizens who were fed up with the indiscriminate bloodshed. Even Israeli president Ezer Weizman, a former air force commander and moderate, called upon Rabin to reassess the negotiations with the Palestinians. "We cannot continue as if nothing happened," he told reporters. "It cannot go on like this."

The latest bombing had come on the eve of final negotiations with the Palestinians over extending the Gaza-Jericho agreement of autonomy to major West Bank cities later in the year. Political debate inside Israel had already been beset by division, malice, and threats of civil unrest. The bombing only added fuel to the existing firestorm.

Bomb squad technicians working the crime scene in Ramat Gan meandered through the mess in order to search for clues and small bits of evidence. Shin Bet teams, having picked through the bloody belongings of more than a hundred people in the last ten months, were exhausted and frustrated. With forensic teams they were able to piece enough evidence together to identify the bomber as twenty-two-year-old Labib Anwar Farid Assam, a student from the village of Karyut, in the foothills of the Jordan Valley south of Nablus. Unlike previous suicide bombers, anonymous faces with relatively blemish-free criminal records on the Shin Bet master computer, Assam had an extensive Shin Bet rap sheet. During the Intifadah, Assam had served as a Hamas instigator, turning demonstrations at A-Najeh University into bloody pitched battles. Shin Bet case agents knew where he had lived, they knew who his cohorts were, and they felt they might be able to learn who had sent him on this kamikaze mission.

* * *

The two black men wearing galabiya robes and munching on a greasy bag of fried sweet honey balls attracted little attention on the side streets of Nablus that sunny fall morning. Nablus was known for its large Sudanese population, and the two men walking arm and arm looked as if they belonged—their clothes were the kind worn by Sudanese descendants, their teeth were a combination of brown and yellow, their afros were nappy and unkempt, and they each carried a colorful yellow-and-red nylon bag filled with fruit and a rolled-up pita sandwich. To the locals passing by on the street or standing in front of the mosque known in the town as a Hamas bastion, the two men looked like job hunters, day laborers in search of construction work inside the Palestinian city. But under their robes, each man carried Israel-police issue Jericho 9 mm automatics nestled in canvas holsters fastened to their inner thighs, and miniaturized communications gear hidden inside towels carried in their bags. To complete the disguise, the two hadn't showered or brushed their teeth in a week, and they had eaten and slept in their robes until they developed the unique aroma of a day laborer with nothing but the galabiyas on their backs.

The two "Sudanese"—actually recent immigrants to the Jewish state from Ethiopia who found a home in the Ya'mas—were carefully watching the comings and goings of the mosque and the northern entrance to the casbah in search of familiar faces. Each of the operators had been briefed extensively by Shin Bet agents who worked with the Ya'mas to identify the men of the Nablus cell who had dispatched Labib Anwar Farid Assam on his deadly assignment in Ramat Gan. The Shin Bet was not interested in capturing a guide or a minor player. In order to make a dent in the Izzedine al-Qassam Brigade's ability to launch attacks against Israel, it was essential that the cell be compromised and captured in a single sweep.

August 19 was one of those hot nights in the West Bank when

people perspire like marathon runners, even though a cool and refreshing breeze was bouncing around the surrounding hilltops. It was hot, West Bank hot. The men on street corners whispering into miniaturized communications devices were sweating, as were men sitting inside a beat-up sedan, windows tinted a concealing purple, who clutched assault rifles and sub-machine guns as they pressed wired receivers into their ears. At just before midnight, Shin Bet agents, supported by a small army of undercover squad operatives and Ya'ma'm operators, checked their watches at a stake-out on Faisal Street, in the northern entrance to the casbah. They were watching an apartment where they had pinpointed an arms cache and safe house used by a Izzedine al-Qassam cell leader. Yet as the agents nervously waited, thinking perhaps that this lead had turned out to be another dead end, a beat-up sedan pulled up in front of the building. The driver appeared happy, almost giggling. As he rubbed his face, he jostled the radio dial in search of a station broadcasting a news bulletin. The midnight news brief was the usual full day of events wrapped up into a five-minute spot sandwiched in between commercials. There were no bulletins. As the man continued to wait inside his car, the Shin Bet agents slinked silently toward the vehicle. In a split second, the driver found himself restrained by a dozen heavily armed men and gagged with duct tape. He was tossed into a car that screeched up to the building the moment the operation began, thrown in the trunk, and rushed off to Jerusalem. The stake-out had been a success.

Abdel Nasser Issa was a twenty-nine-year-old Majd lieutenant and disciple of Yehiya Ayyash. As commander of the Nablus cell, Issa had recruited, trained, and supported four-man teams throughout the city and had masterminded a slew of operations, including the Ramat Gan bombing. It was Issa that recruited Ramat Gan bomber Labib Assam, and Issa who drove him to the Tel Aviv area; a videotape found in Issa's Nablus lair showed Assam bidding farewell to his family and friends before the bombing. Agents found improvised explosive devices inside Issa's flat, as well as fertilizer bombs, vats of chemicals, bomb-making equipment, weapons, ammunition, and, most disturbing of all, a library of forged identity cards and wigs, costumes, even yarmulkes. Bomb disposal officers cleared out the Nablus safe house for booby traps and additional explosives.

The arrest of Abdel Nasser Issa was a coup for the Shin Bet. Issa was a professional who had avoided capture for a long time. He had just returned from the Gaza Strip where he had met with Ayyash and other Izzedine al-Qassam officials. His Majd training had worked, and his countersurveillance techniques were meticulous, though sometimes all the skill and training in the world can't defeat a bunch of red-eyed investigators who, for the first time in a long time, catch a break. After Issa's arrest, nine additional cell members were picked up throughout the Nablus area by special operations teams for once happy not to be sleeping.

It had been a good twenty-four hours for the counterterrorists. Earlier in the day, Palestinian secret service agents arrested Wa'el Nasser, an al-Qassam fugitive suspected of planning several bombings inside Israel. Yet during his interrogation, Issa remained defiant. Knowing Shin Bet agents were on the other side of a two-way mirror, the cherubic-faced Issa sat silently in restraints as he showered his interrogators with a devilish smile that both disturbed and provoked. Looking at his rap sheet and case history, the agents knew the arrogance was inherited—his father, an operative with Dr. George Habash's Popular Front for the Liberation of Palestine, had languished in an Israeli prison for ten years.

Morning had cascaded a brilliant shower of warm orange sunlight over the streets of Jerusalem on Monday, August 21, 1995. The city starts its day early, and by 7:30 A.M., rush-hour traffic from the outer neighborhoods to the city center had been bustling. Motorists swerving in and out of clogged lanes fiddled with radio dials as the morning news programs provided updates, traffic reports, and the occasional bursts of gossip. Passengers on buses thumbed through the morning dailies, and students crammed with textbooks and reading assignments. Jerusalem is a university town, and Hebrew University is a magnet for college students throughout Israel and throughout the world. The No. 26 bus is one of the many lines that ferries students and teachers to Mt. Scopus; as the line passed through the Sheikh Jarakh section and National Police headquarters, the passengers that routinely rode the bus included a mix of cops and college kids.

At 7:45, along a street in the neighborhood of Ramat Eshkol, bus driver Ronen Shmuel had leapfrogged another No. 26 bus heading to Mt. Scopus, a common practice for bus drivers attempting to spread the crowds of strap hangers among buses. The passengers searching through their schoolbooks or munching on breakfast sandwiches appreciated the maneuver; Jerusalem buses are notorious for their sardinelike conditions, and any move that buys breathing room is appreciated. During the ride through the northern neighborhoods of Jerusalem, no one had noticed anything unusual about a young dark-skinned woman clutching a heavy knapsack. Because Jerusalem is a mixed city of Jews and Arabs, natives are often far more security conscious than people living in Tel Aviv or Haifa, though even the policemen riding to work failed to notice the woman; because of Jerusalem's religious sensitivities, it was considered politically incorrect to stare at women, especially Arab women, on city streets and buses.

As Shmuel steered past the other No. 26 bus stopping to pick up a long line of fares, the female stood up and simply depressed a button on her pack. The five kilograms of Yehiya Ayyash's latest pipe bomb detonated. The bus was destroyed at once by the powerful explosion, as was much of the bus adjacent to it. The blast was so powerful that it tossed passengers through the bus windows and onto the street some twenty feet away. The smell of melting plastic and barbecued flesh was nauseating. Limbs and extremities littered the asphalt roadway, which was slowly filling with blood. A headless corpse was tossed to the rear of the bus like a blood-stained mannequin. Five died that morning in Jerusalem, including a police officer and an American teacher from Connecticut. More than one hundred were seriously hurt.

The bombing of the No. 26 bus in Ramat Eshkol was the first "successful" Hamas suicide attack inside Jerusalem—in December 1994, a bomber attempted to board a bus near the central bus station in the city but blew himself up before he could get inside. The No. 26 bombing was one too many—the nation was fed up. "Can we send our kids to school on the bus in the morning?" anguished parents shouted at police who quickly raced to the bomb scene to keep the inevitable demonstration from turning violent. "Will it be my son and daughter killed tomorrow? Enough is enough!"

Support for the peace deal and future concessions with the Palestinians diminished with each Hamas bomb attack. Polls measuring public sentiment for the next elections, scheduled for November 1996—the first to have separate ballots for Knesset and prime minister—showed the Likud coalition's candidate Benjamin Netanyahu tweaking past Rabin. Indeed, right-wing supporters had gathered at the bomb site by the hundreds following the Ramat Eshkol bombing, and news cameras from networks around the world captured the hate, the fear, and the frustration of protesters screaming "Rabin is a traitor, Rabin is a murderer." Rabin had learned his lesson following the Ramat Gan massacre. He didn't bother touring this crime scene, though he suspended talks with the Palestinians and closed the Territories once again. Speaking on national radio, Rabin said, "This is a hard and painful day, but we are determined to fight Hamas and Islamic Jihad terrorism and to continue building the peace with the Palestinians who wish peace with us."

Jerusalem's police chief, Commander Arieh Amit, scores of Border Guard and bomb squad officers, and a steady legion of Shin Bet agents worked the Ramat Eshkol blast. Conditions were brutal. The pounding Judean sun and the smell of the burned flesh turned the stomachs of investigators. The maddening wails of children still crying, hours after the blast, lingered in their ears. For many of those wearing surgical masks and latex gloves that sizzling hot Monday morning, this was their tenth suicide bombing in less than two years.

Inside his cell, Abdel Nasser Issa was no longer defiant. He was joyful. Issa, as per Ayyash's instructions, had built the acetone-based device and, only hours before he was arrested by the Shin Bet, had delivered it to Muhhi a-Din Sharif, an al-Qassam operative in Jerusalem, who had passed the device on to Salem Abdel Rabbo Sabiah Jabarin, a twenty-six-year-old laborer from Dahariya, near Hebron, who volunteered for a martyr operation. Sabiah had been given loose guidelines as to which targets to attack, though he was told to use the device no later than forty-eight hours after receiving the knapsack. In order to avoid detection by police or suspicious passengers, Sabiah had adopted a female disguise.

Shin Bet agents interrogating Issa on Sunday, August 20, knew he was holding back crucial information that could help save lives, but "overt" physical pressure was strictly illegal. Yet in response to Issa's purposeful silence, Prime Minister Rabin gave the Shin Bet some "subjective leeway" in its use of physical force to extract information. Issa was the first subjective victim. Soon the face that had smirked defiantly was displaying the contortions of a man encountering the outer reaches of his physical and mental limits. Issa's breaking point took less than twenty-four hours to reach. Soon additional Hamas operatives were arrested. Shin Bet agents believe that the pressure brought to bear on Issa helped to thwart four suicide bombings and the kidnappings of several Israeli soldiers.

The Nablus cell had been the classic Hamas operation: it was detached, isolated, loosely connected to its commanding echelons, and incredibly effective. The order to bomb the buses in Ramat Gan and Jerusalem had, Israeli investigators believe, come from Damascus, via fax to Izzedine al-Qassam commanders in Gaza; probably the order to initiate the command to strike had originally emanated from Teheran. Orders are forwarded, through encrypted messages, to the regional al-Qassam Brigade commander, who then selects a cell, as well as outside logistical assistance ranging from intelligence gatherers to suppliers of weapons and explosives. With the exception of the regional commander, no two men know each other. Even when aggressive means of questioning can be applied to a captured terrorist, the intelligence dividend from the confessions of one man are minimal.

In Gaza, of course, Palestinian interrogators had far fewer restrictions in the use of physical pressure, and agents did not require permission from Chairman Arafat when it came to torture, beatings, and threats. In the camps of southern Lebanon, in the cells of the Egyptian, Jordanian, Syrian, Iraqi, and Libyan intelligence services, Palestinians had become experts in the use of force on prisoners.

Arafat had condemned the bombings in the summer of 1995, and he personally called Prime Minister Rabin to promise full-fledged Palestinian intelligence and security efforts to eradicate Hamas from Gaza. Arafat realized that his political fate was tied precariously and ironically to his former enemy. In September 1995, Palestinian security services openly began joint cooperation in the hunt for Yehiya Ayyash.[15]

* * *

A day after the blast, Rabin openly discussed the political objectives of the bombings with a group of Israeli reporters as he toured the Golan Heights. "Their purpose is to bring about, by suicide terror activities, the fall of my government," he said. "They see in me, as prime minister, the main enemy because we speak for the continuation of the peace process." Yet Yehiya Ayyash wasn't the only force out to topple Rabin. The fall of 1995 would prove to be one of the most divisive and painful periods in the history of the Jewish state.

Notes

[1]Interview, New York, September 9, 1998.

[2]Barton Gellman, "Israel Renews Talk of Isolating West Bank in Wake of Bombings," *The Washington Post*, January 23, 1995, p. 3.

[3]Raine Marcus, "It Was Like a Slaughterhouse," *The Jerusalem Post*, January 23, 1995, p. 3.

[4]Interview, New York, September 26, 1998.

[5]Ron Levin, "*26 Shanim Be'Shabak, Mi'Lemata A'd La'Tzameret*," *Ma'ariv*, March 29, 1996, p. 3.

[6]Leslie Susser, "A New Era at the Secret Service," *The Jerusalem Report*, March 23, 1995, p. 14.

[7]Interview, New York, September 26, 1998.

[8]John Donnelly, "Israel's Most Wanted: The Elusive Engineer," *The Miami Herald*, December 23, 1994, page 1A.

[9]Interview, August 15, 1998.

[10]On Levy, "Face-Saver for Troubled GSS," *The Jerusalem Post*, January 7, 1996, p. 2.

[11]Jon Immanuel, "Hamas Bomb Factory Destroyed in Gaza Blast," *The Jerusalem Post*, April 3, 1995, p. 1.

[12]See on Levy, "Face-Saver For Troubled GSS," *The Jerusalem Post*, January 7, 1996, p. 2.

[13]Interview, September 6, 1998.

[14]Levy, "Face-Saver."

[15]Alon Pinkas, "Joint IDF, PA Efforts to Capture Ayyash," *The Jerusalem Post*, September 8, 1995, p. 2.

Chapter 6

The Autumn
of the Assassin

A dark blanket of thick purple had settled Rafat into a peaceful slumber on the night of September 21, 1995. By 4:00 A.M. an eerie sense of tranquillity had descended over much of the village. The task force of commando cops and Shin Bet agents had used the camouflaging cover of darkness and the mask of the whipping wind to surround the one-story house. Surprise was key, but it was meant to provide effect rather than tactical prudence. The agents that chilly autumn morning weren't after a terrorist they feared would resist with a barrage of gunfire, nor were they concerned that there were booby traps inside the house ready to explode the moment a trip wire was pulled. They knew the target of the raid wouldn't be armed and wouldn't resist. After all, how much of a fight would a fifty-five-year-old diabetic woman with bad eyes and decaying teeth put up?

Aisha Ayyash had stood up to Shin Bet questioning before. She had sat huddled at the corner of her sparingly furnished home, under a blanket, as agents grilled her regarding her son.

203

Aisha Ayyash was defiant and arrogant. When Shin Bet agents had taunted her, asking her if she wanted her son returned to her in pieces or ground up like chopped meat, she would often respond, "If you can catch him and do that to him, fine, but you'll need to catch him first." She withstood surveillance, harassment, and almost daily visits by the Border Guards and the Shin Bet. On the night of September 21 she would face an interrogation in Jerusalem, under very different circumstances than she had been used to.

There had always been certain unwritten rules etched in the Shin Bet's playbook as to what they could or wouldn't do in counterterrorist operations. Suspects, informants, or any of the other characters that came across their path could be manipulated, threatened, roughed up, and, in some cases, tortured; but a different set of rules had always applied to women, especially Muslim women. In a region of the world where butchery was an accepted practice of settling disputes, sexual respect had remarkably been maintained. Israeli troops and Shin Bet agents were always taught to never touch an Arab woman, and never question her alone, without a chaperone nearby. The rulebook was not always adhered to, but the Shin Bet had a markedly superior record to their Palestinian counterparts who, according to claims made by Amnesty International, had routinely threatened male prisoners that their wives, mothers, and sisters would be raped before their eyes if they did not cooperate, confess or compromise fellow operatives.

Political correctness and cultural sensitivities had not brought the Shin Bet any closer to getting its hands on Yehiya Ayyash, however, and, three years into the chase and some seventy bodies later, it was time for the rules to change.

Aisha Ayyash was dragged out of her house just before 4:00 amid the cries of her family; it was just early enough to avoid a large-scale riot by villagers and the handful of armed Hamas men who lived in Rafatt. The Shin Bet raced the Engineer's mother to its holding facility inside the Russian compound in Jerusalem, where the local police maintained a sprawling headquarters. Investigators interrogated the sickly woman without respite about her son's whereabouts, though they all knew he was, in the best-case scenario, in Gaza, and in the worst-case scenario teaching new pupils in a classroom in Khartoum in Qom. But Aisha's arrest was a maternal pressure point designed to cause Ayyash's insides to buckle. Shin Bet agents wanted Yehiya to think about his mother inside the grueling and inescapable box of a Shin Bet interrogation room, and they wanted him to think about the hands of the filthy and hated Shabakniks touching the matriarch of a family at the center of the Jihad. According to Hamas folklore, Aisha managed to smuggle a note from prison to her son, pleading for justice. "Oh my beloved son," the note elaborated, "they arrested me because I delivered you. They tied me up, burned me, and much, much more!"

On October 29, 1995, the Ramallah Military Court issued an indictment against the mother of the Engineer. The official charge was "utilizing forged documentation to enter the Gaza Strip;" the military prosecutor contended that Aisha had illegally crossed into the Palestinian Authority to meet with her son, and to cooperate with a "hostile terrorist organization."[1] The legal action was designed to elicit a response. Sons have done remarkable things to keep their mothers from harm's way. Shin Bet agents were hoping that Ayyash was man enough to expose himself to the crosshairs.

There were many inside Israel's defense establishment who realized that the autumn would be a time of decisive action. Israeli forces were slated to begin pulling out of five major West Bank towns, and Hamas and the Islamic Jihad had both vowed to do everything in their power to torpedo the peace accords. For the first time in a long time, the Shin Bet was growing concerned that a terrorist faction would target Israel's political leadership rather than ordinary civilians. The thought of a Hamas suicide bomber, wearing an Ayyash-designed device, detonating himself adjacent to Prime Minister Rabin sent shudders down the spines of Shin Bet agents working protective security. Hamas had always sought the spectacular and the gut wrenching, and the murder of an Israeli prime minister or an Israeli president, defense minister, or IDF chief of staff would escalate the war to a level that few wanted to contemplate. With the exception of a failed attempt by Black September to kill Prime Minister Golda Meir with a car bomb outside the El Al terminal at John F. Kennedy International Airport in New York City, Palestinian terrorists had never mounted a serious attempt on the life of an elected Israeli leader. The Shin Bet was determined to keep it that way.

The Shin Bet conducted an in-depth audit of its abilities—and shortcomings—following the Beit Lid blast and the discovery of that third bomb. Immediately after the bombing, a high-ranking Shin Bet official wrote a report in which he pointed to lax security procedures in the protection afforded Israel's political leadership. The report, one of remarkable candor and criticism for an internal Shin Bet memo, disapproved of not only how the VIP Protection Unit safeguarded its principals, but also how it gathered and analyzed intelligence on potential threats. The report was handed to deputy director Gideon Ezra, but Ezra, angered over not being named Perry's successor, resigned when Carmi Gillon was appointed the service's director.[2] Additional Shin Bet veterans, seeing their rise up the ranks squashed by Gillon's appointment, resigned as well.

There were storm clouds looming over the Shin Bet that fall. The Ayyash hunt, internal squabbling, and civil discourse had challenged the agency's tasks and responsibilities like never before in Israel's history. October and November promised to be bloody. Yet, for the first time in Israeli history, there were concerns that the bloodshed would not be directed solely from a Palestinian front.

Threat analysis is, perhaps, the most difficult aspect of dignitary protection work. Is a threat real? Does it justify increased protection, preemptive action, or is the potential of harm so great that a principal's entire itinerary needs to be altered or canceled altogether? As the prime minister of a country entrenched in a dire terrorist conflict, Yitzhak Rabin was, according to U.S. law enforcement officials, considered, along with PLO Chairman Arafat, Egyptian President Hosni Mubarak, Jordan's King Hussein, and President Clinton, among the world's most targeted heads of state. And, with Prime Minister Rabin scheduled to visit the United States twice in the fall of 1995, the Shin Bet's eyes scanned the American landscape for a possible Hamas strike.

The Hamas infrastructure in the United States had, until January 1993, remained invisible. Occasionally in the Israeli press there were reports about the suspicious activities of Muslim groups in the United States collecting money for the Intifadah; according to the reports, Israeli officials complained to the Americans about these "reported" activities, but these reports were never pursued. Then, following the murder of Sergeant Nissim Toledano and the deportation of the "415," Hamas had found itself in disarray; its leaders were deported and the Israelis seemed to have scored a huge success by isolating the ringleaders and the operational masterminds from the legions in the streets.

In January 1993, in an attempt to infuse the Occupied Territories with cash and confidence, Hamas leaders dispatched two Palestinian-Americans, Mohammed Salah and Mohammed Jarad, to travel to Israel and distribute nearly a hundred thousand dollars in emergency cash to Izzedine al-Qassam cells in Ramallah, Hebron, and Gaza. For Jarad, a timid grocery store owner with a bad heart, it was his first trip on behalf of Hamas; Salah had made the trip once before, bringing nearly fifty thousand dollars to Hamas cells in the Territories. That money was used by Hamas to buy weapons and ammunition—material that would be used in the murders of four Israeli servicemen. But both men were arrested by the Shin Bet, and they gave complete and incriminating confessions not only disclosing the objective of their trip to Israel but also evidence of a Hamas network in the United States. The Israelis, outraged at learning that the terrorist movement had operatives in the United States, urged American officials to act. But in this age of political correctness, the administration was unwilling to launch a full-scale investigation into a minority population. "Not all Arabs are terrorists," claimed an outraged representative of the al-Kifah refugee center in Brooklyn on local New York talk radio. American officials, inclined not to publicly indict an entire religious group because of the fanaticism of a few, turned a blind eye to any possible homegrown conspiracy.

The Israelis were dumbfounded by the Hamas network in the United States, grudgingly admiring its foresight and sophistication. Hamas representatives among the Palestinian-American diaspora were well educated, fiery orators, and immersed enough in the American legal system to settle their activities inside the gray area between freedom of speech and religion, and seditious acts on behalf of a terrorist organization. Perhaps most important, they were incredibly successful in raising funds, ostensibly for refugee relief at the height of the Intifadah but really for the military campaign against the Israelis. And, until Hamas was declared a terrorist organization, it was all quite legal.

Following the bombing of the No. 5 bus, however, U.S. Attorney General Janet Reno publicly declared that American law-enforcement would go after Hamas. The test case of this policy in the legal campaign against Hamas in the American heartland was against none other than Musa Abu Marzouk. As head of the political leadership of Hamas, Marzouk was the CEO of an international conglomerate of political offices, financial backers, and military sub-units. He was smart, a master diplomat and tactician, and he had managed to insulate his role as the chairman of the board of Hamas from the attacks perpetrated by Izzedine al-Qassam and Yehiya Ayyash. Although a permanent resident alien, Abu Marzouk's name had been placed on an Immigration and Naturalization Service terrorist watch list; as a member of a terrorist faction, he was subject to the loss of his green card as well as deportation.

On January 25, 1995, Musa Abu Marzouk landed at New York's Kennedy International Airport following a lengthy trip to the Persian Gulf. His name and passport tripped an INS watch list and Marzouk was immediately ushered into federal custody. News of Marzouk's apprehension sparked joy and relief inside the halls of Shin Bet headquarters. Israel wanted him to stand trial for the many men, women, and children he had a hand in murdering. Shin Bet agents wanted a front-row seat at his interrogation.

According to the one-thousand-page Israeli extradition request, Musa Abu Marzouk was linked to ten acts of terrorism, including the Afula, Hadera, and No. 5 bus bombings. On August 8, Marzouk was arrested by FBI agents in his INS holding cell, acting on a warrant issued by an Israeli court. He was remanded to the Manhattan Corrections Center on Pearl Street and Park Row in downtown Manhattan pending a formal extradition hearing.

The Israeli decision to seek Abu Marzouk's extradition was nothing short of remarkable. Engaging in a legal case to bring him to justice was an invitation for Hamas to step up an already bitter war; many police officials feared a new wave of Hamas kidnappings would follow. The American decision to detain and hold Marzouk took courage. FBI officials at 26 Federal Plaza could look out the window at the World Trade Center and recall the first time fundamentalist Muslim terrorists struck inside the United States. According to one New York City law enforcement official involved in counterterrorist operations, "Holding Musa Abu Marzouk was a giant 'kick me' sign plastered all over the five boroughs. After watching CNN and seeing what these guys were capable of, no one here wanted that to happen on the streets of Manhattan."[3]

The Shin Bet had to consider terrorists like Abu Marzouk when planning Prime Minister Rabin's trip to the United States in the autumn of 1995. Rabin's first U.S. stop would be Washington, D.C., for a gala ceremony at the White House on September 28 along with Jordan's King Hussein, Egyptian President Mubarak, and PLO chairman Arafat to sign the Israeli-Palestinian interim agreement. The ceremony was a peacemaker's delight and a security service agent's nightmare, and Rabin's speech echoed both those concerns. "Please take a good, hard look," he said, talking of the leaders of the Middle East assembled together in one room. "The sight you see before you at this moment was impossible, was unthinkable, just two years ago. Only poets dreamed of it; and, to our great pain, soldiers and civilians went to their deaths to make this moment possible." Looking at Arafat, his once hated enemy, Rabin proceeded to evoke the memory and sacrifice of Israeli victims. "The sounds of celebration here cannot drown out the cries of innocent citizens who traveled those buses to their deaths. And your eyes shining here cannot erase for a single moment the sight of the lifeless eyes of the students who were going to their classes and the housewives who were on their way to market when hatred struck them down."

There were fears in Washington that Hamas would attempt a spectacular strike aimed at both Israelis and Americans for any one of a hundred possible reasons, from the arrest of Aisha

Ayyash to the detention of Musa Abu Marzouk. Washington would be safe, though; all public appearances were well coordinated, and the U.S. Secret Service were masters at safeguarding the White House as well as visiting heads of state. New York, one month later, would be another story.

On October 5, at an angry rally in Jerusalem called by the Israeli right wing to protest the interim agreement signed in Washington, tens of thousands gathered to voice their vehement opposition to the land-for-peace proposal. It was a fiery evening, marked by incendiary speeches by Likud and settler leaders, including prime minister candidate Benjamin Netanyahu. As Netanyahu addressed the crowd from a second-story perch, demonstrators gathered on the damp and chilly Jerusalem street began chanting: "Rabin is a traitor!" Placards bearing Rabin's face on the body of an S.S. officer were openly and gleefully displayed.

To the right wing—from low-key Likud supporters to fanatical Kahane-Chai devotees—a government-sanctioned withdrawal from the confines of Greater Israel was tantamount to treason. The betrayal, in their eyes, was not against family or even one's country, but rather an act of sedition perpetrated against the pillars of one's faith. The Oslo I and Oslo II Peace Accords had forced many Israelis to take a sobering look at themselves for the first time. It was a defining moment of a nation's character. The image of the handshake in the destructive wake of Yehiya Ayyash's bombing campaign had convinced many that peace was a deadlier alternative than war.

The shadow of Baruch Goldstein fell over the Israeli political landscape that fall as the rhetoric turned ugly. A leader of the Women in Green movement, a right-wing settlers group, had declared that "This junta is raping the Jewish people;" and, the leader of the Zo Artzeinu settlers movement, Moshe Feiglin, proclaimed that his group would hold the Rabin government responsible "for its crimes against security and Judaism."[4] And, in Brooklyn, New York, the Mecca of righteous Jewish thinking, rabbis openly professed that it would be legal under Jewish law to assassinate the "treacherous" Israeli prime minister. Many Israelis, for the first time since 1948, felt that the country might be going down the path of civil war.

At the end of October, Prime Minister Rabin traveled once again to the United States, this time to New York City for the fiftieth anniversary of the United Nations. UN-50, as the celebration was known, was the worst of all security nightmares. The U.S. Secret Service, the U.S. State Department's Diplomatic Security Service, the FBI, the NYPD, special agents from Customs, the Drug Enforcement Administration, the Bureau of Alcohol, Tobacco and Firearms, the Marshals Service, and even the Internal Revenue Service—plus 152 indigenous secret service and bodyguard "packages" that would protect each leader—had all converged on New York City in a mammoth undertaking to ensure the safety of leaders from the four corners of the planet; New York City had been fortunate enough to host Pope John Paul II ten days earlier as a dress rehearsal security operation. Motorcades bounced up and down the avenues of Manhattan like speeding rockets. Streets were closed and entire neighborhoods were cordoned off while the world leaders met, spoke, and visited the sights of the Big Apple. Even U.S. military special forces were covertly dispatched to New York City to keep the 152 political bull's-eyes safe from assassins.

There was good reason for safety concerns. In September an armored limousine had been stolen from a diplomatic mission in New York City, prompting fears that terrorists might rig the stolen vehicle with a ton of explosives and then ram it through a barricade or a wall of police. Specific concern centered around the Israeli prime minister. At a special dinner for Rabin at the World Financial Center in downtown Manhattan, hosted by

New York Mayor Rudolph W. Giuliani, the NYPD's Emergency Service Unit for the first time deployed sanitation trucks filled with sand at key intersections as a means to barricade cross streets from a suicide car bomber. Everywhere Rabin went, in fact, he was followed by NYPD and Secret Service CAT, or Counter-Attack Teams, following behind motorcades and ready to pounce on a threat with a flurry of rifle and machine-gun fire; countersnipers and observers manned an eagle's-eye vigil over most of Rabin's arrivals and departures.

It was of course the ultimate in Middle Eastern ironies. Inside a high-security tier on the sixth floor of the Federal Bureau of Prisons' Manhattan Corrections Center, or MCC, Musa Abu Marzouk, the Hamas political chief, watched the local news and reports of Rabin's formal affair downtown as he sat on a hard plastic chair wearing his bright-orange jumpsuit that all federal prisoners wear behind bars. The potential for Hamas staging some grandiose act of terrorism was too real to ignore.

There were other threats that American law enforcement officials had to take seriously. After all, much of the religious rhetoric supporting the assassination of an Israeli leader who traded land back to the Arabs had come from the great center of Jewish thought: Brooklyn. The Jewish Defense League, Kahane Chai, and a small litany of right-wing groups called the United States home.

Yet in New York, with the potential for assassination so high during the frenzied festivities, the Shin Bet handled Rabin's package with a unique form of tunnel vision. It placed great emphasis, and sometimes none-too-friendly attention, on individuals of Middle Eastern descent who happened to be at the wrong place at the wrong time near Rabin's hotel, or at any of the sites his entourage would visit. Jews, on the other hand—even protesters hurling epitaphs and saliva at Rabin as he walked to and from his awaiting limousine—were allowed to get dangerously close. When Secret Service or NYPD officials would suggest the possibility of certain security situations to the Shin Bet details, the Israeli agents would often raise their heads, click their teeth in disdain, and say, "Yehiyeh Be'Seder," "It's OK, don't worry!"

American law enforcement officials could not comprehend that attitude, nor did they accept it. Their sole objective was to safeguard Rabin while in New York City; if anything was going to happen, they wanted it to happen as far from the five boroughs as possible. "You had a bad feeling that somewhere, someone was gunning for one of these leaders, especially people like Rabin or Arafat," reflected Lieutenant Bob Sobocienski, commander of the ESU countersniper team that had many of Rabin's movements covered with a long-range rifle team of marksmen. "You just were determined to make sure that nothing was allowed to happen here in this city and not on my watch."

But the assassins were busy at work that October.

Yitzhak Rabin returned to Israel from the UN-50 gala celebrations in New York City facing the political fight of his life. Opinion polls on the peace process split the country right down the middle, polarizing the nation into two camps with fixed views based on a combination of fear and ideology. The Labor-led coalition was in trouble, and the Likud party leader and candidate for prime minister, Benjamin Netanyahu, was solidifying his support among the right wing by pinning blame for the summer of bloodshed and failure squarely on Rabin's shoulder and on the shoulders of Rabin's partner in peace, Yasir Arafat. Connecting the two leaders into an almost indistinguishable image would prove to be a potent political tool for Netanyahu, and a mighty obstacle to overcome for Rabin. Politically, the terror had to stop if the Rabin government—and the peace process—was to endure.

In late October the pieces of the punitive puzzle came together on the Mediterranean island of Malta, a sun-scorched and mysterious country known more for being a haunt for Libyan sailors in search of liquor and hookers than ground zero for the back-alley killings of the Arab-Israel conflict. It is hard to view assassination as a tool of ballot politics in Israel, but in October a seemingly golden opportunity presented itself to Israel's spymasters. The man responsible for several deadly Islamic Jihad attacks, most notably the Beit Lid massacre, Dr. Fathi Shiqaqi, had suddenly become vulnerable and available.

Dr. Shiqaqi was, in the world of Middle Eastern politics, fair game, indeed; any leader of an organization that executed suicide attacks inside Israel warranted biblical justice. He had also become sloppy in the art of guile and disguise. According to intelligence reports, Dr. Fathi Shiqaqi traveled to Tripoli, Libya, in late October 1995 along with three other Palestinian terrorist leaders: Abu Mussa, the secretary general of the Fatah Intifadah; Talal Jani, the executive director Ahmed Jibril's Popular Front for the Liberation of General Command; and Abu Ali Mustapha, the number two man in Dr. George Habash's Popular Front for the Liberation of Palestine.[5]

The trip to Israel was, according to reports, a fundraising sortie—a plea for cash for opposition movements that suddenly found themselves with a serious cash-flow problem. The meetings in Tripoli with Libya's interior minister were not successful; Libya, with U.N. sanctions following its role in the destruction of Pan Am 103 over Lockerbie, Scotland, in December 1988, was reducing its overt monetary support for the Palestinian resistance movements. In fact, the plea for money was so acute that the two other men in Shiqaqi's party left Tripoli early so that they could inform their bosses in Damascus of the bad news in person.

On October 28, 1995, Dr. Fathi Shiqaqi arrived in the Maltese capital of Valleta on the daily ferry service that ran from Tripoli. The usually bearded Shiqaqi was clean-shaven for the trip. He carried a forged Libyan passport that Colonel Qaddafi's Mucha-barat had generously supplied him with—a newly printed travel document in the name of Ibrahim Shawish. Shiqaqi was, how-ever, a creature of habit. Whenever he traveled to and from Libya, Shiqaqi stayed in the Diplomat Hotel in the Valleta sub-urb of Slima. He felt comfortable and secure in Slima, and in the modest sand-colored five-story hotel, his routine had become a matter of interest to nearly half a dozen Middle Eastern intelli-gence services that monitored the movements and activities of the Palestinian Islamic Jihad.

Malta was something of an intelligence clearing station in the Arab-Israeli conflict, resembling Lisbon as a neutral port of call for spooks of all religious persuasions and paymasters. As one old Middle Eastern hand in the game of espionage described it, "It wouldn't be uncommon on the streets of Malta to stumble across a group of Libyan sailors actually working for Cairo while eating at an outdoor café run by Moroccan intelligence and at the same time bumping into a team from Langley, Vir-ginia, and strolling along the waterfront next to a Mossad-trained man-and-woman team."[6]

Early on the morning of October 29, 1995, Shiqaqi left his room, number 616. Making sure that he wasn't followed, he ate a hearty breakfast and headed into town for a shopping spree along Tower Road. The main thoroughfare was fairly quiet that fall morning, and Shiqaqi was able to buy some shirts for his children without having to worry about crowds. It was a chilly morning, uncharacteristically cold for an October in Malta, and the winds snapping from the north caused many of the town's residents to wear their heavy sweaters and jackets. Shoppers walked briskly with hands inside their coats, and one man, who had become a fixture on the streets, had buried his face inside a dark-colored jacket as his eyes danced around the street in search of his mark.

Shiqaqi headed back to the hotel clutching his packages and

bags and paid little notice to the surrounding landscape. As he arrived, the young man in the dark jacket who witnesses describe as owning a uniquely "Middle Eastern" appearance walked up to Shiqaqi and, in a flurry of 9 mm fire, pumped six bullets into the body of the Islamic Jihad leader. The first bullet, a 9 mm round to the head, killed the forty-nine-year-old terrorist chieftain. Two additional head shots followed, as did three well-aimed clusters to the heart. Before local merchants or any other witnesses could stop the killer, he escaped on the backseat of a motor scooter heading at top speed toward Valleta. The entire operation lasted all of fifteen seconds. Shiqaqi, the mild-mannered terrorist chieftain who had sanctioned several large-scale suicide bombings, lay dead in a pool of flowing blood.

Officials from the Pulizija tá Malta, the oldest police force in all of Europe, realized that they had what one official called "a sensitive case" on their hands. The hit was a professional operation, and the perpetrators had long since departed the island.

Assassination as a national policy is a confused and sometimes constrained element of Israeli national security. Israel's intelligence services do not enjoy carte blanche when it comes to killing. Nor do they admit to selective strikes aimed specifically at terrorist leaders. But according to experts and published accounts, the operation in Malta bore the classic signature of a Mossad operation: fast, furious, and unforgiving. The professional aspects of the hit suggested that it was not an impromptu operation put together in haste, as Mossad operations officers were leaving their offices for a long weekend. The hit required preparation, it required planning, and it required a logistics infrastructure that guaranteed the principal would, indeed, end up dead, and those involved in the operation would be able to make a clean getaway. The Mossad knew it would be implicated in the assassination regardless; it didn't want an agent languishing in a Valetta jail cell affirming those suspicions.

According to published reports, the Mossad operation in

Malta was an all-inclusive endeavor. Agents were already in place, though news of Shiqaqi passing through Malta prompted additional teams from the Metzada division, which handles selective strikes and assassinations, to be dispatched to the Mediterranean island nation. A hit team usually consists of two triggermen—or triggerwomen—supported by between ten and fifteen operatives.[7] They are considered the cutting edge of Mossad operations and are among the busiest of all agents within the secretive organization. Since 1972, dozens of high-ranking officials in the various Palestinian terrorist factions have found their throats slashed, their bodies peppered by magazine-emptying bursts of machine-gun fire, or their cars, houses, phones, and apartments blown up around them.

The strike team allegedly arrived via private boat, making passport control and telltale bits of evidence unnecessary. They were transported by waiting cars to a safe house that the Mossad had rented; following the assassination, reports were issued that seven cars were mysteriously rented from a garage in Mosta.

Once in country, the Mossad contingent maintained constant visual surveillance of Shiqaqi; he could not leave his room and certainly not the hotel without an Israeli tag team following behind. On October 29, when the opportunity to pull the trigger was at hand, the operative simply shouted the name "Shiqaqi" while walking before the target just in front of the hotel at 173 Tower Road; then, when Shiqaqi was frozen in that split second of realization that his life was about to come to an end, the operative unleashed his six-shot barrage. A Yamaha EXY motorcycle, bought in France and brought to Malta long before the operation commenced and bearing a license plate stolen more than five years earlier, was an ideal escape vehicle.

The hit team—which, according to published accounts, consisted of some forty operatives—left no trace of their presence. The gunman picked up the spent shell casings and abandoned the motorcycle nearby. The team was driven to a waiting speedboat that, according to reports, ferried them to Sicily. The safe house in Valetta had been stripped clean of evidence, including fingerprints, before the first police cars responded. A special squad of agents, the best actors in the Mossad repertoire, reportedly remained behind, posing as tourists and eyewitnesses, to offer their "full and complete assistance" to the Maltese police in assembling information and even composite sketches of the killers. In fact, Maltese investigators, picking through the crime scene in white overalls, scratched their heads in disbelief over how little evidence, other than the squashed slugs that had snuffed out Shiqaqi's life, remained.

The Shiqaqi assassination was, according to reports, the first Mossad liquidation in nearly seven years—the last was the brilliantly planned and executed termination of Arafat deputy Abu Jihad, gunned down in his Tunis bedroom in April 1988. According to reports, the mission that terminated the career of Dr. Fathi Shiqaqi was code-named Operation Caesarea. It had been similar to other Mossad operations in Paris, Rome, Beirut, and Tunis. In the always burning lights of Mossad HQ, news of Shiqaqi's six-shot swan song was met with mixed emotion. A man who had blood on his hands was now dead. Prime Minister Rabin, speaking at an economic conference in Amman, was briefed on the operation's success. Retribution was expected to be swift and bloody.

On the night of October 29, 1995, on a remote stretch of a military airfield in the Syrian capital of Damascus, a full military honor guard greeted the arrival of a chartered Tunisian aircraft ferrying the body of Dr. Fathi Shiqaqi. In the city's Yarmouk refugee camp, more than forty thousand Palestinians shouting "Death to Israel" lined the narrow streets demanding vengeance for the murder as they paid honor to the martyr Shiqaqi; a Hizballah honor guard, wearing black fatigues and masks and with dynamite attached to their assault vests, raised their AK-47s in salute as the motorcade inched its way along unpaved streets. A Palestinian marching band led the funeral celebration, joined by Syrian political and military leaders, Iranian and Libyan diplomats, and representatives from the pro-Iranian Hizballah group. In downtown Teheran, more than ten thousand people staged an animated anti-Israel, anti-America rally to coincide with the Shiqaqi funeral procession.[8] Dignitaries, speaking in both the Damascus and Teheran marches, publicly vowed revenge for Shiqaqi's murder.

Revenge came swiftly and in an explosive package. On November 2, 1995, suicide bombers blew up two cars a minute apart in the PLO-ruled Gaza Strip, injuring eleven Israelis. The attacks were attributed to the Islamic Jihad.

There was little that was remarkable concerning Shiqaqi's murder—a violent end was, after all, not a surprising fate for one of the region's most active terrorist factions. Shiqaqi himself had once told a member of Palestinian chairman Yasir Arafat's Fatah faction that he "had helped plot the assassination of Egyptian president Sadat," and that "a leader who is not baptized with blood and fire is no good."[9] What did catch many by surprise, however, was the man chosen as Shiqaqi's successor—the man at the head of the line of his funeral procession. On Monday, October 30, 1995, the Islamic Jihad formally announced that Ramadan Abdullah Shallah, a thirty-eight-year-old academic, had been unanimously named as Shiqaqi's successor during secret consultations between leaders of the Islamic Jihad in the Palestinian Authority's Gaza Strip, leaders of the Israeli-occupied West Bank, and other Islamic Jihad leaders abroad.

Ramadan Abdullah Shallah, a soft-spoken British-educated professor, was one of the founders of the Islamic Jihad. Yet what many in Western intelligence and American law enforcement found most troubling in regard to Shallah's ascension to the helm of one of the Middle East's most active terrorist factions was the fact that from 1993 to just before he succeeded the assassinated Dr. Shiqaqi, Shallah had taught at the University of South Florida in Tampa, where he cochaired several university-affiliated think tanks that, evidence would later implicate, were involved in terrorist activity. While teaching at the university, Shallah was the operations director of the Islamic Jihad, coordinating attacks inside Israel from his university offices in Tampa. The revelation of Shallah as Islamic Jihad commander, in fact, indicated that for years the Islamic Jihad had run a significant aspect of its international operations directly from the United States under the guise of various religious think tanks and mosques ostensibly functioning to promote religious freedom and political moderation. Public moderation ended once he left the United States. As the funeral for Shiqaqi continued down the streets of Gaza City, an Islamic Jihad spokesman declared, "This ugly crime will make every Zionist, wherever he may be on the face of the earth, a target for our amazing blows and our bodies exploding in anger."[10]

After nearly two years of failure in the hunt for Ayyash and the key leaders of Hamas and the Jihad, the Israeli intelligence community had finally scored a major coup. They finally had reason to pat one another on the back. But retribution was expected. In a fiery sermon issued hours after Shiqaqi's Damascus funeral, Islamic Jihad leader Shallah issued the following warning: "We say to Rabin you will pay dearly. We have a rendezvous with you, you cowards who assassinated Shiqaqi in the back when he dared face you. We are addressing you, you assassins, and we say to you Rabin, listen closely, you have triggered a tough war!"[11]

The mood in Israel that November was not optimistic. Shiqaqi's murder was a victory for the intelligence services, but many feared retribution would not be limited to isolated attacks in Gaza. There weren't many residents of Jerusalem or Tel Aviv who felt secure as they drove to work, walked the major thoroughfares, or rode the city's buses. Pensioners, the old men who sat in front of shopping malls and cinema entrances and checked all those coming in for bombs, were increasingly wary that autumn. Something was about to happen. Something had to happen. Everyone just hoped that *when* it happened they were nowhere near it.

For Israeli Prime Minister Rabin, the exhaustive struggle to maintain the peace process amid the bombings and amid the growing political challenge from the right wing was taking its toll. Opinion polls throughout the country were split fifty-fifty in support of the peace process, but an even draw was no way to bring the nation forward through the vision of Oslo. Some sort of national consensus would be needed—peace with security had to be achieved. Right-wing opposition to the peace process was vehement and it was ugly, even by the fratricidal, no-holds-barred rules of Israeli political mudslinging. The images of an angry and pale Rabin wading through pools of blood fit brilliantly into the right-wing agenda to paint the Labor-designed Oslo Accords as suicide for the Jewish state. Each bomb attack swayed public opinion away from what both Rabin and Peres viewed as the window of opportunity for the Middle East's next two thousand years. Each right-wing rally, where activists openly called Rabin a traitor and murderer and some even openly waved banners of the Israeli premier in an S.S. uniform, brought the level of civil discourse in Israel to dangerous levels. Many Israeli political analysts had always realized that the country, a patchwork of a hundred-plus cultures and agendas, would always find unity in its struggle for survival against the Arab threat. But what would happen if that threat were removed or diminished? Would the harsh and unbreachable differences between Israelis, between the European Ashkenazim and Middle Eastern Sephardi communities, boil over into open hostility? Would the divide between secular Israelis and the orthodox movements erupt into civil war? The country was confused and divided, and the situation was dangerously coming to a head.

In an attempt to jump-start the peace process and win public support for the gamble the Jewish state had entered into with Arafat, an alliance of left-wing and Peace Now groups organized a massive rally for the heart of Tel Aviv, in Kings of Israel Square, with the city hall skyscraper as a backdrop. The Israeli prime minister, Labor Party officials, and many of the country's top entertainers had signed on to appear together, unified on a single stage, to squash the cries of traitor and murderer. It would be a night that Israel will never forget.

November 4, 1995, was a warm and comfortable night in Tel Aviv. A humid haze had engulfed much of the city, and a cooling, though ominous cloud cover had drifted in from the Mediterranean. The cinemas, outdoor cafés and even the sprawling Dizengoff Shopping Center, usually packed with couples and soldiers ending their weekend leaves, were empty that Saturday night. It was Kings of Israel Square that was packed with young men and women, parents with children, even seniors, all attracted to the carnival-like atmosphere created by the lively music, the political speeches, and the heartfelt pleas to "give peace a chance." A hundred thousand people had assembled in the massive city square to lend a supporting song to Rabin and his two-year campaign of peace in a rally labeled by organizers as the Yes to Peace, No to Violence peace rally.

The who's who assembly of politicians, dignitaries, movie stars, and singers gathered on a stage facing the filled-to-capacity square. At 8:30 P.M., Prime Minister Rabin, appearing relaxed and confident, addressed the crowds. "Permit me to say that I am deeply moved. I wish to thank each and every one of you, who have come here today to take a stand against violence and for peace." Rabin praised the enthusiastic crowd visible in a sea of PEACE NOW and GIVE PEACE A CHANCE banners. "This government, which I am privileged to head, together with my friend Shimon Peres, decided to give peace a chance—a peace that will solve most of Israel's problems. I was a military man for twenty-seven years. I fought so long as there was no chance for peace. I believe that there is now a chance for peace, a great chance. We must take advantage of it for the sake of those standing here, and for those who are not here—and they are many. I have always believed that the majority of the people want peace and are ready to take risks for peace."

Perhaps speaking on a premonition, Rabin continued. "In coming here today, you demonstrate, together with many others who did not come, that the people truly desire peace and oppose violence. Violence erodes the basis of Israeli democracy. It must be condemned and isolated. This is not the way of the state of Israel. In a democracy there can be differences, but the final decision will be taken in democratic elections, as the 1992 elections which gave us the mandate to do what we are doing, and to continue on this course."

After months of touring buses bombed by Ayyash's explosive devices, and following nearly a year of venomous right-wing taunts and threats, the outpouring of affection at the rally overwhelmed Rabin. Standing next to Shimon Peres and singer Miri Aloni, he even—unprecedentedly—agreed to sing in public. Following the speech, the monotone Rabin joined the assembled musicians in "Song for Peace," one of Israel's most popular ballads. This outpouring of support for the peace accords was, according to Leah Rabin, one of the happiest moments of Yitzhak Rabin's life.

A hundred feet away from the stage, at the parking spot in between city hall and the Gan Ha'Ir Shopping Mall on Ibn Gvirol Street, another man was experiencing the happiest day of his life. He was twenty-five years old with a dark complexion and a beguiling smile. He had, quite innocently, managed to hover around the prime minister's limousine without attracting even the slightest of suspicion. His name was Yigal Amir.

The security package surrounding Prime Minister Rabin that night was, in the words of a retired Israeli police lieutenant, "bizarre and unusual," especially considering the fact that threats that had been made against his life by both Arab and Jewish extremists. Security was not evenly applied that night—it was tight in some areas, criminally lax in others. Spotlights were brought in to scan the nearby rooftops for potential snipers; some apartments surrounding Kings of Israel Square were searched; parking to area residents was limited; and a heavy uniformed police presence was everywhere. Yet around Rabin and the areas of access to and from the stage, security was virtually nonexistent. He was protected by only a handful of plain-clothed Shin Bet agents. Many captains of industry, movie stars, and even sports figures move about with larger security details.

According to reports, weeks earlier Shin Bet director Gillon had personally informed Rabin that the extremist elements of the right wing were plotting to assassinate him. On October 10, 1995, a rabbi was arrested when he tried to attack the prime minister as he gave a speech at the Wingate Institute near Netanya. Three days later, on October 13, Itamar Ben-Gvir, a man known to the Shin Bet as a Kach activist, was arrested for vandalizing Rabin's armor-plated Cadillac by stealing the hood ornament. "The same way we got to the hood ornament," he said, "we can get to Rabin."[12] Shin Bet officials had increased the size of his security detail and urged Rabin to wear a lightweight bulletproof vest, but he refused. Reportedly he told his Shin Bet shift leader that he felt secure in Israel.

Yigal Amir had been stalking Yitzhak Rabin for nearly a year. On January 22, 1995, Amir had ventured to Jerusalem, to the Yad Vashem Holocaust Memorial, to kill Rabin as he addressed an assembly commemorating the fiftieth anniversary of the liberation of Auschwitz. Rabin never made it to the ceremony—he was diverted to the Beit Lid carnage following the early morning attack. In September, Amir once again stalked Rabin, attempting to kill the prime minister as he dedicated a major traffic interchange at Kfar Shmaryahu just north of Tel Aviv; Amir would later admit he was deterred by the heavy Shin Bet presence.

The second of ten children, Amir was a veteran of the 1st Golani Infantry Brigade and a law student at the religious Bar-Ilan University near Tel Aviv. He had worked as an emissary in Riga, Latvia, and, as a result, learned to shoot handguns at a Shin Bet-run range. An Orthodox Jew whose father hand-wrote holy scriptures for a living, he was a member of an extremist right-wing group called Eyal, an offshoot of the outlawed Kach movement, founded by Rabbi Meir Kahane, who was murdered in New York City in 1990 by an Islamic terrorist cell. And, as a member of Eyal, Yigal Amir was known to the Shin Bet. In fact, Eyal was a Shin Bet creation meant to serve as a magnet for right-wing militants who might be prompted to commit terrorist acts so that all those displaying a propensity for seditious violence could be monitored and checked. Eyal's leader and Amir's mentor, Avishai Raviv, was a provocateur whose Shin Bet code name was "Champagne." According to reports, several months before that fateful night, Raviv is said to have told Amir, "You have no balls. You're not a man. If you're a man, shoot Rabin."[13]

The Shin Bet had been informed of Amir's intention as far back as June, when a man named Shlomo Halevy informed the Shin Bet of a plot to kill the prime minister after a mutual friend overheard a conversation in a men's room. Halevy informed the authorities of the plot as well as the fact that the assassin might be a twenty-five-year-old short man with dark skin and black hair who was a member of Eyal. Unlike the U.S. Secret Service, which investigates virtually *every* vocalized threat made against the president of the United States, the Shin Bet simply chose to ignore the warnings.

* * *

Yigal Amir was the ultimate insider—the ideal assassin. He was completely unthreatening; in fact, many said the young man who helped old ladies in the neighborhood with their groceries looked like everyone's next-door neighbor. On the night of November 4, Amir was able to enter the ostensibly impenetrable "sterile area" surrounding Rabin's limousine *precisely* because he looked so familiar and unassuming. Removing his black yarmulke as to avoid the potential suspicion of being an Orthodox Jew at a Peace Now rally, he used his personable charm and friendly demeanor to convince one of the Shin Bet agents that he was the driver for pop star Aviv Gefen. Instead of hiding from the Shin Bet agents and police officers assigned to the area, he engaged them in friendly conversation. Not one of the police officers or Shin Bet agents around the limousine bothered to search him, and not one of them bothered to ask Amir to present identification. Nobody bothered to get him out of the area. But why would they show undue concern? Amir was an Israeli— one of them. And, after all, the Shin Bet was on alert and at the ready to respond to any Arabs in the area.[14]

Gideon Ezra, now a Member of Parliament and a former head of the Shin Bet Protective Security Division, told Israeli TV that, "Rabin's security detail was naturally more psychologically alert when he visited Nablus than when he was in Tel Aviv." In the wake of the Hamas suicide bombings and the assassination of Islamic Jihad leader Dr. Fathi Shiqaqi only one week earlier in Malta, the Shin Bet was focused on an "Arab" threat. The Shin Bet had, for the better part of fifty years, indoctrinated its agents that the principal threat to the Jewish state was an Arab one. It was a blinding tunnel vision that had left a clear field of fire for a Jewish assassin.

At 9:40 A.M., as Rabin made his way down the podium stairs to his limousine, Amir walked behind the Israeli premier, removed a Beretta double-action semiautomatic pistol from the

small of his back, and pumped three hollow-point dumdum bullets into Rabin's back. Two of the bullets penetrated the seventy-
three-year-old leader in an explosion of flesh and blood; the
third seriously wounded Yoram Rubin, an agent on his Shin Bet
detail. The unthinkable had finally happened. A Jew had shot
an Israeli leader. In a split second, an assassin had forever
changed the Jewish state.

The Shin Bet collapse had been absolute. People at the staircase
were able to get within five yards of the prime minister. The
Shin Bet detail never even identified Amir in the area; in fact,
of the three agents who surrounded Rabin and the three supervisors walking alongside the prime minister, only one noticed
Amir approaching Rabin.[15] The Shin Bet agents surrounding Rabin in an inner circle never even drew their Jericho 9 mm semiautomatic pistols—even after the gunfire. Nor did they subdue
or arrest Amir. He was pinned to a wall by an alert police officer
who tackled the gunman seconds after the shooting and
whisked him away in a waiting patrol car. Amir would later tell
police that he acted alone on God's orders and that he had no
regrets. He also told police that he couldn't believe how easy it
was to get to Rabin.[16]

The commander of the VIP Protection Unit was present at the
Kings of Israel Square rally and personally supervised the security package around Rabin. A former head of security for the
Israeli consulate in New York City, he has been described as a
highly motivated individual who personally has drafted former
commandos from Sayeret Mat'kal, Sayeret Golani, and the
Cherry undercover squad onto the ranks of his unit. They were
cocky, confident, and very young. In early 1995 a controversial
Shin Bet directive removed all agents thirty-five years of age or
older from the VIP Protection Unit; many of these agents who
were bounced to other divisions were extremely experienced
hands at the delicate and unforgiving science of safeguarding a

principal from harm.[17] But the former commandos froze. "The men in this unit train specifically for these kinds of events," a senior Shin Bet officer told a German newspaper, "but they failed in the ultimate test of reality." The Shin Bet decision to replace cunning and experience with brawn and firepower had tragically backfired.

Although wounded himself, Yoram Rubin pushed Rabin into his waiting Cadillac and ordered driver Menachem Damti to "floor it to Ichilov Hospital," located just a thousand feet from the steps at city hall. But here, too, the Shin Bet fell down on the job. The agents had not prepared an evacuation route in case of tragedy, and Damti found himself boxed in—a gridlock of people made it impossible to move. In fact, in what one U.S. law enforcement official called "the classic Israeli cluster-fuck," a desperate Damti was forced to argue his way through a police roadblock. He was forced to take a roundabout route to Ichilov Hospital, wasting valuable time in getting the mortally wounded Rabin to the emergency room. Shin Bet agents at the scene did not communicate directives or updates of the situation to advance teams, nor did they phone the emergency room at Ichilov to warn of Rabin's impending arrival. The trip to the hospital should have taken seconds but ended up lasting more than three minutes. Prime Minister Rabin lost consciousness thirty seconds after being hit.

When the Cadillac pulled up to the emergency room entrance, a trauma team was not waiting—in fact, a police officer and Rabin's bodyguard hoisted the mortally wounded premier onto a stretcher and brought him into surgery.

Surgeons in the emergency room at Ichilov Hospital worked feverishly on Rabin, but the damage caused by the two dum-dum rounds had been far too extensive. The two bullets that struck the prime minister punctured both lungs, permitting air to leak into his chest cavity and place enormous pressure on his failing heart. Doctors inserted a tube into his chest cavity to release air and alleviate the pressure, but Rabin had already suffered massive brain damage from his heart pumping oxygen, instead of blood, to his brain. He died ninety minutes later.

Foreign Minister Shimon Peres, President Ezer Weizman, Chief of Staff Shahak, and Leah Rabin had all assembled inside the Ichilov Hospital emergency room. Veterans of Israel's wars for survival who had walked through walls of fire appeared humbled by the split-second turn of events. Men who had spent long dark nights in enemy territory began to cry. They knew that the country had been dealt a lethal blow. At 11:14 P.M., Rabin's confidant and speechwriter Eitan Haber emerged to a sea of anguished journalists to announce, "With horror, grave sorrow, and deep grief, the government of Israel announces the death of Prime Minister and Defense Minister Yitzhak Rabin, murdered by an assassin."

A veil of innocence that had separated Israel from other nations evaporated in the muzzle flash of a Beretta 9 mm pistol. The unthinkable had happened. Israel's armor of Kevlar had been penetrated, and it had been compromised not by an Arab terrorist but by a Jewish zealot. Shock—on the streets of Tel Aviv, and inside homes in Jerusalem, Haifa, Beersheba, Carmel, Nahariyah, and Ashqelon, only shock. A horrible nightmare had become reality, and dread of an uncertain future became a daunting fear of the next day. On Ibn Gvirol Street, where Rabin's blood still lay moist on the littered pavement, the young and old wept. On television bulletins broadcast live from Kings of Israel Square, a young father clutching a toddler could barely hold his emotion as he wept the tears of a battered nation. An Orthodox soldier, an M-16 assault rifle slung over his shoulder, removed a small prayer book from his fatigue pocket and began to chant a psalm. Men nervously searching for an answer began to scream in anguish over what had happened to their beloved Israel. "I've fought in three wars," said a man on the street, "and I think we've just lost the biggest battle of our lives." A young girl, her hair spread wildly in golden bronze curls and wearing a Shalom A'chshav, or "Peace Now," T-shirt, closed her eyes in disbelief as her hands, cupped over her tan cheeks, trembled uncontrollably. According to former Russian dissident and Knesset member Natan Sharansky, "More than a person had been killed, the nation has been desecrated."[18]

International reaction came swiftly. President Bill Clinton viewed Rabin, the elder statesman and warrior, with the high regard sons usually reserve for their fathers. Clinton was openly bewildered by the assassination and privately feared the effect it would have on the Middle East peace process. Less than an hour after Rabin's death was announced, President Clinton, holding back his tears, addressed reporters from just outside the White House. "The world has lost one of its greatest men, a warrior for his nation's freedom and now a martyr for his nation's peace." He concluded his brief remarks saying, "Yitzhak Rabin was my partner and my friend. I admired him, and I loved him very much. Because words cannot express my true feelings, let me just say 'Shalom Chaver.' Good-bye, friend."

Yasir Arafat, completely shocked by Rabin's death, offered words of condolence and compassion to the Israeli public. With tears in his eyes, Arafat praised Rabin as a great leader of peace. "I am very sad and very shocked for this awful and terrible crime against one of the brave leaders of Israel and the peacemakers." But Arafat was as concerned about his own safety as he was about the teetering peace process. Hundreds of heavily armed Force 17 loyalists surrounded the Arafat compound immediately after news of Rabin's death reached Gaza. In the Hamas strongholds of the refugee camps, hundreds of plainclothed Preventive Security agents patrolled the teeming neighborhoods in force—just in case. After all, it was Arafat, not Rabin, who many Middle East insiders thought would be killed by one of his own.

On the other end of the emotional spectrum was the response of many in the Occupied Territories and in areas under the control of Arafat's various police and secret police agencies: There was great joy in Rabin's murder and an ironic sense of justice in the fact that a right-wing Jew, "another Goldstein," had turned the nation inside out and at war with itself. In Jenin and in Nablus, Hamas supporters wearing facemasks and black Ninja outfits danced in celebration as they fired their AK-47 assault rifles into the cool autumn night. But beyond their joy was the sense of foreboding. In Rabin they knew who they were battling, and they knew that although he was the man who issued the infamous "break their bones" order to Israeli forces in the Intifadah as a means to stop the uprising, he was perhaps the sole man in the Israeli political system with whom they'd have a fair chance of doing business. The sense of foreboding was also a bitter confession to the bloody reality of the Arab-Israeli conflict. Murder was never an end to a means in the war over Israel and Palestine, it was simply a spasm of inevitable violence that promised only greater suffering.

In the Ein el-Hilweh Palestinian refugee camp in southern Lebanon, men fired wild bursts of machine-gun fire into the air when news of Rabin's assassination reached Lebanese radio. Hizballah guerrillas, celebrating the murder of the Israeli leader as if their soccer team had just won the World Cup, launched RPG grenades into the darkened Lebanese night, vowing that this was the first step in a holy path that would bring them to Jerusalem. Ironically, those sentiments were echoed in Brooklyn, where many Kahane-Chai supporters greeted news of Rabin's murder with relief. "I'm thrilled," shouted an old lady with a coif of bright red hair, "one traitor is down. Thank the Lord." Other women sold buttons in order to raise money for Yigal Amir's defense. "Help raise funds for our heroes and prisoners," one woman said. Local residents snatched up hundreds of the improvised ornaments in a matter of hours.

*   *   *

Few in Israel slept that painful Saturday night. Most listened to the radio or watched CNN or Israeli TV for bulletins. The radio airwaves were filled with sad songs usually reserved for Memorial Day, and news reports reviewed Rabin's illustrious military and political career. The fear that had permeated the country after each of Ayyash's suicide bombs turned a bus into a deathtrap was far less than the anxiety and foreboding that had struck almost every Israeli household. They knew that, as Israelis, they were all targets of Arab terrorism. And, perhaps had Prime Minister Rabin been assassinated by a man carrying a knapsack full of Acetone-3 mixture and shouting "Allahu Akbar," the public sense of national collapse might have been far less. But Rabin was killed by a Jew. A neighbor from next door. And the principles of the fabric that had held the besieged country together were quickly eroding.

Foreign Minister Shimon Peres, a man who had spent the past thirty years as Rabin's rival and, finally, ally, was named acting prime minister. He faced an insurmountable challenge not only to salvage the peace accords but to somehow re-cement the adhesive bond that was coming undone inside Israel. The mood inside the country wasn't one of anger or rage but of reserved shock. "I do not think there is anything I need to say," Peres told a special cabinet session immediately after Rabin's death. "I feel that all of us, together, will do everything we can to render him, not our last respects, but rather eternal honor. His life was cut short, but not his work. His spirit has left him, but this spirit has not abandoned us, nor the process in which we are engaged. We are all determined to continue on this great path—to serve the people, to serve the state, as a country strong and secure, true to its pursuit of peace. That is all we can do after this terrible tragedy."

Peres had, of course, also been targeted by Yigal Amir that night. Amir had hoped to kill both Rabin and Peres that fateful night, but Rabin had stopped to talk to event organizers and pop star Gidi Gov and Peres had walked down the stairs minutes before the prime minister.

Rabin's body arrived in Jerusalem, at the Knesset, at 2:00 on the afternoon of Sunday, November 5. His simple wooden casket, draped with the Israeli flag, lay in state as hundreds of thousands of Israelis joined the Rabin family to pay their final respects. Leah Rabin, who had been at the rally with her husband the night before, could barely contain her grief and sorrow. By the end of the day nearly one million Israelis had passed by the coffin of the first Jewish leader to be assassinated since biblical times.

Carmi Gillon, who had been in the United States at the time of the shooting, took the next plane to Tel Aviv—straight into the eye of the storm. The Shin Bet had little opportunity to reel back and assess its incredible failure. Rabin's funeral promised to be an international gathering the likes of which had never before been seen in the Jewish state—presidents, prime ministers, kings, queens, princes, and representatives from nearly a hundred nations would be flocking to the Jewish state in the next forty-eight hours to pay their respects. It was the type of international recognition that both Rabin and Peres could have only dreamed about when they embarked on the Oslo "backdoor" to the Palestinians, yet both men had dreamed of such international gatherings assembling for economic conferences, trade fairs, sporting events, and even religious observances.

The security for Rabin's funeral rivaled the massive veil of protection cast over New York City for UN-50, but the badly battered Shin Bet and Israeli National Police did not have two years to prepare their contingency plans. They had all of forty-eight hours. From the perspective of Carmi Gillon and the senior division heads, the Rabin funeral was an enormous terrorist target of opportunity. Israel was already crippled by the Rabin murder—the country could have been decimated, perhaps beyond repair, by a spree of suicide bombings or an assassination attempt made during the funeral proceedings. Security forces sealed the West Bank and Gaza, preventing Palestinians from entering Israel, but even a conservative estimate placed hundreds of Hamas operatives inside Israeli territory. How many Ayyash-built bombs were there in circulation? How many shaheed were in safe houses in East Jerusalem, Haifa, Tel Aviv, or Netanya awaiting the order from the cell commander to martyr himself? What were the directives racing in via fax from Teheran and Damascus to Islamic Jihad and Hamas commanders in Gaza and the Sudan?

Shin Bet commanders realized they also had to contend with the possibility that Yigal Amir was not the self-professed lone gunman manipulated by Eyal, Avishai Raviv, and his Shin Bet handlers. Was there a larger right-wing Jewish plot out attempting to seize control over the remnants of the Israeli democracy? In Jerusalem, only blocks from where the funeral procession would pass, Kach supporters spray painted an ominous threat: "Rabin, a Victim of Peace, Peres the Next in Line!"

Advance teams from the U.S. Secret Service and State Department's Diplomatic Security Service, along with teams of French, Jordanian, German, Egyptian, and British secret service agents, had preceded their principals to Jerusalem. They were jittery and prepared for anything. The top-secret threat-analysis reports that they had read on the flight to Ben-Gurion International Airport had highlighted the last eighteen months of suicide bombings, undercover squad shoot-outs, and kidnappings. Their Shin Bet liaisons, still reeling from the Rabin murder, would be too preoccupied to provide them with an up-to-date portrait of known threats on the ground; and, many of the advance agents knew, the Shin Bet was not in a state of

mind to analyze the latest strands of intelligence in any com-
prehensive or reliable manner. The foreign details would be on
their own in Jerusalem.

More than ten thousand policemen and soldiers were summoned to safeguard the international assembly of world leaders
and mourners. Undercover squads from Gideon, the elite coun-
terstrike force of the Jerusalem police, infiltrated areas of Arab
East Jerusalem to monitor potential security concerns. Police motorcycle counterterrorist squads, high-speed bikers with M-16s
slung across their shoulders, stood fast awaiting any potential
sign of danger, and police and army choppers flew overhead to
monitor rooftops and the funeral procession route. Shin Bet
agents, some openly wielding mini-Uzis, patrolled key thoroughfares and intersections. The Ya'ma'm and Sayeret Mat'kal
stood at the ready—just in case a worst-case scenario once again
reared its ugly head. Nothing could be left to chance anymore
in the new Israel of November 1995. The constantly changing
rulebook had changed once again.

At just after midday on Monday, November 6, 1995, nearly a
thousand dignitaries from more than a hundred nations assembled at Mt. Herzl National Cemetery. The mourners included
U.S. President Bill Clinton, First Lady Hillary Rodham-Clinton,
former Presidents George Bush and Jimmy Carter, Secretary of
State Warren Christopher, U.N. Ambassador Madeleine Al-
bright, National Security Adviser Anthony Lake, Middle East
Peace Coordinator Dennis Ross, Speaker of the House Newt
Gingrich, Senate Majority Leader Robert Dole, Senators Al
D'Amato and Edward Kennedy, as well as congressmen and a
contingent from New York, Rabin's last hosts, including Governor George Pataki, New York Mayor Rudolph Giuliani, and
former Mayor Ed Koch. Egyptian president Hosni Mubarak,
who for security reasons chose not to attend the U.N. jubilee in

New York, ventured to Jerusalem for the Rabin funeral; Mubarak himself had been ambushed in Addis Ababa, Ethiopia, on the way from the airport to an Organization of African Unity summit and barely escaped with his life. Mubarak's visit to Israel would be the first time that an Egyptian head of state had visited the Israeli capital since Anwar es-Sadat's epic pilgrimage of peace in 1978. King Hussein of Jordan, Rabin's true partner in the process and a friend who was an icon of the region's pursuit of a peaceful future, ventured to Jerusalem in a somber pilgrimage to honor the slain Israeli leader. Jordanian mourners included Queen Noor, Crown Prince Hassan, and Prime Minister Zeid Bin Shaker. Israel's inroads to the Arab world, the grand regional vision made possible by Oslo, were evident by the fact that Morocco, Oman, Tunisia, and Qatar sent high-level delegations to the funeral.

It was pageantry—and foreboding—the likes of which the state of Israel had never seen before. One after one, the leaders of the Western and the Arab worlds addressed a worldwide audience, eulogizing the slain Israeli leader as a hero of war and a champion of peace. President Clinton spoke of Rabin's courage and vision.

Jordan's King Hussein, returning to the city where his grandfather had been assassinated, appeared wounded by the loss of a comrade in arms. "You lived as a soldier, you died as a soldier for peace." In closing, and perhaps scanning across the martyred landscape of peacemakers in the regions and thinking of his own fate, Hussein continued. "He had courage, he had vision, and he had a commitment to peace, and standing here, I commit before you, before my people in Jordan, before the world, myself to continue with our utmost, to ensure that we leave a similar legacy. And when my time comes, I hope it will be like my grandfather's and like Yitzhak Rabin's."

Noa Ben-Artzi Philosoph, Yitzhak Rabin's eighteen-year-old

granddaughter, brought tears to the eyes of the gathered and the world in a soul-wrenching eulogy written at her grandfather's desk.

Less than two weeks after Rabin's assassination, Prime Minister Shimon Peres toured the Palestinian city of Jenin, days before the city was to be handed over to the Palestinian Authority, a first "fact on the ground" that the Oslo II Accords, signed in Washington, would be implemented to the letter. As Peres descended from the IAF chopper, he was seen wearing a bulletproof vest underneath his field jacket; a phalanx of Shin Bet agents, young men with shaven or close-cropped heads openly clutched mini-Uzi submachine guns with their fingers on the triggers. For once it would not be business as usual with the Shin Bet. The five Shin Bet agents who surrounded Peres covered him, quite literally, like a security blanket—they remained one step ahead of him and one step behind. "Yehiye Be'Seder" could no longer be Standard Operating Procedure.

Commentators all agreed that Israel would never be the same country again. The Shin Bet, too, was changed forever. To reclaim its birthright as a domestic security force to be reckoned with, the Shin Bet sought to reestablish its image, its direction, and its ability to protect and to serve the citizens of Israel against the enemies that lay in wait. Shin Bet officials knew that the embattled intelligence agency would need a spectacular operation, an Entebbe of its own, to reclaim its birthright as a force to be reckoned, and to win back the Israeli public's confidence. To achieve this task, the Shin Bet looked south, to Gaza, and to the one man whose smirk had, before Yigal Amir, been the true personification of evil. Irony had once again claimed victory in the muddled world of the Middle East. Yehiya Ayyash would salvage the reputation and, possibly, the future of the Shin Bet.

Notes

[1]"Mother of 'Engineer' Faces Forgery Charge," *The Jerusalem Post*, October 30, 1995, p. 2.

[2]Alon Pinkas, "Internal GSS Report Warned About Lax Security Months Ago," *The Jerusalem Post*, November 28, 1995, p. 1.

[3]Interview, Queens, New York, October 7, 1998.

[4]Margo Lipschitz Sugarman, "A Chronology of Hate," *The Jerusalem Report*, November 30, 1995, p. 6.

[5]"How Killers Got to Shiqaqi," *Intelligence Newsletter*, no. 276, November 23, 1995.

[6]Interview, Amman, July 29, 1997.

[7]Ron Mivrag, "*Kach Po'alim Ha'Mechaslim*," *Ma'ariv Mosaf Shabbat*, November 3, 1995, p. 8.

[8]"Slain Palestinian Head Buried," Associated Press, November 1, 1995.

[9]"Slain Jihad Leader Remembered," Associated Press, October 29, 1995.

[10]Louis Rene Beres, "Assassination of Terrorists May Be Law-Enforcing," Purdue University On Line, October 31, 1995.

[11]"Thousands Mourn Slain Jihad Chief," Agence France Press, November 1, 1995.

[12]Sugarman, "Chronology of Hate."

[13]Nadav Shragai and Gideon Alon, "Witnesses: Raviv Told Amir 'If You're a Man, Shoot Rabin'," *Ha'aretz*, October 14, 1998, p. 3.

[14]Alex Fishman, "*Re'idat Adama Be'Shabak*," *Yediot Aharonot*, November 10, 1995, p. 2.

[1]Moshe Zunder, "Kach Hifkarnu et Rosh Ha'Memshala," *Ma'ariv Sof Shavu'a*, September 27, 1996, p. 4.

Chapter 7

Payback

Saturday was festive in Gaza—there was genuine joy in the air. December 16, 1995. The eighth anniversary of the founding of Hamas. Looking like the Rose Bowl during a college championship game more than a dumping ground for refugees, Gaza City was alive with color, music, and pageantry. Colorful balloons of green and white filled the sky, as did the smell of gunpowder and the occasional ear-popping explosions of AK-47s being fired on full auto. Small children ate deep-fried Awami treats as they sat on their father's shoulders and watched masked men dressed in black wave razor sharp swords that sparkled in the cheating stabs of sunlight that managed to break through the rain clouds.

In Gaza Stadium, where the applause and cheers made it seem like a pop concert more than a religious revival, Hamas activist Mohammed Taha fired up the crowd by promising the ten-thousand-plus in attendance that Hamas would, indeed, continue killing Israelis. In the crowd, men frenzied with rage and devotion shouted "Kill them by the busload!" There were colorful murals on display surrounding the main podium, including depictions of Hamas activities such as stabbing and stoning Israeli soldiers. Palestinian policemen wandering outside the stadium appeared amused by the celebrations.

Souvenir hawkers sold trinkets and flags, T-shirts and banners. Bootleg audiocassettes were a particularly lucrative concession, especially a tape of popular songs entitled *The Engineer.* Selling for about 80 cents, or three hours wage for the average Palestinian laborer, the tape celebrated the handiwork of Yehiya Ayyash. "Strike, oh engineer. You're the lion that scares the enemy. Plan, strike, and return the land of our grandparents. With an explosive belt you make glories."

The line to buy the tape was long, as were lines to buy T-shirts bearing the image of Yehiya Ayyash and posters of his face emblazoned over a fireball and the skyline of the Old City of Jerusalem. Mostly, small kids and teenagers bought the poorly produced, high-decibel tapes, but there were also a few older gentlemen on line with cash in hand. Most of the vendors thought them to be agents of one of Arafat's security entities; after all, they openly wore pistols, poorly cut polyester blouses over black cotton pants, and shoes that appeared too tight. Only spies or security agents could dress so shabbily.

On the night of November 8, 1995, less than ninety-six hours after the two rounds exploded inside the chest of Israeli prime minister Yitzhak Rabin, Yasir Arafat did what many Israelis thought even more far-fetched than a Jew killing an Israeli premier—he traveled to Tel Aviv. The Shin Bet had argued against Arafat attending Rabin's funeral on security grounds, and there were many in Force 17 who echoed those sentiments. There was also the problem of imagery. The sight of the Palestinian president visiting Jerusalem only two days after the assassination of the Israeli premier was too much, many Israeli insiders felt, for the public to tolerate. Arafat's presence would provoke far more than it would console. It would certainly have created a bizarre theater of the surreal, this new Middle East. Nevertheless, Arafat had been overwhelmed by Rabin's assassination—he had spoken to the Israeli prime minister only two hours before Amir's bullets were fired. Aides told reporters that Arafat had cried when he learned that Rabin had been shot in the back.

Arafat was flown to Tel Aviv courtesy of an Israel Air Force chopper. Under a tight veil of secrecy, and under the watch of Israeli special forces and Shin Bet agents, Arafat paid a condolence call on Rabin's widow, Leah. Sipping a cup of tea in a ceramic cup, Arafat looked sullen and remorseful. His anguished face reflected the dark clouds looming over the horizon of the peace accords. Arafat stayed with Leah Rabin for ninety minutes. He was flown back to Gaza after midnight, and news of the visit was not released until late the following day.

Arafat's call on Rabin's widow was arranged by Yossi Ginnosar, a former Shin Bet official who was instrumental back in 1986 of forging the then illegal back-door contacts with Arafat and his security apparatus. Ginnosar had a brilliant career in the Shin Bet cut short as a result of two scandals that rocked the agency in the mid-1980s. He had survived dark spasms of Shin Bet history before, though the state of affairs at Shin Bet HQ in the wake of Rabin's assassination was the darkest they had ever been. In fact, it was the worst crisis within the ranks of an Israeli intelligence service since October 1973, when A'man failed to predict the impending invasion by both Syria and Egypt.

The mood in the Shin Bet was one of utter despair. There was no controversy surrounding the tragedy, and no top-secret security blanket with which to cover the terrible blunders. The organization had failed in one of its basic and most sacrosanct missions. The country was teetering as a result. The agents not involved in the fiasco, those not complicit in the collapse, nevertheless shared the shame of the VIP Protection Unit. The mood of failure was infectious. If there is one thing that penetrates the skin of an Israeli more than anything it is the notion of a *friyer*, the slang term for sucker. The Shin Bet was now a national joke—and a national concern. Preventing the next wave of Hamas bombings through aggressive fieldwork, the tradecraft that the Shin Bet was legendary for, would be next to impossible as public scrutiny of the agency's most humiliating chapter was bound to compromise its ability to intimidate and manipulate.

On November 8 the Shin Bet launched an extensive internal investigation. The investigating committee, chaired by three former Shin Bet division heads, was tasked with examining: (a) preparation for the Peace March operation; (b) intelligence gathering for the event; (c) the coordination of intelligence assets with security inputs; (d) coordination of the security for the event with the National Police, the Ya'ma'm, paramedics, event organizers, and others; and (e) the performance of the VIP Protection Unit during the peace rally. Many inside the Shin Bet knew that careers would be ruined and lives possibly destroyed; there was even talk about bringing charges of criminal negligence against the Shin Bet agents who had allowed the assassin to get so close. Already, Shin Bet officials had gone public with charges of neglect against the police for failing to maintain a sterile area around Rabin's limousine; the police closed ranks with charges of their own. Former heads of the Shin Bet joined the fray, pointing fingers and laying blame; some even called for Gillon, still only identifiable as "Kaf" in the press, to resign. Even former agents of the U.S. Secret Service were interviewed in the Israeli press sharing their criticisms and opinions; after all, the Secret Service had withstood the storm of the Kennedy assassination and, some seventeen years later, would once again have their methods reviewed following the failed attempt by a lone and crazed gunman to assassinate President Ronald Reagan.

The airing of a top-secret agency's dirty laundry in public was

a dangerous game for a country that had just lost a leader—
especially a Middle Eastern nation battling an incredibly forceful
terrorist offensive. The orgy of recriminations, many in the intelligence community feared, would significantly weaken the
agency's ability to recover. On the streets of Tel Aviv, however,
Shin Bet self-pity was of little significance. Many of the young
people who flocked to the spot where Rabin had been murdered
to sing songs of peace, light candles, or weep thought that the
storm surrounding the Shin Bet inconsequential and childish.
All they wanted to know was that no other leader would end
up assassinated and no buses would blow up in the immediate
future.

Hamas did not know how to react—operationally—to the Rabin assassination. The closure of the Territories, and increased
vigilance by Arafat's secret services, significantly restricted the
list of options. Was it the right time to initiate a major offensive
against Israeli cities, when the enemy was humbled and badly
fractured? Or was it prudent to wait until world sympathy
faded? Hamas chose prudence over wholesale slaughter. With
resourcefulness and patience, they opted to wait out the storm
and see what—and who—was left standing when the clouds
cleared.

The Palestinian Authority was equally concerned with the
state of affairs at Shin Bet headquarters, as well as the mood
inside Israel. The Rabin assassination could have resulted in an
immediate suspension of the implementation of Oslo II, as well
as a return to the state of siege mentalities that many Israelis—
and not necessarily hard-core right-wing fanatics who preached
Greater Israel—found hard to shake. The future of the growing
Palestinian Authority, and any hopes for Palestinian sovereignty
to extend to additional cities, towns, and villages in the West
Bank, was entirely dependent on the Israeli citizen's sense of
security. One more suicide bombing, one repeat of the No. 5 bus
after-blast scene, and Arafat might very well have to settle for

Gaza and Jericho. Arafat's security forces could not bring back Rabin, but they could do the next best thing.

By November 1995 it was accepted as common knowledge among the Shin Bet, as well as the Mossad and A'man, that Yehiya Ayyash was holed up somewhere in Gaza. Although Arafat had publicly—and privately—promised Rabin that the Palestinian security forces were doing all within their legal power to hunt Ayyash down, the Palestinian Authority was maintaining regular contacts with the elusive Engineer.[1] According to reports, General Musa Arafat, Military Intelligence director and Chairman Arafat's nephew, maintained a regular personal dialog with Ayyash. General Arafat was reported to have suggested to Ayyash that he thinks of a life overseas—in Syria, the Sudan, Iran, or even in hiding in Europe or in North America, anywhere—far away from the trigger fingers of the Israeli security forces.

In fact, when Shin Bet officials would raise the issue of Ayyash's whereabouts with their liaisons in Chairman Arafat's office, they were often told that the Engineer was far out of *their* reach, in the Sudan.[2] For Ayyash, such a solution wasn't an option. While the distance between Rafatt and Gaza on a map constituted a mere two-hour drive, in reality they were political light-years apart. Smuggling Ayyash in and out of Gaza might have been a major achievement for Hamas and the special operations protective services of the Islamic resistance, but bringing his entire family to the Strip was virtually impossible. Yet the Israelis were scheduled to return additional cities and towns to Palestinian Authority control that winter, and Ayyash had hoped to seek refuge in Palestinian-controlled areas in order to maintain contacts with his parents, his wife, and his children.

The Shin Bet's worst-case scenario was that Ayyash ends up in Iran, Syria, the Sudan, or some other distant Arab police state where he would be virtually invulnerable. Shin Bet officials wanted Ayyash close to home—close enough where they might be able to one day watch him die, or sit and smile in the interrogation room as proper pressure was applied. Arab Desk officials, left bruised but not completely humbled by the Rabin assassination, understood the merits of proactive response—not only in operational terms, but in elevating morale inside a counterterrorist and counterespionage entity that had, for too long, been seeking an enemy it could not locate. There was, after all, relief in Israel following Shiqaqi's six-shot farewell in Malta. Yet Yehiya Ayyash was the prize that many coveted. To the men—and women—who spent those dark and sleepless nights in observation posts around Rafatt on the hunch that Ayyash might return home, eliminating Shiqaqi had all the appeal of taking one's sister to the prom. Ayyash was the target. Ayyash was the terrorist who they all wanted to see expired.

In the operational scheme of things, the fact that Ayyash was inside the confines of Gaza was a source of comfort to the Shin Bet agents hunting the Engineer. Unlike the West Bank, with its vast stretches of terrain and endless caves, wadis, and groves, Gaza was basically an imprisoned slum-state without the expanses of forests, mountains, plains, or lowlands. Gaza's one window to the sea, its Mediterranean shoreline, was constantly watched by the vigilant eyes, and 20 mm cannons, of Israeli Navy patrol boats. It was doubtful that the Egyptians would allow Ayyash to cross the Rafath checkpoints into Sinai; Mubarak, after all, had learned his lesson in providing safe passage to terrorists who had killed Americans following the bungled Achille Lauro seajacking. And, even if he made it to the West Bank, it would be doubtful if the Jordanians would not arrest him on sight. Ayyash was trapped. He was hiding inside a city of squalor and prying eyes. He had been swallowed up by the mysterious depths of an angry and volatile human sea. But that human sea was desperately poor, and it routinely gave up its most valued resources if the price was right, or if the pressure points were squeezed just tight enough.

The Palestinians had turned a blind eye to Ayyash's presence in Gaza, as well as to much of the Hamas infrastructure that openly strutted it's power and potential inside the Strip's myriad refugee camps. Blindness had been prudent. Ayyash was merely a nuisance to be tolerated in Gaza. But November 4, 1995, changed everything. Rabin's death made Ayyash expendable. Suddenly, counterterrorist cooperation between the Palestinians and Israelis, sometimes at the behest of the CIA station chief in Tel Aviv, began to flourish.

In an interview with the daily newspaper *Ma'ariv*, former deputy director of the Shin Bet Gideon Ezra described the hunt for Ayyash as more of a challenge than an obsession.[3] One of the most beguiling aspects of the challenge was the search for the one Achilles' heel that would betray Ayyash and provide the Israeli hunters with an "in." Once an "in" had been established, the remaining aspects of any operation, whether it be an arrest, a kidnapping, or an assassination, were merely technical in nature and limited to the scope and flair of the case agent's imagination. Finding an "in" with Ayyash was incredibly difficult. "He was one of the most paranoid individuals I had ever come across," claimed an Israeli police special operations officer who hunted Ayyash, "and paranoia sparked intuition, and that intuition drove him to be incredibly careful." Yet paranoia is a pitfall for life ruled by fear—especially for someone who was determined to live for his wife, son, and future-born. Ayyash's life on the run turned him cold, bitter, sad, and tired.[4] His life on the run became a jog instead of a dash. He stopped sleeping in a different bed every night. He began to trust confidants and school chums. He provided the Israelis with the "in."

Yehiya Ayyash had, as a result of his "larger-than-life" reputation inside the West Bank and Gaza Strip, enjoyed the hospitality of a good many anonymous strangers eager to do their part in the struggle by hiding him for a night, providing him with identity papers, or trekking to Rafatt with gifts and notes for his family. The help provided by the owners of the safe houses was greatly appreciated, but it could not be trusted. Noble gestures are, after all, often suspect in a guerrilla war. In Beit Lahiya, in Gaza, Ayyash came across Osama Hamad, a Hamas operative and close friend from his days at Bir Zeit University who offered him a place to stay, apartment 4 in one of his uncle's houses, a two-story building at No. 2 Shaheed al-Khaluti Street. The shelter wasn't luxurious, but it was far from prying eyes.

Ironically, Hamad's house was located only fifteen hundred yards from the Israeli frontier at the Erez checkpoint. It must have given Ayyash considerable satisfaction to be able to wake up in the morning and look directly into Israel and realize he was untouchable. The house on Shaheed al-Khaluti Street was also only fifty yards from one of the largest Palestinian police stations in Gaza. He assumed the name of Abdullah Abu Ahmed and communicated with his Hamas commanders through messenger—and with his parents, courtesy of cellular phone.

When news of Ayyash's new identity and new landlord reached Shin Bet HQ, through a surreptitious route of information that remains classified, the name "Hamad" set off alarms. Searching through the massive Shin Bet computer database, agents came across Osama's uncle, Kamil Hamad, a forty-three-year-old real estate broker, car salesman, and jack-of-all trades who had managed, quite miraculously, to build a small fortune in one of the poorest spots in the world. Hamad was also a merchant in that always-valuable Gaza commodity known as information—he had been a low-level Shin Bet informer for nearly twenty years.

In exchange for information and other amenities, the Israeli authorities, at the Shin Bet's request, had helped Hamad grow wealthy in Gaza, often excusing him from paying taxes, duties, and other forms of required levies that broke the back of many an honest businessman. It was a lucrative relationship for Hamad, and he became a useful asset for the Shin Bet. But the Palestinian Authority was clamping down on tax dodges and demanding exorbitant sums from Gaza's richest citizens. Hamad's profits decreased and the riches were dwindling. Only those in the Arafat inner circle had any hope for riches in the new and autonomous Strip.

Hamad had attempted to court key individuals in the security services, and he was seen at lavish dinners with General Musa Arafat as well as the offices of military intelligence officials.[5] Hamad had, through his contacts with General Arafat, arranged the release of Osama after he was arrested in the Strip following the summer bombing wave in Ramat Gan and Jerusalem. Izzedine al-Qassam commanders were intrigued by his connections and wary of his clout. Hamad became a VIP in Hamas circles. He was a man to be trusted—and protected.

Kamal Hamad was a character straight out of an espionage film. He was, claims a former A'man officer, "worthy of a John Le Carré novel." Rich enough to maintain two armed and well-dressed bodyguards and three wives ranging in age from forty-two to twenty, Kamal Hamad had fathered eighteen children and, reportedly, was involved in raising fifteen "luxurious" apartment blocks in the sands of Gaza. But instead of investing in real estate, where the savvy made a killing in Arafat's Gaza, Hamad invested heavily in building on other people's properties. His expenses skyrocketed. His line of credit with banks in Israel, and the Cairo-Palestine Bank in Gaza, diminished. His building projects were stopped cold in their tracks—often incomplete and with a trail of investors demanding their money back; the flats he was building, which he often sold to the well-connected and powerful in Gaza, ended up as nothing more than drywall cubes without running water or electricity. Hamad was in trouble. Former Shin Bet informants with a fondness for Mercedes sedans, English-tailored suits, and trips to Europe with pretty young women walked a tightrope when they teetered on financial ruin. He would be lucky to survive, let alone keep any sliver of his empire.

To the majors, colonels, and generals of the Palestinian intelligence services, Hamad was a cash cow who would secure them fancy homes and penthouse apartments at a fraction of the going price. To the Israelis, he was an asset, a screw to be turned. He was the "in."

One sunny and unseasonably warm afternoon, Kamal Hamad ventured into Israel to retrieve two Mercedes sedans he had purchased and was waiting to clear through customs at an Ashdod dockyard; one car was to be a bribe to General Musa Arafat, and the second was to serve as a "family" car. As he dealt with the bureaucracy of his customs paperwork in a secluded port office, Hamad was approached by several Shin Bet agents. The contact was reestablished—an old working relationship rekindled. Before Hamad left Ashdod, he found an envelope with several thousand dollars in the glove compartment of his car and a bill for one shekel—less than thirty cents—that he owed customs for the two cars. Business was back to normal.

According to reports, the Shin Bet had been slowly turning the screws on Kamal Hamad as far back as early 1995 when they learned that he had, through his real-estate holdings, been helping Hamas fugitives in Gaza find shelter and work.[6] In October 1995, Hamad met with a high-ranking Shin Bet official responsible for the southern command known only by his nom de guerre of Abu Nabil. Abu Nabil, a veteran of the counterespionage games in Gaza, was after information—detailed information. Hamad wasn't opposed to becoming a shill in the Israeli hunt for Ayyash, although he wanted a contract with the Shin Bet in which the General Security Service would guarantee Hamad's safety and, most important, his fortune. He also

wanted Israeli identity cards for himself and his wives. The Shin
Bet didn't cut contracts with informers, even invaluable ones,
and Abu Nabil bargained hard with the Palestinian developer,
realizing that Hamad had little choice and few options. If he
refused to help the Shin Bet, all it took was an anonymous tip
to Hamas, the jihad, or even the Palestinian Authority, that Hamad was a long-standing helper of the dreaded Shabak and he
was as good as finished; all the gold in Gaza didn't protect a
traitor from a horrid death. The Shin Bet was not in the mood
for demands and requests. The agents wanted information and
access.

With the "in" in their hands, the agents on the trail of the Engineer needed to assemble an accurate dossier on Ayyash and
a plan on what to do with him. Kamal Hamad was asked to
provide his handlers with an incredibly intimate portrait of
Ayyash. Where did he sleep? When did he wake up? When did
he shower? When did he go to the bathroom? Who visited him?
How did he communicate with the outside world? The Shin Bet
was looking for the one chink in the Ayyash armor that could
technically be exploited.

Ayyash had, true to form, lived the life of a pious fugitive.
Most of his days were spent in prayer, or at work, teaching the
basics of improvised bomb-making to classes of new cell commanders being prepared for the continuation of the struggle.
Life on the run must have been lonely and boring for Ayyash.
Separated from his wife, his son, and his parents, telephone conversations with his family at Rafatt were his only contacts. Because land-line communications were most certainly monitored
by the Shin Bet, as well as the Palestinians, the Ayyash family
maintained a link by cellular phones.

Israelis called them *Pelephones*; the Arabs, unable to pronounce
the letter *P*, called them *"Bilephones."* With more than two million cellular telephones in use inside Israel and the West Bank,

it is an obsession that Jew and Arab shared equally. The addiction to the small phones originated with the old socialist monopoly that once controlled phone service in Israel. Israelis often had to wait a dozen years for a phone line—service was erratic, expensive, and light years behind the United States and Western Europe. In the Territories, phone service was a hundred times worse. When cellular phone service came to Israel, anyone could finally have a phone—no waiting list and no payoffs. In fact, cellular phone rates were sometimes cheaper than land-line charges, and the connection was far clearer. Cellular phones became an Israeli obsession. Bathers in the Mediterranean carried phones with them into the chest-high surf, and couples on double dates often communicated with one another, at opposite ends of a cinema, by a cellular phone. In the West Bank, cellular phones were often the sole means of communication between villages left without phone service by the Israeli authorities. Ironically, Ya'akov Perry, following his retirement from the Shin Bet, became CEO of Cellcom, Israel's most successful cellular carrier.

The cellular phone was the one means by which Ayyash could be monitored, tracked, and, if possible, eliminated. If he carried the phone with him at all times, the Israelis could electronically track and trace his movements; knowing the phone's number, the Israelis could monitor his conversations and, perhaps, be waiting for him in a dark alley one night instead of a Majd team transferring him to another safe house. It was even possible to booby-trap a cellular phone with a small explosive charge that, when placed to the head, would shoot fire and shrapnel into the target's brain.

Rigging a phone with explosives was nothing new—in fact, it was a Mossad innovation that had been used with lethal results. On January 9, 1973, Dr. Mahmoud Hamshari, the Black September commander in France, answered the telephone inside his second-story apartment in a middle-class Paris neighborhood.

"May I please speak with Dr. Hamshari?" the voice asked with a distinctively native Parisian accent. "This is Dr. Hamshari" was the firm reply. A switch igniting a high-frequency signal connected to a detonator and a hundred grams of Grade A plastique put an end to the call. The explosion was a relatively small one, but the results were major. Hamshari, one of the architects of Black September's 1972 Munich Olympics massacre, died hours after much of his face had been blown off.

The prospects of rigging a cellular phone were intriguing—and challenging. The explosive charge would have to be very small. It would also need to be a shaped charge, concentrating the maximum destructive force into one intended area. The device would also have to be small enough in order not to interfere with the day-to-day functions of the phone, and it needed to be light enough so that the person clutching the deadly device to his ear would not be suspicious. For the planners of the operation, there was also a significant—and all-important—consideration. Only the target was to be harmed—innocent civilians killed or wounded in the collateral blast would not be acceptable. The device would be outfitted with a safety to ensure that a radio signal from a walkie-talkie or a kid's remote-control toy did not detonate it. The planners needed to be absolutely certain that it was the target placing the phone to his head seconds before the explosion. The phone that Dr. Hamshari was holding when it exploded was rigged with a safety device which was disabled only after the assassin had made absolute voice confirmation of the target's identity. Hamshari lived with his wife and small child and it was imperative that they were to be spared from harm.

In getting to Ayyash through a cellular phone, the operational challenge was not what to do with the phone: that was technical. The main obstacle was getting their hands on his phone.

For the operation to succeed, it was crucial for Hamad to believe that the cellular phone ruse would be used only for eavesdropping purposes. "Listen," Abu Nabil is reported to have told Hamad, "we know he sometimes spends time in your house and we know that he communicates with other Hamas big-shots from your property. All we want to do is for you to help us eavesdrop on Ayyash. That's it. This way we can intercept the bombers before they kill lots of women and children. You don't want to see more innocent people die, do you? We know that every few weeks he changes his cellular phone number. Just let us know the next time it happens, and we'll take care of the rest."

According to former Shin Bet deputy director Gideon Ezra in an interview with Israeli television, operations targeting an individual aren't openly sanctioned—or ordered—by the higher political authorities, but rather handled at the operational level and approved by management. Approval usually required a foolproof plan as well as an opportunity. January 1996 was seen as the ideal time to handle this lingering matter. Elections in the Palestinian Authority were scheduled for January 20, and many in Hamas would be more occupied with the political campaign waged against Arafat for the ballot box, than in the security of a man who, though teaching a future generation of craftsmen and martyrs, had outlived his operational usefulness.

Paranoia had been the staple that kept Yehiya Ayyash alive for a remarkable three years on the run. Paranoia had made him savvy, smart, and successful. Ayyash knew the Shin Bet was still gunning for him, no matter how demoralized the service might have been over the Rabin assassination. Yet there were reasons for concern, even from within the ranks of Hamas. Political infighting had turned ugly inside the political hierarchy, inside the al-Qassam cells, and inside the Majd. The detention of Musa Abu Marzouk and the continued Israeli adherence to Oslo II, even in the aftermath of the Rabin assassination, persuaded many of the Young Turks that the time was ripe for an all-out suicide campaign to settle the score once and for all. The politicians in Damascus and Teheran, however, opposed wanton bloodshed. Assets had to be deployed as needed, not in one massive show of bloodshed that was bound to backfire politically. Hamas, for the first time in its successful terrorist campaign, had begun to splinter, and there was even talk of an armed conflict between opposing camps. Ayyash now had to watch his back from the men he had so faithfully served, while also guarding against Arafat's men and, of course, the Shin Bet and Mossad.

By January 1996, with his wife and son safely smuggled into Gaza and living in a safe house a kilometer away, Yehiya Ayyash began to settle into a routine existence, although he was still suspicious and extremely careful. When he would visit Heyam, he never came at the same time or announced his visits; according to his wife, he often came to the door in costume, dressed as a woman.[7] If there was one weakness he displayed that winter, even after his wife and son were safe and sound in the Strip, it was his longing for Rafatt and his parents. He phoned them regularly and at regularly scheduled times. "You can take the bomber out of the village," commented a Jordanian intelligence officer, "but you can't take the village out of the bomber." Ayyash was a prisoner of his longing for his mother and father—and he was concerned about the incessant Shin Bet attention the family received.

The phone calls home lasted longer and longer. Even men responsible for the deaths of nearly ninety women and children get homesick. The calls were made about once every two weeks. Ayyash had spent a long time on the phone with his father on December 25, after Heyam had given birth to a bouncing baby boy. Ayyash was proud and happy; he wanted his father to see the newest addition to the family. The next conversation was scheduled for the morning of January 5.[8]

Ayyash had always suspected that the Shin Bet was listening in to his phone conversations, and he would change the phone he was using once every few weeks. From time to time the clarity of the calls would go from okay to terrible. Static would fill the lines, as would weird high-frequency sounds.

At the same time, Kamal Hamad had purchased a cellular phone for Osama at the Nabil's electronics store in Gaza City— the phones came from Israeli dealers who marketed them through local agents. Hamad's phone, ostensibly, was to be used for the nephew to communicate with his uncle when working at one of the family's properties, or when Hamad traveled on business to Israel or the West Bank. Osama routinely allowed his friend in college to use the phone; in fact, Ayyash used the phone with such frequency that he passed the number, 050-507497, to his father, Abdel-Latif Ayyash, as *the* number by which he could be reached. Yet before handing off the Motorola telephone to his nephew, Hamad brought it to his Shin Bet handlers. It is widely believed that Hamad Kamal had no clue what the handlers would do with the phone. He probably thought they'd plant a microchip eavesdropping device somewhere in the circuitry that would enable men with earphones on their heads to pick up, with great clarity, everything that Ayyash told his parents and his comrades in the Izzedine al-Qassam Brigade. When Hamad received the phone back, it looked exactly as it had before. It was still in off-the-shelf, out-of-the-box condition: it didn't smell any different or weigh any more and, most important, it worked well.

By January 1996 the Shin Bet had suggested to Hamad that he take a brief leave of absence from the Gaza Strip. There was nothing suspicious about Hamad leaving the beauty and splendor of the strip on a dark and cold winter's night. He had managed to get through the frontiers during closures and during firefights before. Business was business, and in the gray no-man's-land between Israel and the Palestinians, money talked louder than gunshots.

*　　*　　*

January 5, 1996. Dawn broke with a gray mist over Tel Aviv. Here and there small tweaks of sunlight attempted to fight through the thick cloud cover. At the base of the stairs at Tel Aviv's city hall, the spot where Yitzhak Rabin was shot had been turned into a Berlin Wall-like memorial: graffiti of grief covered an otherwise bland wall that had forever been engraved into the Israeli psyche. Hundreds of small memorial candles were left daily by citizens refusing to accept what the past two years had brought on their country. The memorial candles had long since been removed from the corner of Dizengoff and Queen Esther Streets. Worse things had happened to the nation since that bloody morning in October.

Inside the American embassy, on Ha'Yarkon Street, men from Washington, D.C., who wore small gold shields on their belts, had assembled as the advance team for the upcoming visit to Israel by Vice President Al Gore and Secretary of State Warren Christopher. The Secret Service and State Department Diplomatic Security Service special agents had been to Israel before— quite a few times, in fact, in the last year—but this trip concerned them. The quiet after the Rabin assassination had to end sometime, and they wanted their principals to be as far away from the trip wire as possible. The Shin Bet also worried them. The liaisons appeared preoccupied, aloof. They were reeling from what had happened and what might occur. The American special agents reviewed intelligence files, CIA profiles, and material gathered from libraries and magazines. Protective intelligence—heading off a threat before it materialized—was how the Americans executed the precarious trade of dignitary protection.

Yehiya Ayyash had been working odd hours that January, mostly at night, residents of the street recalled. Night work, intelligence sources believed, was a sign that Ayyash was preparing a new wave of bombs that would be unleashed after the Palestinian elections. Zinab Hamad, Osama's forty-seven-year-old mother who lived downstairs, recalled that Ayyash was quiet and modest; she did not recall him bringing any "work" home.

On January 5, Yehiya Ayyash returned home at 4:30 in the morning. Darting down the alleys of Beit Lahiya to shake any Israeli—or Palestinian—surveillance, Ayyash passed garbage cans and stray cats. He was dressed as a woman, cradling his Glilon assault rifle under his gown. Once home, Ayyash prayed, then munched on a light snack at a table adorned with a map of Tel Aviv next to a smaller table topped with electrical tape, wires, pipes, and circuits. Before laying his head on a plush mattress adorned with three large pillows, he checked the table to see if Osama Hamad's Motorola phone was on.

Wearing nothing but a pair of purple briefs, Ayyash slept for a few hours, the way he had slept for the past three years: with one eye open and one ear listening for the ominous sound of footsteps. A small transistor radio had been turned on, the volume knob angled as low as it would go so the news broadcasts were still audible. The first rays of daylight had yet to emerge from the dark purple-and-orange skies that foretold of an impending rainstorm. Rain did not mix well with the Gazan landscape. Unpaved roads turned to mud, poorly constructed roofs leaked, and the stench of uncollected trash and open sewage lines were stirred up in the cruel harsh rains of January. Winter in Gaza made any West Bank native long for the open splendor of plush green hills and the smell of olive trees and citrus groves.

At a command post just outside the barbed wire forest that separated Gaza from the rest of the world, near the Erez checkpoint some fifteen hundred yards from the house at No. 2 Shaheed al-Khaluti Street, a group of men wearing blue-and-green winter parkas juggled field radios, cellular phones, black boxes, and field glasses. The men were impatient. The sound of a small-engine prop-driven plane flying was heard overhead. Eyes scanned the frontier into Gaza through field glasses that had been carried on endless stakeouts in front of the house in Rafatt and the safe house in Nablus.

At 8:40 A.M., Osama Hamad's Motorola cellular phone rang. Rushing to his worktable, Ayyash rubbed his eyes and grabbed the ringing phone with his right hand. Majd officers had warned Yehiya that cellular communications were easier to monitor. Ayyash's father had tried to reach his son on the regular phone in the Hamad house, but mysteriously the line had not been working properly all week—most people trying to reach the residence heard a busy signal. So, with a backup number at his disposal, he tried the cellular phone.

Abdel-Latif Ayyash had told his son that he had been trying, since 8:00 A.M., to call on the land line but it had been busy. As the two men spoke, the low-flying plane that had been buzzing Beit Lahiya leveled at a cruising altitude. The plane was nondescript, a trainer it appeared, and bore no markings linking it to any nation. The passenger, cradling a black box with a switch, a red light, and a green light, listened attentively to his headset as it relayed a link to the command post down below.

Father and son spoke in brief and affectionate sentences. "How are you father?" was the last words heard at the end of telephone number 050-507-497. When Abdel-Latif Ayyash tried the number again, all he received was a recording from the connecting service informing him that the line was unavailable.

The Engineer would have appreciated the technical mastery involved in the construction of the bomb that killed him: its lightweight simplicity, its miniaturized might. Fifty grams of RDX explosives molded into the battery compartment of a telephone had been designed to kill only the man cradling the phone to his ear. The force of the concentrated blast caused most of the right side of Ayyash's face to implode around his jaw and skull; shrapnel and energy raced into his brain. A slab of flesh hung over his premolars; a burnt and smoldering nub of flesh had replaced his ear. The booby-trapped cellular phone had been so ingeniously built, and so target specific, that the left side of Ayyash's face had remained whole. The right hand which held the telephone was neither burnt or damaged.

Yehiya Ayyash, "The Engineer," the most wanted man in modern Israeli history, was dead.

Zinab Hamad was cleaning her living room when she was startled by a small explosion coming from apartment number four. Hoping it was nothing more than a round let off by mistake, she entered the room to find the white walls sprayed with blood, brain matter, flesh, and hair. Zinab saw the tenant, Yehiya Ayyash, hunched on his back, with blood pouring out of the right side of his head. Zinab did not scream or cry. She didn't want to alarm neighbors, many still sleeping on the Muslim Sabbath, that something had happened inside No. 2 Shaheed al-Khaluti Street.

From another telephone in the house, Osama Hamad immediately phoned his contacts in the Izzedine al-Qassam Brigade to tell them the news. Majd crews arrived immediately, though they parked their cars several blocks away to avoid arousing suspicion. The men, with long beards and AK-47s, surveyed the scene, standing over their murdered icon. The Majd team then wrapped Ayyash's lifeless body inside a bedsheet and quickly placed it into the trunk of a waiting sedan. All of Ayyash's belongings were gathered into a laundry bag. Only an hour after the blast, all physical hints linking Yehiya Ayyash to the apartment on Shaheed al-Khaluti Street had vanished.

Majd officers ordered Osama not to tell anyone what had happened that morning. Ayyash's body was going to be taken to an icebox for safekeeping until the political leaders could figure out what to do with him. Hamas leaders had thought of hiding the body, to encourage the legend that the Engineer had turned into a ghost that would wreak havoc inside the heart of the Israeli enemy.

The masterminds behind the death of Yehiya Ayyash would not have their fifteen minutes of brilliance denied them. Men who had for the better part of their careers shunned the press suddenly began to give radio correspondents exclusive scoops. Israelis driving home from half-days at work suddenly had something to smile about when the hourly updates broadcast that, according to "unofficial channels," Yehiya Ayyash, the master bomb maker known as the Engineer, had been killed by unidentified assailants in the northern half of the Gaza Strip. Palestinian intelligence, who learned much of what went on inside the Strip from Israeli radio, was shocked. Why hadn't they been notified?

By mid-afternoon on January 5, in the middle of a driving rain the likes of which hadn't been seen in Gaza in nearly a decade, Beit Lahiya was inundated by Palestinian intelligence squads and heavily armed policemen in search of the mysterious house. Hamas supporters were rounded up and a curfew imposed over most of the refugee camps. When, finally, the house in Beit Lahiya was found and subsequently searched, intelligence teams found nothing. As inspecting lieutenants were replaced by majors, colonels, and even deputy directors, including Muchabarat head Mohammed Dahlan, small droplets of blood and later tiny shards of bone were found on the floor and in between the marble tiles. When the room was completely turned over, they found additional evidence that someone had met a gruesome end only hours before.

Osama Hamad was immediately arrested and taken to the police station only a stone's throw from his home. With an election only two weeks away, Arafat's men were unwilling to tolerate any Hamas shenanigans, especially involving explosives and a figure as charged as Yehiya Ayyash. The pressure applied to Osama Hamad was enormous—and effective. In less than an hour he retraced the entire chain of events. Calls went out to Hamas commanders in the Strip—Ayyash's body was to be returned *forthwith* to the Palestinian police.

The body of Yehiya Ayyash arrived at Palestinian police headquarters in Gaza just before dark. The rain had intensified, and the men with the beards and Browning high-power automatics strapped to their waists cautiously handed custody of the martyr's corpse to men who they knew they would soon oppose on the battlefield. Ayyash's body was immediately identified and then rushed to Shifa Hospital.

Just after 4:00 A.M., two special agents from the U.S. State Department's Diplomatic Security Service were eating lunch at a popular café near the embassy. During this break from the hectic preparations preceding Vice President Gore's and Secretary of State Christopher's visit the following day, their cellular phone rang. One of the agents, posted to the embassy as the assistant regional security officer, had maintained close links with his counterparts in the Palestinian Authority—he recognized the voice of the caller at the other end. It was General Nasser Yusef, head of the Palestinian police, and he needed help. The Palestinians had little experience in crime scene investigations and the safe transport of evidence; after-the-fact criminal work was, after all, rarely needed in a department that usually obtained confessions.

The two federal agents of course were concerned about the bombing. The possibility existed that Gaza and even the streets of Tel Aviv and Jerusalem were about to be littered with the bodies of those caught in terrorist crossfire. Preventative intelligence standard operating procedure dictated that any security development that might effect the ability to safeguard a principal needed to be investigated. After contacting Washington and the U.S. ambassador, the two trekked south, to Gaza, and a crime scene both men would never forget.

By nightfall, Gaza was awash in a torrential downpour. Power was out in much of the Strip. Streets were flooded with up to five feet of water, and the two had to hitch a ride with the local policemen to Nasir Yusef's office. Following the obligatory Byzantine requirements of sweet tea and mint leaves, the two were driven to Beit Lahiya to survey the blast area. One of the agents brought with him an improvised evidence-gathering kit of plastic zip-lock bags and cotton swabs. The agents, veterans of America's global precinct, had thought they had seen it all, but this was different. Ayyash's body had been left completely intact by the blast, with the exception of the right side of his face. The agents, with their Palestinian hosts, photographed the corpse and jotted down notes. They feared what would happen in the next few hours—and the next few days.

The drive back to Tel Aviv, some ten hours later, was a long and anxious one. It was a bad time for the VP and Secretary to be coming, both agents thought. Hamas would not let this killing pass quietly. Both special agents were convinced that Hamas retribution would be harsh and brutal.

It was a quiet Friday night in Israel. News reports of Ayyash's death were the headline-grabbing lead on the nightly broadcasts. Families throughout Israel began their Sabbath meal with a blessing on the wine and on the bread; they prayed that, perhaps finally, the bloodshed would come to an end.

In a nondescript building somewhere in Tel Aviv, it had been a remarkable day but the mood was not festive. On the contrary, emotions of anxiety, foreboding, and self-doubt prevailed. Yehiya Ayyash had been one of the few Palestinian terrorists who, many of the security operatives who pursued him admitted, was smarter than the men who had hunted him. According to one special operations official, "He was a cold-blooded killer, but that didn't make him unique. We get paid to hunt ruthless murderers who think nothing of taking human life. But he was a master at deception, disguise, and disappearance. He was every-where and nowhere. He was a God-like hero to his people and the very mention of his name attracted a flock of men willing to strap his devices to their torsos and turn themselves into hu-man bombs. He taunted us and challenged us, and we often came up short. We knew that each time we failed to kill him, we faced the danger of waking up the next morning to learn that another dozen had been killed by one of his contraptions. Our battle with him was a race against time measured in blood and coffins, and we were always just a few seconds off the mark, always just a step behind. He was the most dangerous man we have ever had the task of hunting down."[9]

Israel did not formally accept responsibility for the death of Yehiya Ayyash—the state of Israel never admits to its role in the selective termination of terrorists—yet few doubted that there was an Israeli smoking gun to such a professionally mas-terful elimination. And hints of official complicity did emerge. According to former Shin Bet deputy director Gideon Ezra, in an interview on Israeli television, the operation was "Gillon's means of extinguishing the Engineer."[10]

There were few celebrations inside the halls of Israel's intel-ligence communities that night; too many people had died in the past three years for anyone to show the slightest glimmer of joy. The investigation, pursuit, and eventual assassination had exhausted many veteran agents, some of whom had been chas-ing terrorists since Ayyash was in diapers. For the men who led the hunt it was the end to a pursuit that had cost many inno-cents their lives, that had claimed highly regarded comrades, and that had caused the country to be rocked to its very foun-dation. For Carmi Gillon, his office already a chaotic clutter of boxes as he removed his personal effects, the death of Ayyash was a positive conclusion to what had been one of the most short-lived and tumultuous tenures of command in the Shin Bet's history.

*   *   *

On Saturday, January 6, 1996, in one of the largest funerals ever staged in the history of the Gaza Strip, a hundred thousand people assembled around the Palestine Mosque in Gaza City. The mood of sorrow and anger had been building since the night before as loudspeakers atop mosques and electrical poles announced the death of the Engineer: "Hamas is reporting that our hero, the hero of all the bombings, is now a martyr" was the taped message that resonated throughout the echo chamber of the Strip until morning.

As dawn broke, and the multitudes walked to the city square, the mood turned from grief to rage. One by one, Hamas officials spoke to the crowd in a furious barrage of speeches and threats. "The Engineer did not die," one speaker boasted, "he left behind him a newborn, as if he wants to tell that the struggle has begun anew." And another: "The martyr Ayyash was a great man who contributed to the death of Rabin by exposing the gaps in the Israeli security services." Throngs of young men and children, stepping over those unable to meet the dash, trampled one another to touch the passing coffin. Women ululated in a dizzying cadence of grief, as young men wearing black masks fired bursts from their AK-47s into the gray sky; several bystanders were seriously hurt when the rounds came crashing back to earth.

Ayyash's mother, wearing the long black veil of a woman mourning the murder of her son, was guest of honor at the mass funeral in Gaza. Carrying a photo of her son, Izzedine al-Qassam supporters inserted a .45-caliber pistol into her hand. Forced to fire the weapon, Aisha was rocked by the recoil as the assembled mourners wailed in joyous relief that the Ayyash matriarch was firing her vengeful rounds into the heavens.

Majd officers searched the crowd for foreigners and Israeli intelligence agents, perhaps posing as journalists, who might have infiltrated into the Strip to photograph and film. Ayyash's death had raised the stakes of the covert war.

The size and scope of the funeral compelled Hamas and the Palestinian Authority to shut down much of the Gaza Strip for three days. Arafat's police force maintained energetic patrols through Gaza City and the refugee camps, though the streets were empty. The writing was on the wall for a bloodbath. Ayyash's killing was a beginning—rather than an end—to a new and potentially uncontrolled level of violence foreign even to the previous killing zones of the Arab-Israeli conflict. Israel had lost a prime minister and the Palestinians had lost a cult hero. Speculators realized that all bets were off.

Official Palestinian reaction to the assassination of Ayyash was causing controversy and concern in Israel. On Friday evening, as Palestinian police officials were cleaning up the crime scene and glancing over photographs of what remained of Ayyash's head, Yasir Arafat paid a condolence call to Hamas spokesman Mahmoud Zahar in his Gaza office before heading to Bethlehem to celebrate the Greek Orthodox Christmas. Arafat later called Ayyash a martyr and even sent an honor guard of Palestinian policemen to Ayyash's funeral; the cops, in their dress uniforms with badges polished for the event, stood and saluted as Ayyash's cloth-draped body was lowered into the ground at the Shajaiya cemetery. They stood by as an Izzedine al-Qassam ceremonial guard fired thousands of rounds of ammunition into the air, despite a ban on public displays of weaponry by the Palestinian Authority. "What would you say if an IDF officer would salute over the grave of Baruch Goldstein?" an Israeli radio reporter asked Sufian Abu Zaide, a Palestinian Authority official, during a live debate on the stalled peace process. There was no reply.

Inside the camps of Gaza, inside tents planted deep in the

Sudanese desert, and inside air-conditioned offices in Teheran, the means of vengeance was being plotted. Men who moved about with bodyguards and prices on their heads assembled targets, intelligence files, and operational plans to submit to the organization's political chiefs for approval. Days after Ayyash's burial, Hamas issued an ominous communiqu: "Every child is crying for revenge. Ayyash did not die, but left behind a new Jihad. The gates of Paradise have not been closed and the chain of martyrs will not stop. Listen Peres, don't be so happy. We are coming."

Islamic Jihad leader Sheikh Nafez Azzam joined in the saber rattling. "There is blood in our mouths which we want to spit in the face of this unjust world."[11]

Days before Yehiya Ayyash was killed, a well-dressed gentleman sporting a beige suit and carrying a WELCOME TO ISRAEL travel bag reportedly boarded a flight at Ben-Gurion International Airport. Carrying an Israeli passport identifying him as a Jew from Haifa, Kamal Hamad and two Shin Bet bodyguards took their first-class seats for the ten-hour flight to the United States. Once across the ocean, Hamad was rushed through customs and immigration like a visiting dignitary, and his Shin Bet companions handed him over to several waiting agents who took Hamad into the anonymous world of new identities, safe houses, and the fear of always having to look over one's shoulder for the bullet or bomb with one's name on it.

Although Hamad had escaped with much of his extended family, his nephew and niece were held in Palestinian Authority custody for months. An arrest warrant was issued by the Palestinian Authority's attorney general, though most knew that a bullet between the eyes would be the only form of due process Hamad would receive should he ever return to Gaza. Under the care of the Shin Bet, Hamad had lost the most precious portfolio of his empire: his wealth and stature.

For Carmi Gillon, the death of Ayyash marked the end of a remarkable and failed tenure as the head of the General Security Services. Historians will debate Gillon's, and the Shin Bet's, failure in protecting Rabin, as well as the root causes behind the agency's many blunders leading up to that fateful Saturday night in November. Nevertheless, Ayyash's death was the high point on which he could resign. Bright and early on Monday morning, January 8, 1996, Gillon submitted his resignation to Prime Minister Peres. The note was brief and direct, though Gillon made a point of mentioning that "One of the key challenges facing the agency was the struggle against Hamas and the other Islamic radicals." Gillon ended the letter of resignation by stating that he he was now "confident that the agency is on the right track and ready for all its missions."[12]

Shin Bet commanders were sure that the streets of Tel Aviv would be visited shortly by men wearing lethal backpacks. The only questions were where, when, and how many would have to die.

Notes

[1]Nadav Ha'etzni, *"Ha'Mehandes Mitkaven Lachzor Ha'Baita,"* *Ma'ariv Sof Shavu'a*, October 27, 1995, p. 11.

[2]Jeffrey Bartholet and Tom Masland, "Spooking the Spooks," *Newsweek*, March 18, 1996, p. 37.

[3]Tzvi Galit, "Rabin Hura 'Lisgor et Ha'Sipur'," *Ma'ariv Mosaf Shabbat*, January 12, 1996, p. 7.

[4]Ehud Ya'ari, *"Ha'Mehandes Sulak, Nisharu Lo Me'at Technaim,"* *Ma'ariv Sof Shavu'a*, January 12, 1996, p. 6.

[5]Anat Tal-Shir and David Regev, *"Kablan Be'Malkodet,"* *Yediot Aharonot Shabbat*, January 12, 1996, p. 6.

[6]Alex Fishman, *"Ha'Mehandes Chusal, Ha'Kablan Yachol Lalechet,"* *Yediot Aharonot Ha'Mosaf Le'Shabbat*, November 21, 1997, p. 22.

[7]Nadav Ze'evi and Moshe Zunder, "*Kach Husal Ha'Mehandes*," *Ma'ariv Sof Shavua*, August 22, 1997, p. 21.

[8]Ibid.

[9]Interview, New York, October 1, 1998.

[10]Ibid., p. 20.

[11]Serge Schmemann, "Palestinians Vow Vengeance at Gaza Funeral of Terrorist," *The New York Times*, p. 10A.

[12]David Horovitz, "Shin Bet Chief Steps Down," *The Irish Times*, January 9, 1996, p. 5.

Chapter 8

Ghosts

The death of Yehiya Ayyash was front-page news in
Israel when the papers came off the presses on Sunday,
January 7. The kiosks carried extra copies of *Yediot
Aharonot*, *Ma'ariv*, *Ha'aretz*, and the *Jerusalem Post* that
chilly winter's morning, though news of the operation warmed
the spirits of many in the country who now hoped the carnage
had come to an end. In the hummus restaurants of Jaffa, where
laborers filled their stomachs with a hearty breakfast, eyes were
transfixed on the first accounts of the ingenious cell-phone termination of Israel's public enemy No. 1. It was the prime topic
of conversation that Sunday morning. The death of the Engineer
was seen as a national victory—an end to an ordeal that began
one cool November morning in Ramat Efal.

In the Knesset, where Prime Minister Peres was attempting to
salvage what remained of the peace process, the death of
Ayyash was a hopeful beginning to the new work week. Those
sentiments were shared in the hallways of the Kirya, the sprawling IDF HQ, the Ministry of Defense complex in the heart of

downtown Tel Aviv, and the offices of the Shin Bet and the Mossad.

Prime Minister Peres was told of the operation moments after the explosives shot through the Engineer's brain. Peres was in the Defense Ministry that rainy Friday morning, reviewing intelligence files and attending to the routine business of a man who was both the leader and the defense minister of his country. Peres was informed of Ayyash's demise by Carmi Gillon.[1] The operation was a turning point—a means to put the tumultuous three years of war against Hamas, with all its victims, to rest.

Gillon's sole request to Peres—amid the resignation caused by the Shamgar Committee's investigation into the conceptual breakdown of Shin Bet protection of Prime Minister Rabin—was that he be able to recommend a successor. For the Shin Bet to recover its esprit de corps and operational integrity, the agency would need an iron man whose courage, determination, and track record were beyond reproach. It needed a national icon, a figure of moral character who could redirect the agency while at the same time cleaning house. Carmi Gillon wanted Rear Admiral (Res.) Ami Ayalon, the one man, he believed, who could restore the agency to its previous standing and glory.

Rear Admiral Ayalon was a former commando in the Israeli Navy's Flotilla 13 naval special warfare unit, as well as a former commander of the unit and of the IDF/Navy. He was a highly decorated combat officer who had served on covert assignments that will remain classified fifty years after the fact. In a commando raid on an Egyptian island in 1969, then Lieutenant Ayalon became one of but a handful of men in Israel to earn the Medal of Valor, Israel's highest commendation for combat courage. Eventually rising up the ladder of command to serve as a naval vessel commander and commander of Flotilla 13, Rear Admiral Ayalon served as commander of the IDF/Navy from 1992 to 1995. Many thought that if he could overcome his disdain for the media and his habit of speaking no more than one sentence at a time, the lanky kibbutznik was headed for a grand future on the national scene. According to one former comrade, "Under the word *charisma* in the dictionary there was a photograph of Ami Ayalon."

According to reports, Ami Ayalon, upon his retirement from the Israeli military, had eyed the post of Mossad director and apparently was uninterested in the Shin Bet. The Rabin assassination changed his perception. Ayalon was a fixer: a man who liked to play a role in units desperately attempting to reinvent and rehabilitate themselves; he had assumed command of Flotilla 13 in 1979, following a tragic training accident that greatly strained the morale of the unit.

Ayalon's appointment was received with an enthusiastic show of support in the Israeli cabinet. Even many of the Shin Bet's midlevel and senior supervisors, the bureaucrats and division subdirectors who could sabotage or support any appointment, welcomed new blood from outside the organization and gave their support to Ayalon. He would be the first director of the Shin Bet whose identity was not a state secret of the highest order. The Shin Bet had to disrobe a few layers of its secretive armor if the Israeli electorate would once again be able to trust its abilities to protect the country from terrorists and spies. Ayalon's public persona and presence would be needed, even though it would take him a while to get his feet wet with the inner workings of the agency—from counterespionage operations and stings to VIP protection.

Israel had always underestimated Hamas and its ability to rewrite the rules of engagement. Many Israeli intelligence and security officials viewed the Hamas zealots as primitive fanatics. Suicide bombing was, after all, a low-tech form of warfare. Israelis did not understand the fiery will of the Hamas operatives, and they allowed their own racial prejudices and hatreds to misgauge the lethal skills of an enemy who on more than one occasion had been as cunning, brutal, and unforgiving as any the state of Israel had ever faced off against. Few in the Israeli intelligence and defense community hierarchy properly valued the tradecraft mastery that Hamas and its invisible legions had displayed. Perhaps only the soldiers in the field, the operators in elite army reconnaissance formations and the police special operations units who had battled Hamas and had hunted Ayyash with M-16s and booby-traps throughout Gaza and the West Bank, truly appreciated—and feared—what they were up against. When Hamas threatened vengeance for the martyrdom of Yehiya Ayyash, the men on the front lines braced themselves for attack and urged their intelligence chiefs to do the same.

Inside the Gaza Strip, at the secretive offices of the Hamas political apparatus and the Izzedine al-Qassam Brigade, life had not returned to normal following the assassination of Yehiya Ayyash. The anger and the plotting had consumed days and nights of men who were under Palestinian surveillance and, they realized, potentially next on Israel's extensive hit list. Hamas commanders never clutched a cellular phone, a walkie-talkie, or a laptop computer the same way again.

Hamas wanted to destroy what remained of Israel's frayed sense of security. The next military campaign had to be concentrated and without respite. Prime Minister Peres had called for elections in the spring of 1996, with voters for the first time in the nation's history to directly elect a prime minister. There was much debate over whether the peace process made the average citizen safer—or feel more at risk—than before the handshake between Rabin and Arafat. Israeli politics was a brutal, frank blood sport, and Hamas realized that they could, under the guise of seeking vengeance for Ayyash, alter the scope of the new Middle East to go beyond the abilities of the conventional armies of Syria, Egypt, and Jordan.

Yehiya Ayyash had been a loyal soldier who had carefully

planned for the future. Thanks to Yehiya Ayyash, there was no shortage of men skilled in the assembly of explosive devices and operationally savvy enough to know how to select the most damaging targets. Thanks to the martyrdom of Yehiya Ayyash, there was no shortage of men in Gaza, and in Ramallah and Hebron, who were willing to flip a switch and venture to paradise in the name of the holy war and vengeance. In many ways, Yehiya Ayyash was more dangerous dead than he had been alive.

At 6:40 on the morning of Monday, February 26, 1996, the No. 18 bus in Jerusalem was in the middle of the first of many crosstown runs through the interlocking boulevards of the Israeli capital. It had been cold in Jerusalem, and a bone-numbing drizzle made the brief Israeli winter miserable. Jerusalem might bill itself as the City of Gold, but in the winter it is often dark, cold, and dreary. Throughout the city, those having to be at work were grudgingly trudging their tired bodies through damp streets, chasing down buses already packed to capacity with commuters.

As the No. 18 proceeded toward the corner of Jaffa and Sarei Yisrael Streets, near the central bus station, a passenger sitting in the front of the bus carrying a large kit bag detonated a twenty-kilogram device of homemade explosives, nails, bullets, and ball bearings. The blast incinerated much of the bus in a spasm of fire and blood. The inside of the bus transformed instantly into a smoldering ruin of charred skeletons and the melted remnants of seats and advertising posters. Witnesses standing on the crowded sidewalk remember a fireball followed by a ferocious boom. The bomb was designed to be a fragmentation device, to spread a rain of death in a 360-degree radius.

The damage done to the dead and dying was horrific. Even veteran police and bomb-squad officers, men who had walked through the human debris before, found this attack particularly unnerving. The blast had sent bodies flying into the air. Bits of skin and flesh showered down on the Jerusalem neighborhood; body parts landed on the fifth-floor windowsill of a young couple's apartment. Twenty-five people were killed that morning, including two Americans and the son of Nachum Barnea, one of Israel's most respected journalists. Another eighty were seriously wounded.

Prime Minister Shimon Peres, like Yitzhak Rabin before him, was forced to make the macabre walking tour of the bomb scene. For Peres, who lacked the charisma and military background of Rabin, the bombing was a blow to his ability to sell the peace accords to an Israeli electorate already at the brink. The sight of a stone-faced Peres surrounded by a phalanx of jittery Shin Bet agents, guns at the ready, did little to reinforce a sense of security to the Israeli public. By the time Peres arrived, crowds of demonstrators had already gathered, waving banners and hurling epithets at police and Magen David emergency medical workers. "Death to the Arabs!" the crowd chanted as Peres walked by. "Rabin is waiting for you!"

Many inside the Israeli government called for the disruption of the negotiations with the PLO, although Peres was adamant about riding out the storm. "The alternative to peace is another Bosnia in Israel," Health Minister Ephraim Sneh told reporters, echoing the sentiments of Peres.

Bosnia, however, *had* come to Israel that morning.

News of the No. 18 bus bombing had yet to filter throughout most of Israel by 7:00 A.M. To passengers sitting on board commuter buses, or to soldiers at roadside hitchhiking stations heading back to their military units following the Sabbath leaves, February 25 was like any other Sunday in Israel. At just after 7:30, at Ashqelon Junction in southern Israel, soldiers were carrying kit bags, gym bags full of fresh underwear and snacks, and M-16 assault rifles slung over their shoulders. Some of the soldiers were still half asleep. None of those seeking a ride that morning noticed anything odd about a soldier with a relatively fair complexion who was walking about in IDF fatigues and large olive parka. The soldier looked hip: confident, cocky even, with a small earring. He looked like any other conscript headed straight from an all-nighter at a disco, a pub, or the warm embrace of his girlfriend back to the grind of another week of military duty. But this soldier was different. He was wired with ten kilograms of explosives. As a car pulled up to the curbside station to pick up passengers heading south, the soldier tripped the electronic detonator, causing the pipe bomb he was wearing under his jacket to explode. The force, the blinding flash of light, and the deafening blast turned the hitchhiking station into a bloody patch of hell. Soldiers were decapitated, their limbs torn off, their bodies pierced by the spray of shrapnel. One witness, a motorist about to pull up to the stop to see if his brother was waiting for a ride, told Israeli radio that there was a flash, followed by a female soldier crashing through his car window with her body flying in one direction and her head in another.[2]

The Shin Bet had known that Hamas would strike, but it hadn't guessed that the blow would be a double-barreled salvo. Israel had closed the Territories on February 12, the end of the forty-day period of mourning, but there were no attacks and the frontiers were once again opened. Yet February 25 should have raised red flags: it was the second anniversary of the Hebron Massacre.

Later that morning, a man telephoned Israeli radio and, in Arabic, claimed responsibility for the attacks on behalf of the Izzedine al-Qassam Brigade. "The attacks were a painful blow to those who ordered the assassination of Yehiya Ayyash," said a Hamas pamphlet distributed throughout the West Bank.

Fearing that the bombers had come from Gaza, Yasir Arafat ordered his police and secret service into action in a massive dragnet designed to show the world—and most importantly the Israeli public—that the Palestinian Authority was doing its share to fight Hamas terrorism. Throughout that afternoon and evening, plainclothes agents of Force 17, the Preventative Security Service, and the other Arafat intelligence services kicked down doors and dragged Izzedine al-Qassam operatives and commanders to police stations and interrogation rooms. Arafat's law-and-order display looked good for CNN cameras, but it was too little too late. And, as it turned out, the bombers weren't from Gaza; they hailed from the Al-Fawwar refugee camp near Hebron.

For Shin Bet investigators, the carnage on Jaffa Street and at Ashqelon Junction was like bad déjà vu. They were facing an enemy that was more reptilian than human: every time a limb was sliced off from the beast, it grew a new one. The man whom the Shin Bet and A'man believed was behind the attacks in Jerusalem and Ashqelon was another Hamas hero named Mohiyedine Sharif, known in Izzedine al-Qassam circles as "The Electrician."

Originally from Hebron, Mohiyedine Sharif was one of Yehiya Ayyash's prized pupils and protégés, organizing numerous cells in and around his hometown of Hebron, as well as in East Jerusalem. Sharif had been on the Shin Bet most-wanted list since the Ramat Gan and Ramat Eshkol bombings in the summer of 1995; according to the Shin Bet, Sharif had acted as an intermediary between Ayyash and the suicide bombers involved in the two deadly attacks. Shin Bet commanders were determined not to publicize "The Electrician" as the heir apparent to Ayyash's legacy, but they were determined to stop him before he would unleash the next wave of suicide bombers.

At 6:20 A.M. on Sunday, March 3, exactly one week after the No. 18 bus erupted into a ball of fire on Jaffa Street, another No. 18 bus full of wary passengers proceeded along Jaffa Street, past the city's main post office in the business district. It was a bright morning, one that promised to shower golden sunshine upon the city. Instead, a firestorm of death rained down from the heavens. At 6:22, a young man with a light complexion dressed as a typical Israeli in Western clothing gazed out the window, staring at a group of Romanian workers brought in to replace Palestinians barred from entering the Territories; they were cleaning up the nearby sidewalk. Without warning, the rider unzipped his heavy parka and flipped the detonator on a fifteen-kilogram pipe bomb he carried on his waist. The blast tore through the bus with force and fire. The roof of the bus was torn off its frame like a tin-can cover. Buses were designed to carry people and survive potholes and traffic—they weren't constructed to withstand the rage of a suicide bomber.

The Jerusalem emergency medical services, by force of habit one of the most battle-savvy in the world, had sixteen ambulances at the scene less than four minutes after the bus bomb went off. The bomb maker had taken special care to inflict the maximum death toll, and he had achieved lethal results. Survivors wandered around in a wide-eyed daze. A man covered in blood, his head smoldering from the flames, walked in circles as emergency medical crews tried repeatedly to get him into an ambulance. Policemen cried as they pulled the wounded to safety; Border Guards, some of them recent arrivals from Ethiopia who had survived an arduous test of humanity in order to get to Israel, were stunned to see the destruction. A veteran bomb-disposal officer, his bloodshot eyes forced once again to witness the ravages of explosives and shrapnel on tissue and bone, suited up in a Kevlar wrapping as he gingerly stepped through the dead and debris to see if the bus was, perhaps, booby-trapped with additional explosives. "This isn't Jerusalem," one of the bomb-squad cops uttered, "this is fucking Belfast!"

The bomber was identified as Mohammed Abdo, a twenty-four-year-old laborer from Hebron. Abdo had been a student at Bir Zeit University and, like many of the students, had become an adoring admirer of Yehiya Ayyash. Ayyash would have been proud of Abdo's dedication. Nineteen people were killed that morning in Jerusalem and another two dozen seriously injured.

In a leaflet faxed to news agencies throughout Israel and the Middle East, the Izzedine al-Qassam Brigade claimed responsibility for the carnage in Jerusalem, stating that the operation was in retaliation for the assassination of Yehiya Ayyash. The leaflets also stated that the attack would be the last for three months.[3]

It was a cruel and masterful ruse. Israel had just over twenty-four hours to relish the promise that the bombings would stop.

Prime Minister Peres, his political promise dwindling each time an Israeli voter boarded a bus, vowed to take measures to put an end to the Hamas bombings. The IDF would deport anyone suspected of masterminding or supporting an attack, and the homes of bombers would be dynamited. In Gaza, in a show of force, Arafat ordered armored cars into the streets to stand at the gates of refugee camps. Heavily armed special operations police units, wearing black fatigues and carrying assault rifles with telescopic scopes, walked provocative patrols through Hamas and Islamic Jihad strongholds, challenging the fundamentalists.

So too did the IDF. On the morning of March 4, IDF infantry and special operations units entered the al-Fawwar camp in an operation designed to punish those responsible for the three recent bombings. Collective punishment was something of a West Bank specialty—the Ottoman Turks, the British, the Jordanians, and the Israelis all had successively punished the community for the crimes of a select few, and this morning would be no different. Residents were ordered at gunpoint into their homes and locked in. Snipers ringed rooftops and helicopters knocked the solar panels off many homes as they flew low and fast over the terrified camp. The homes of the Jerusalem and Ashqelon bombers were sealed shut; their families, who days earlier had thrown parties to honor their shaheed, were now homeless, living with their meager possessions on dirt roads; their homes would be blown up in a matter of days. As the sun rose over Hebron, the Israeli units patrolling the narrow alleyways in a determined show of force took solace in the fact that they had punished a community that had sent three of its sons on murderous missions inside Israel.

But collective punishment wasn't an IDF exclusivity that morning. Inside the cabin of a truck heading from the West Bank to Tel Aviv, a twenty-four-year-old man from Ramallah, dressed like an Israeli college student, sat silently as he listened to the Arabic news service. The driver of the truck, an Israeli Arab, was paid handsomely for transporting the man from Ramallah to Tel Aviv, though he didn't ask—nor did he want to know— the purpose of the stone-faced individual's reason for breaking into the Territories to enter Israel. The man from Ramallah sat silently as the truck barreled down the Jerusalem-Tel Aviv Highway heading north, past the Latrun Interchange, past Ben-Gurion International Airport, toward the Ayalon Freeway.

Even after the No. 5 bus bombing and the murder of Yitzhak Rabin, there was something about Tel Aviv that made Israelis forget the hell and sorrow of where they lived. Tel Aviv was chic, fast-paced, and lively. Motorists cared little about the peace talks or the political situation in Syria when they tried to get through gridlocked avenues and side streets; pedestrians, walking past stores with the Sony, Nike, NBA, and Coca-Cola logos, didn't think of themselves as being in the Middle East—they could have, after all, been walking in Rome, London, or New York. And of course, even combat soldiers on leave in Tel Aviv could easily forget security duty inside southern Lebanon when walking along the streets of the city where voluptuous almond-eyed beauties strutted their stuff in that so very alluring Tel Aviv manner. Dizengoff Center was the epicenter of this escape from Israel's reality. It was the country's first shopping mall and it remains its most famous. It is, courtesy of places like Pizza Hut, the Hard Rock Café, and McDonalds, a safe haven from regional woes.

Afternoons are the busiest for both halves of the sprawling mall, split in half by Dizengoff Street. Close to 4:00 P.M., as workers begin to sneak out of work they converge on the shopping plaza for a chance to spend money, eat at a café, or just be part of the Tel Aviv scene.

At 3:55 P.M. on March 4, 1996, Dizengoff Center was packed with a combination of shoppers, pedestrians, and partygoers celebrating the Purim holidays. Children, many wearing Power Ranger and Disney costumes, clutched the hands of their parents as they held balloons and bags full of sweets. Previous Purims had been more festive. Taking the security situation into consideration, Tel Aviv mayor Roni Milo canceled many official Purim parties throughout the city, and he ordered additional police patrols.

The man from Ramallah had been aware of the increased security precautions as he walked alongside the entrances of the mall, probing its defenses in search of a weak spot. Standing next to the Bank Leumi on the corner of King George and Dizengoff Streets, the man from Ramallah was about to enter the mall when he noticed two policemen standing in front of one of the gates he thought of entering—his handlers had told him that the gate was usually crowded with kids packed around a video arcade. It was better to detonate himself indoors, he was told: explosions are far more lethal when concentrated inside four walls. His eyes wandered around the dizzying intersection looking for an "in"; the man from Ramallah sought out the best spot to ensure his mission would be a success. At exactly 4:00 he noticed the Bank Hapoalim branch across the street and a crowd of people impatiently hovering around an ATM machine. Crossing the street at the light, he walked slowly and carefully toward the curb, scanning the faces that surrounded him. At 4:01

the man from Ramallah pressed a small button inside his coat that ignited the forty pounds of explosives inside his backpack.

The explosion was horrific. A bustling streetcorner had been turned into a kill zone. The force of the blast tore bodies in half and hurled victims hundreds of feet into the air and shattered display windows hundreds of feet away, sending a lethal shower of needlelike glass shards slicing through the spring air. Ambulances, police units, and bomb squad personnel raced to the scene, as did scores of Shin Bet investigators and high-ranking army officers who had heard the bomb go off in their offices ten blocks away. Citizens on the street provided emergency medical care to those who could still be saved, and covered the dead, the burned, and the mangled with their jackets. The carnage had been absolute. In all, fourteen would die that afternoon in Tel Aviv, and nearly a hundred were seriously wounded. The dead ranged in age from fourteen-year-old Dana Gutman of Moshav Mishmeret to eighty-two-year-old Rachel Sela of Tel Aviv. Many of the wounded were small children whose white costumes of lace were now soiled with blood and soot.

Phone lines in Tel Aviv jammed as worried parents, husbands, and wives phoned hotlines to see if their loved ones were among the dead and wounded; many of the concerned simply raced into their cars and drove to emergency room receiving wards to find out if their loved ones had been at the scene. People who had been tempered to tolerate the intolerable were now grasping at the last fibers of their sanity in order to get through the day. Everyday life in Israel had become an insane game of Russian roulette.

Prime Minister Peres, Internal Security Minister Moshe Shahal, and Police Commissioner Assaf Hefetz toured the bomb scene shortly after the blast to an audience of angry and scared citizens who shouted a chorus of "Death to the Arabs!" and "Revenge!" The ministers and police officials walked carefully through the minefield of shattered body organs and broken glass. They looked dour and clueless: Peres looked daunted; his Shin Bet security package struggled to keep the angry mob at arms length. Four bombs in eight days was a siege and it had to end. Shin Bet director Ami Ayalon, surrounded by a phalanx of agents wearing snug police caps, looked horrified as he walked through the carnage. In his career as a naval commando, Ami Ayalon had seen almost everything there was to see, though he had never witnessed an Israeli streetcorner turned into a morgue. Once again, Bosnia, Belfast, and Beirut had cast their shadows on Israel's Mediterranean jewel.

As darkness fell over the corner of Dizengoff and King George Streets, a crowd of people assembled behind the crime scene tape to stand a silent, tear-filled vigil. Orthodox volunteers collected blood and tissue with cotton balls, and police investigators, standing side by side, crouched to pick up every bit of forensic evidence they could gather. There was no urgency to the investigation; Hamas had already identified the man from Ramallah as twenty-four-year-old Salah Abdel-Rahim Ishaq. Hamas, and the Islamic Jihad, took credit for the blast. Even a rookie bomb technician could recognize the device as classic Ayyash.

The handiwork of the ghost of a man that had been killed three months earlier had, in four days, killed fifty-seven men, women, and children. That man had changed a nation forever, and now he was impacting the entire world.

On March 12, 1996, Egyptian president Hosni Mubarak, at the behest of President Bill Clinton, convened the remarkable Summit of the Peacemakers in the five-star Movenpick Hotel on Sinai's southern coast, at Sharm es-Sheikh. The summit was a regional and international gathering of world leaders and their intelligence chiefs tasked with devising an international strategy to combat terrorism while at the same time bolstering the Jewish state—and Prime Minister Peres—with high-profile support. Joining Presidents Mubarak and Clinton were Prime Minister Peres, King Hussein of Jordan, Chairman Arafat, as well as Morocco's King Hassan II, Russian President Boris Yelstin, Britain's Prime Minister Major, German Chancellor Kohl, and the premiers and leaders from France, Italy, Spain, Norway, Canada, Turkey, Mauritania, as well as, incredibly, the leaders or foreign ministers from Bahrain, Algeria, Kuwait, Saudi Arabia, Yemen, and the United Arab Emirates.

In all, twenty-eight nations were represented inside the ornate ballroom in Sharm es-Sheikh; for many of the Arab ministers, it was the first time that they had sat in a room with a delegation from Israel. Prime Minister Peres was speechless as thirteen Arab states pledged their commitment to ending the carnage. "From all around the world we have come to deliver one simple unified message," President Clinton told the assembled leaders. "Peace will prevail."

President Clinton remained in the area one more day following the historic conference. He traveled to Israel, where he met with Prime Minister Peres, sat in on a cabinet meeting, visited the graves of Prime Minister Rabin and murdered corporal Nachshon Waxman, and met with high-school students in Tel Aviv whose lives had been touched by terrorist bombs. Clinton pledged a hundred million dollars to help Israel fight terrorism. In fact, Israel that day was busy fulfilling pledges of its own.

A small group of Shin Bet officials, IDF commanders, and police officers watched as a squad of combat engineers wired a one-story house in Rafatt with enough explosives to obliterate the structure in a cloud of dust. Many of those who gathered on the plush green hills of Rafatt that chilly morning had been there before—on all-night stakeouts, intelligence-gathering missions, and, once, a late-night call to the Ayyash family for a ten-hour question-and-answer session. Rafatt had become a dot on a scarred map, and many there that morning had hoped that this was the last time they'd ever step in that cursed village. They hated the faces of the residents who cheered with each explosion; they hated the village's smell and its primitive piety. Most of all they hated the monster that Rafatt nurtured and protected.

The men awaited the home's demolition, praying that the destruction of the Engineer's nest would once and for all exorcise his ghost from the Arab-Israeli battlefield. The hated Ayyash had proven to be an elusive foe. He had stymied the region's most capable counterintelligence entity and terrorized a nation. He was, in many regards, the terrorist who won.

Notes

[1] Nachum Barne'a, "*Kach Shichne'a Kaf et Ayalon,*" *Yediot Aharonot Mosaf Shabbat,* January 12, 1996, p. 4.

[2] Nicholas Goldberg, "A Return of Terror and Tears," *New York Newsday,* February 26, 1996, p. 4A.

[3] Nicholas Goldberg, "Another Bloody Sunday," *New York Newsday,* March 4, 1996, p. 5A.

The Stopwatch of Borrowed Time

Benjamin Netanyahu was elected prime minister of the state of Israel on May 29, 1996, in a too-close-to-call election with incumbent Prime Minister Peres. The two-pronged election, one for prime minister and the other for representatives in the Knesset, was a national referendum on the issue of security. Voter turnout was high, the rhetoric inflammatory and challenging. Prime Minister Rabin's widow told supporters that if Prime Minister Peres lost to Likud challenger Netanyahu, her husband's killer would be handed a victory; and, in an ironic twist of fate that could only happen in the muddled, often jumbled, surf of the Israeli political sea, convicted assassin Yigal Amir voted behind bars at the maximum-security wing of Beersheba Prison.

In the end, the Israeli electorate chose anything but the status quo—the status quo, that is, of suicide bombings. Benjamin Netanyahu's Likud party, and the right wing and religious fringes that promised to flock to any government Netanyahu would attempt to broker, were adamant about their will—and now ability—to slow down the peace process. The new government demanded security guarantees first, and they wanted much more than pledges on paper and weekly sit-downs between Shin Bet and A'man officials and their Palestinian counterparts. Politically, to placate a fractured right wing and religious coalition, the new government sought the preservation of the status quo. The supporters of Greater Israel and of expanding Israel's West Bank settlements were eager to grind the gears of the peace process to a halt.

The suicide bombings that winter and spring had sealed Peres's political fate. Israelis wanted peace, and they wanted to see Rabin's vision of the country's next fifty years of independence come to pass. But they didn't want to just survive and endure any more. They wanted to flourish. They wanted cable TV with a hundred stations; they wanted brand-new Japanese sedans; and they wanted two trips abroad a year. Life could not continue with men incinerating themselves in the streets and buses of Israeli cities.

The Hamas bombing campaign of February and March 1996 was far different from the Ayyash-inspired spasm of violence that had answered the Hebron massacre. Ayyash's bombing spree was a prolonged attempt to break down Israeli resolve through attrition. The post-Ayyash campaign was a blitz of human bone and suicidal resolve designed to alter the mood of an Israeli electorate. Hassan Salameh, the man who masterminded that campaign, was not an angry engineering graduate who turned his faith and skills with wires and chemicals into wholesale slaughter. Salameh was a player, in the terrorist vernacular; an operative and a skilled warrior trained in the best terrorist training centers in Damascus and Teheran.[1] Salameh, arrested in a fluke of luck by Israeli military units in Hebron and indicted on seventy counts of terrorist acts and forty-five acts of murder, told reporters that he had no intention of affecting the upcoming Israeli elections; rather, his goal had been simply to kill Israelis.

Yet Salameh's bravado, especially his request to be executed, was a smoke screen. Salameh had been personally dispatched by the elusive and invisible Mohammed Deif, the commander of the Izzedine al-Qassam Brigade, at the behest of the political leadership. Hamas had redefined the Israeli and, for that matter, Middle Eastern political agenda, and it was intent on beating its foes into submission.

The security partnership with the Palestinians had done little to quell Israeli concerns. Israelis were not impressed by reports, in the days following Ayyash's assassination, that the Palestinian intelligence and police services had thwarted some *eighty* suicide attacks on targets inside Israel in 1995 alone. Israel's shattered nerves were no less soothed by scenes on CNN of Palestinian police officers, wearing flak vests and carrying American assault rifles, kicking down doors in Gaza in search of the masterminds of the next bombing campaign. Nor were Israelis shocked or surprised to learn that many Izzedine al-Qassam activists, even those that the Shin Bet managed to identify as complicit in suicide attacks, were working for the Palestinian intelligence services or the Palestinian police.

Israelis simply wanted a breather from the peace process and separation from the Palestinians, and the Palestinian Authority, and Hamas. In the end, the electorate felt that safeguarding their children from the shrapnel of a pipe bomb was far more symbolic than safeguarding the legacy of Yitzhak Rabin. A paper-thin majority felt that Netanyahu would be able to keep Hamas off the streets.

It was just after noon on Friday, March 21, 1997, and the Apropo Café on the corner of Adam Ha'Cohen Street and Ben-Gurion Boulevard was packed with Tel Aviv residents taking full advantage of a warm spring start to the weekend with a relaxing bite of food and some good espresso in one of the city's more fashionable outdoor eateries. The temperature was cool but not chilly, and the sun's warming rays made spring jackets unnecessary for those sitting outdoors on the second-story terrace. Lovers talked over piping-hot glasses of Kafe Hafooch, and mothers spoon-fed small children sweet blintzes. It was Purim, after all, and the ghosts of last year's carnage were shuttered away in the secure vaults of Tel Aviv's consciousness.

The café was crowded and no one paid attention to the thirty-year-old man eyeing the crowd as he sat next to a small knapsack. He seemed out of place but not threatening. At 1:45 P.M. the man exploded a seven-pound pipe bomb crammed with TNT and wrapped in nails and ball bearings. The blast was ferocious, and the havoc wreaked on the outdoor café, located only a block from the main Tel Aviv police station, was enormous. Three women, including a pregnant doctor, were killed in the blast; forty-eight people, including the six-month-old daughter of one of the fatalities, were seriously injured. The bomber, Moussa Ranimat of Kfar Tsurif near Hebron, was not the typical Hamas suicide bomber. He was married and the father of four children. His orange identity card, as well as the smoldering stumps of his feet, were found near ground zero. Dozens of police and bomb-disposal units raced to the scene. Tel Aviv emergency service personnel were becoming experts at the design and aftereffects of the Ayyash patent built under license by Mohiyedine Sharif. Peace and security, the call to war of Netanyahu's campaign for the office of prime minister, had proven to be nothing more than translucent hyperbole.

In a call to Israel's Channel 1 television station, the Izzedine al-Qassam Brigade claimed responsibility for the attack. The attack had taken many in Israel by surprise—especially Shin Bet commanders, who had hoped for a respite from the bombings. There had been intelligence floating around field offices that Hamas would, indeed, attempt an isolated attack somewhere in either Jerusalem or Tel Aviv. The Apropo bombing frightened many in the cabinet and in the intelligence community, to the point that two weeks later, on April 3, the state of Israel formally withdrew its request to have Musa Abu Marzouk extradited to Israel. The citizens of Israel braced for more madness. Israelis would have four long months to wait and try to guess when and where the next device would explode.

On Wednesday, July 30, 1997, at 1:00 P.M., Jerusalem's Mahane Yehuda Market was packed with midday shoppers carrying plastic bags filled with the day's groceries. The colors of the Oriental bazaar flowed under the narrow gaps of corrugated metal roofing that covered many of the stalls selling olives, vegetables, meats, and bread. Spices from the entire Middle East filled the air with an aromatic bite. Merchants shouted amusing songs meant to entice shoppers to sample their prices, and savvy shoppers, in true Byzantine fashion, bartered them down as far as they'd go. Mahane Yehuda was Jerusalem's Jewish market, and it was a lively, unassuming, shoulder-to-shoulder shoving match that had its unique charms.

At 1:15 A.M., two Hasidic Jews, wearing the characteristic white shirt and black trousers, were dropped off in front of the market; wearing yarmulkes and sporting long, flowing beards, the two men aroused little interest from the Border Guard policemen stationed at the market's main entrance off Jaffa Street. The men walked in together but took up positions fifty yards from each another. The first bomber pressed a button on his attaché case, detonating ten kilograms of TNT wrapped in nails. As the throng of panic-stricken shoppers raced away from the blast in a mad dash for safety, the second man pressed a button on his attaché case. The carnage was indescribable. The dead lay scattered amid pulverized produce. In all, 16 people were killed that afternoon, another 150 seriously wounded.

Israeli police officials, molding latex gloves to their hands for the grim task of recovering evidence, no longer worried as to when the carnage would end. They only wondered where the next attack would occur.

On September 4, 1997, at just after 3:00 P.M., four young Arab men dressed as Israeli teenagers detonated themselves at strategic spots around Jerusalem's bustling Ben Yehuda Street shopping promenade. The men wore wigs to disguise their dark hair and carried small devices inside knapsacks. Miraculously, for a shopping plaza crowded with thousands of people, the death toll had been tempered. Four victims of the blast were killed, another 150 were seriously wounded.

The bombers in both the Mahane Yehuda and the Ben Yehuda bombings were all from the village of Azira Shamalya, a Hamas stronghold near Nablus with a population of seven thousand. The village was in Area B, under Israeli security control, though Shin Bet agents were certain that the directives for the operations came from Area A, under Palestinian control and across the Jordan River, out of the Hamas political office flourishing in Amman, Jordan.

The Apropo killings and the two Jerusalem bombings were a sign to the Netanyahu government that Hamas had embarked on an all-out war designed to kill as many Israelis—and Jews—as possible. Netanyahu was adamant about not repeating the fate of Prime Ministers Rabin and Peres. He was not going to sit out the storm of flying human debris until the country demanded a political change, or until the Palestinian Authority cracked down on the extremists. He was going to take decisive preemptive action against the political leadership of Hamas. It would be one of the most tragic episodes in the history of Israel's intelligence community.

Assassination as a tool of military strategy is a double-edged sword in the fight against terrorism; repercussions can sometimes be even more severe than the desire for retribution and the desired results of deterrence and preemption. As Shin Bet director Ayalon learned firsthand in the spring of 1996, few in Israeli intelligence had predicted that Hamas revenge for Yehiya

Ayyash's killing would be so severe. Is vengeance always worth the risk? Is killing one terrorist leader worth risking an important regional strategic partnership? Can the intelligence agency tasked with the hit guarantee success?

The target selected for Israel's wrath was Khaled Mashaal, the Hamas political leader in Jordan. Israeli intelligence was certain that Mashaal was behind the bombings in Jerusalem that summer; Mashaal, in interviews and in statements, did little to dissuade Israeli suspicions. Like Ayyash, and the Black September warlords before him, Mashaal was a justified Israeli target—he had blood on his hands. But Mashaal wasn't living in a Tunis lair, nor was he hiding in a Gaza safe house. He worked and lived in Amman, the capital city of Israel's sole ally in the Arab world.

In fact, Jordan was far more than merely an Israeli ally: it was a strategic partner poised for unprecedented joint projects ranging from counterterrorism to cultural exchange. In fact, cooperation on the counterterrorist and intelligence-gathering fronts reached new heights, with the Mossad even opening a "station" in Amman that served as Israel's espionage eye to the east. The close relationship between King Hussein and Prime Minister Rabin was heartfelt and meant to guide both nations into a strategic partnership well into the next century. King Hussein had tolerated the fundamentalists, but he kept them under stringent controls and constant military and Muchabarat surveillance. Killing Mashaal on the streets of a friendly capital, especially one involved in such an intimate and precarious alliance, was risky business. In order for the mission to succeed, the operation would have to be carried out successfully, surreptitiously, and without Israeli involvement ever becoming known.

Late in the evening of September 19, 1997, two men carrying Canadian passports in the names of Sean Kendall and Bob Bears landed at Queen Alia International Airport, some forty minutes south of Amman. The two men traveling together took a cab to

the Jordanian capital and checked into the Intercontinental Hotel. They paid in cash, stayed clear of the exotic restaurants, bars,
and belly-dancing entertainment, and spent their days touring
the city in a rented Hyundai sedan. Negotiating the treacherous
traffic of Amman required skill and courage—and the instinct
of a Le Mans champion. Armed soldiers, policemen, and security detachments were everywhere in the city. Brand-new Mercedes Highway Patrol cars raced through traffic circles with
lights and sirens ablaze, and heavily armed police officers, wearing a bluish camouflage scheme, patrolled key intersections on
Land Rovers ferrying mounted .50-caliber machine guns.

There was reason for the security concerns in Amman. On
September 22, two Shin Bet agents assigned to the Israeli embassy were ambushed as they reconnoitered a motorcade route
to be taken by the Israeli ambassador. A day later, King Hussein
sent a message to Prime Minister Netanyahu through the Mossad liaison desk at the Israeli embassy offering to personally
broker a cease-fire between Hamas and the Israeli government.
King Hussein, concerned about the deteriorating Israeli-
Jordanian relations over the crumbling peace process, had
hoped to buy some time by keeping the Hamas bombers home.
The message, however, was lost inside the bureaucracy of Mossad HQ for some seventy-two hours.

On September 25, 1997, at just after 10:00 A.M., the two "Ca-
nadians" stood at the ready outside Khaled Mashaal's office.
Lurking in the lobby of the office building, the two men noticed
their target, and with the innocence of two bodies brushing up
against the other, one of the agents sprayed Mashaal's ear with
an experimental toxin, a synthetic opiate called Fentanyl, which,
when absorbed by the skin, killed within forty-eight hours without leaving even the slightest of chemical traces; death by poison, it was argued in Mossad headquarters, a slow and painful
demise of convulsions and vomiting, could be attributed to med-

ical reasons and was far more deniable than a .22 round between the eyes.

Yet the agents did not make a clean escape—this was not the well-oiled machinery that eliminated Dr. Fathi Shiqaqi in Malta, or the same technical genius behind a Motorola flip-phone packed with fifty grams of explosives. Mashaal's personal chauffeur and a security guard chased the two agents down through the bustling traffic of downtown Amman, until they were eventually beaten and then apprehended by Jordanian police. Murphy's Law had struck with a vengeance. A risky intelligence operation designed to kill a terrorist warlord had ended in disaster. Israel's spies, and their spymasters, were always daring and arrogant, yet arrogance needs to be tempered with restraint and vision.

News of the botched operation reached Prime Minister Netanyahu as he visited Mossad headquarters during the obligatory New Year greetings that Israel's elected leaders often personally deliver to the anonymous warriors of Israel's intelligence services. Netanyahu had hoped to break bread with the agents and analysts and congratulate them on a year of dedication and dangerous service. Yet as Netanyahu emerged from his armored limousine, Mossad director Major General (Res.) Danny Yatom, a former Sayeret Mat'kal commando, took the prime minister aside and told him that the operation in Jordan had gone very bad; Yatom had learned of the fiasco through a coded message sent by a Mossad support team that managed to make it back to the Israeli embassy unscathed. The extent of the bungled affair was apparent to all. If Netanyahu and the Mossad did not confess the details of the hit personally to King Hussein, the fate of the two seized operatives, along with the future of Israeli-Jordanian relations, were threatened. Netanyahu ordered Yatom to Amman and directed him to personally hand-deliver the toxin's antidote to King Hussein.

Inside the plush comfort and beauty of Amman's Raghadan palace, King Hussein met with the anxious Mossad chief. The Jordanian monarch sat stone-faced and livid throughout Yatom's detailed description of the operation gone wrong. Yatom's personal apologies for dispatching hit men on the streets of the Jordanian capital were not warmly accepted. King Hussein was outraged. He immediately ceased all intelligence cooperation between the Israeli and Jordanian intelligence communities. The furious king refused to meet directly with Netanyahu following the operation, and went so far as to tell a Saudi newspaper that "A man decides to open his home generously to a foreign guest; the host enjoys this and the guest is even happier. But when the host turns his back a moment, it turns out the guest has exploited this reception to rape the home owner or his daughter."[2] King Hussein warned Netanyahu that if Jordanian demands weren't met, or if Mashaal died, the two captured agents would stand trial for murder, and if convicted would be hanged.

In a desperate attempt to soothe the battered friendship, help elevate King Hussein's status in the eyes of the fundamentalists, as well as extinguish any concern that His Majesty was complicit in the operation, Israel also promised to release Hamas founder Sheikh Yassin.

For the next week, angry high-level negotiations among Jerusalem, Amman, and Washington went on to determine the details involving the Sheikh's release, the safe return home of the jailed Mossad agents, and the release of some fifty Hamas operatives, including Jordanian citizens held in Israeli prisons. The man who brokered much of the arrangement was Ephraim Halevy, a senior Mossad official and ambassador who had, in his twenty years of service with the espionage agency, helped forge intimate links between Amman and Jerusalem. Halevy's handling of the affair was nothing short of masterful, and the sixty-year-old spymaster would be rewarded for his contacts and foresight months later when he was asked by Netanyahu to succeed Yatom and restore confidence and direction to the troubled espionage service.

At just after midnight on the morning of October 1, 1997, Sheikh Yassin was woken from a deep slumber inside the maximum security wing of Ramla Prison's medical facility and readied for an imminent release. An hour later a Royal Jordanian Air Force SA332 Aérospatiale Super Puma landed at a remote airfield near the prison. The Jordanian chopper, carrying a compliment of men clad in black from the Royal Jordanian Special Forces SOU 71 counterterrorist squad, landed for only a brief moment as both Jordanian and Israeli special forces secured the human transfer. Days later, Yassin was received by tens of thousands of adoring supporters back in Gaza. The man who had sparked one of the bloodiest terrorist campaigns in modern history had scored an impressive public relations victory. "The aim of the operation," an unapologetic Netanyahu would say later at a press conference, was to "cut off the head of the snake of Hamas." Though with Yassin back in Gaza, Israel lost an invaluable trump card in any future dealing with Hamas. Morale inside the ranks of the Izzedine al-Qassam Brigade swelled with fervor over Yassin's release. They vowed more attacks, more bloodshed, more moves on the path to liberating Jerusalem and all of Palestine in the name of Allah.

Israeli security officials had braced themselves for violence that warm and tumultuous July. It had been too quiet in Jerusalem for a summer of rhetoric, few tourists, and a peace process stalled to the point of nonexistence. Senior police officials were concerned that it was only a matter of time before there was an "incident," as the suicide bombings were known: either inside a crowded market, in a shopping plaza, or on board one of the city's always crowded buses. There was a quiet sense of heightened awareness along the outer perimeters of the Old City, as well as along the Ben-Yehuda thoroughfare and the Mahane Yehuda Market. "Hamas was like any seasoned criminal," claimed a U.S. law enforcement official, "who liked to return to the scene of the crime." They also relished anniversaries.

On the morning of July 19, 1998, a year to the Jewish calendar day of the July 30, 1997, Mahane Yehuda Market blast, a man driving a Fiat Ducato tried to do what many Jerusalem drivers do—drive as if the road belonged to him. Caring little for the eastbound traffic racing past him in the adjacent lane, the driver veered around a crowded bus nervously trying to avoid contact. He was unsuccessful. The Fiat at first scraped his fender against the bus, then reversed straight into a station wagon behind him. By the time police units responded to take the report, they noticed that the man was smoldering from a small fire leading from his blouse, through his trousers, to a line leading to the rear of the van. There, police officers were even more surprised to find some six hundred kilograms of flammable liquid connected to propane gas bottles and bags containing thousands of carpenter nails. The front license plate did not match the rear tag. As the bus driver showered the man with a blast from his fire extinguisher, a state of alert was sounded. As the bomb squad raced to the intersection, a four-block radius was evacuated. Tragedy had been averted by only a matter of seconds.

For the next six hours, bomb squad officers worked under the beating summer's sun as they removed plastic canisters filled to capacity with petrol and gingerly disarmed booby-trapped propane tanks. The improvised van bomb was a suicide device. The driver was supposed to light a fuse and then erupt in a furious fireball. In fact, if the driver hadn't set himself on fire while attempting to ignite the massive device, Shin Bet investigators and police officials attempting to prepare prosecution charges might very well have been sifting through the human debris of an explosion's wake.

The driver, burned to the bone on his torso and upper thigh area, was a man the Shin Bet had known for some time. Twenty-nine-year-old Jalal Rahman Sirhan was a "documented" second-tier Hamas activist who had served time in Israeli jails for hurling Molotov cocktails at Israeli forces during the Intifadah. He was reportedly on a list of high-risk security offenders forbidden to enter Israel. Security into Jerusalem from Area A, under complete Palestinian Authority control, was also lax—the fact that a car driven by a known terrorist with two different license plates had been allowed into the Israeli capital was seen as effectively looking the other way.

The device lacked the intricate design of the first Hamas car bomb that Yehiya Ayyash had introduced at Ramat Efal, and it was not as mechanically reliable as Ayyash's Afula creation. Yet, according to Israeli police estimates, the bomb blast produced by a van crammed with more than six hundred liters of flammable agents, propelled by propane, could engulf an area two hundred square feet. A device of that size, as estimated by charts perfected by the U.S. Treasury Department's Bureau of Alcohol, Tobacco and Firearms following the April 1995 Oklahoma City bombing, could launch glass and shrapnel nearly three thousand feet. The van bomb, had it detonated on a crowded Jerusalem intersection, could have killed hundreds.

In the summer of 1998, Sheikh Ahmed Yassin returned to Gaza following a fund-raising junket through the Middle East. Conservative estimates place the cash dividends of Yassin's trip at anywhere between fifty and three hundred million dollars; some reports even claimed the money raised in the Gulf States and in Iran to be closer to five hundred million. "No matter what the amount," claimed an American law enforcement official working a federal joint terrorist task force, "it buys you a lot of death." Money has never been an operational consideration for Hamas, however, nor is it likely to ever be. "You'd be surprised what a punch a ten-inch piece of pipe packed with nails and TNT can do to a madhouse like this," a U.S. counterterrorist official commented to an Israeli counterpart in Tel Aviv. "Imagine how many of those you can buy with five hundred million dollars."

Two men who were destined to benefit from the fortune gathered by Sheikh Yassin were Adel and Imad Awadallah, two brothers and high-ranking commanders in the Izzedine al-Qassam Brigade's West Bank apparatus. Adel was the more talented of the two. He had killed by long distance, sending well-disguised bombers into the Mahane Yehuda market and the Ben Yehuda pedestrian mall. Imad, one of the most feared Hamas hit men, killed both Jew and Palestinian; eliminating suspected collaborators inside the Palestinian Authority was his specialty. In fact, in an internal feud over money and policy, Imad Awadallah shot Yehiya Ayyash's protégé and successor, Mohiyedine Sharif, twice in the chest and once in the thigh, and then rigged his Fiat Uno with a time bomb, to make it look like the Electrician had died in a work accident. Arrested by the Palestinian Authority, Imad Awadallah escaped from a Palestinian jail on August 15, 1998. "You know he was evil," an Israeli special operations officer said, "when even Arafat's cops were afraid of you!"

On September 8, 1998, an IDF patrol was sent to the village of Khirbet Teibeh, east of Hebron, to examine reports of men firing guns and setting off explosions near the summer home of Akram Maswada, a wealthy Hebron entrepreneur with no known ties to Hamas or the Islamic Jihad. Automatic fire and hand grenade explosions were a part of the Hebron landscape, but with the Jewish settlement of Telem only five hundred yards away, the commander of Israeli forces in the West Bank, Brigadier General Yitzhak Eitan, thought it prudent to investigate further.

Spotters and undercover operatives were dispatched to the village to establish covert observation posts around the targeted cottage. Observer teams reported that two men armed with AK-47s were holed up in the small building, and that they spent their days readying equipment and gear into knapsacks and kit bags. A'man officers and Shin Bet agents were summoned to the village and, following a photo ID and the testimony of village residents dragged to questioning, including Akram Maswada, it was clear that the IDF had stumbled across the Awadallah brothers. Realizing that taking down the two Hamas terrorists would be a risky undertaking, Brigadier General Eitan summoned the Ya'ma'm.

On September 10, 1998, as dusk blanketed the Hebron hills with a soothing crimson glow, Israel's counterterrorist specialists were ordered to attack. The assault plan was cruel though brilliant. Attack dogs trained to lunge at a suspect's groin led the assault by jumping through the open windows and lunging at the two brothers who, the Ya'ma'm knew, would be taking a nap. The shock and pain of the dogs' jaws clamping down on supersensitive extremities would prove to be an ideal diversion. By the time Ya'ma'm operators burst through the barricaded door, the brothers had no time to reach for the AK-47 assault rifles they slept with. Both were cut down in a flurry of automatic-rifle fire.

Inside the hideout, Israeli investigators uncovered weapons, ammunition, grenades, explosives, plumber's pipe, wigs, forged identity cards, and other Hamas paraphernalia. Israeli military intelligence agents were convinced that the two were preparing a new wave of suicide attacks against targets in Israel. Israeli fears were reinforced a month later in Hebron, when, on October 1, Palestinian Preventive Security agents, acting on a tip, arrested a Hamas activist and former chemistry major for storing nearly a ton of homemade explosives in his house. Only three days earlier an explosive-laden car, apparently being readied for a suicide mission in Israel, exploded prematurely.

In 1999, Israeli voters, eager for peace, elected Ehud Barak, Israel's most decorated soldier—who had seen much of the Middle East covertly while leading commando squads—to finalize a peace deal with the Palestinian Authority. Perhaps Barak was the man capable of leading Israel to the end of its war with the Palestinians and making the painful, gut-wrenching decisions needed to forge a final peace.

Few prime ministers before him had such impeccable military credentials. Perhaps no one in the State of Israel had displayed more courage on the field of battle. That courage would be sorely needed. Motivated by a battlefield commander's vision, Barak knew that the winds of war would quickly sweep the region into full-scale conflagration if a final peace deal were not achieved. The battle for peace would be the one confrontation Ehud Barak would not win. His position was eventually outflanked and overrun.

Barak also hoped that the legacy of Yehiya Ayyash would be diluted by the progress of peace. Israeli voters, eager—in the words of one counterterrorist unit commander looking forward to the World Cup—to put the ball in the goal, had decided to vote Prime Minister Benjamin Netanyahu out of office and install a government dedicated to the mission of peace. In May 2000, Ehud Barak walked into the tail end of the Oslo peace process. Barak, unwilling to waste further time and barter with lives the way store owners in the *suq* bicker over shekels, presented Arafat with what the prime minister thought was the deal of a lifetime: 95 percent of the West Bank, permission for some Palestinian refugees to return, and even the hint of a Palestinian capital in East Jerusalem, in exchange for a full and binding peace.

Under tremendous pressure from both President Clinton and Barak to accept the deal, Arafat still balked. He was unwilling to accept anything less than all of the West Bank and Gaza, the right of return for all Palestinian refugees, and Palestinian sovereignty over East Jerusalem. Both sides returned to the Middle East bracing for the violent uncertainty of what might follow.

Arafat had bolstered his forces for war, establishing links and weapons shipments from the Islamic Republic of Iran. Israel, too, braced for conflict.

Word of Barak's offer, especially the very suggestion of any compromise on Jerusalem, sparked outrage among the Israeli right.

On September 28, 2000 Ariel Sharon, leader of the Likud Party, ventured to the Temple Mount, in the shadow of the al-Aqsa Mosque and the Wailing Wall, to reassert Jewish sovereignty over a small piece of sacred ground, touching off a firestorm of violence.

What Arafat could not win at Camp David, he would try to win by war. The next day, Palestinians rioted in East Jerusalem. The violence quickly spread to the frontier areas separating Israeli and Palestinian lines in the West Bank and the Gaza Strip. The al-Aqsa Intifadah had erupted.

Fighting between Israeli security forces and Palestinian militants quickly escalated. Gasoline bombs and rocks thrown by spontaneous gatherings of men and women expressing their rage were soon replaced by deliberate acts of murder perpetrated by Hamas, Islamic Jihad, elements inside Fatah, and Arafat's own security and intelligence forces. Palestinian policemen, trained by the Jordanians, the Egyptians, and eventually the CIA to maintain law and order, were soon lobbing mortar shells into Jewish neighborhoods in Jerusalem. Less than two months after the Intifadah erupted, car bombings rocked Jerusalem and Hadera. On March 4, 2001 a Hamas suicide bomber killed three Israelis in Netanya. In July 2000, in the shady splendor of Camp David, Maryland, President Bill Clinton convened a summit between Barak and Arafat to deal with the thorny, final status issues that had been left out of the Oslo accords. But in early 2001, elections in Israel remained frustratingly in the present.

On March 7, 2001 Ariel Sharon took office as prime minister, shepherding a national unity government. Sharon, the burly former general who promised security to the people of Israel, found himself in the same shoes once worn by Yitzhak Rabin and Shimon Peres, wading through the blood-soaked aftermath of buses, restaurants, shopping centers, and cafés hit by Hamas and Islamic Jihad suicide bombers. The frequency and scale of the suicide bombings that have hit Israel since the onset of the al-Aqsa Intifadah are mind-boggling. The terrorists, at first the Islamic militants and then secular suicide squads belonging to the Tanzim, a militia in Arafat's Fatah party, would gladly give their lives over real estate sacred to both Arab and Jew. Sharon's visit, led by a security entourage of Shin Bet agents and policemen, was the spark that many inside the Palestinian Authority were looking for to unleash a wave of violence.

Unlike the first primitive but lethal devices that Yehiya Ayyash had built from store-bought materials, the explosive belts and cases the terrorists used this time around were built of TNT, RDX, Semite, and C4, which had come from sympathizers in Lebanon, Jordan, Egypt, and even Iran.

The results were devastating. On May 18, 2001 five Israelis were killed by a powerful explosion set off by a suicide bomber outside a shopping mall in Netanya. Fourteen days later, on June 1, twenty Israelis, mostly teenagers, were killed and nearly a hundred others were wounded when a Hamas suicide bomber detonated his explosives outside a crowded discothèque in Tel Aviv. Two months later, fifteen were killed by the Hamas suicide bombing of a Sbarro pizzeria at a busy Jerusalem intersection.

The suicide bombings continued and intensified even after the September 11 attacks on New York and Washington, D.C., when Yasir Arafat pledged to fight terror. In a twelve-hour period on December 1 and 2, 2001 over twenty-five Israelis were killed and nearly two hundred wounded in three separate bombing attacks in Jerusalem and Haifa. The bombings would continue in Hadera, Tel Aviv, Netanya, and Jerusalem. Over five hundred Israelis would die. The al-Aqsa incident had quickly developed into a full-scale war over Israel's very existence. Israeli voters were in no mood to discuss peace. They fretted over the very survival of their nation.

Ehud Barak had been elected prime minister on a platform looking forward to a permanent peace. To many Israelis, this now seems impossible.

Since the booby-trapped cellular phone tore open the head of Yehiya Ayyash, many of The Engineer's disciples have also been killed or captured by the Shin Bet, the Israeli National Police, or the IDF. Israeli policy, albeit unwritten and often tempered by political dynamics, has been to assassinate terrorists wherever they are found. This policy was expanded during the al-Aqsa Intifadah, when many Arab terrorists—including many of Yehiya Ayyash's disciples and Fatah militia commanders—were killed in a series of spectacular, high-tech attacks using weapons that ranged from booby-trapped car seats and public pay phones to fusillades of antitank missiles launched from miles away. Often, these Israeli assassination strikes would be used as an excuse by the terrorists to launch more attacks of their own.

By May 2002, Israeli security forces had either arrested or assassinated all the men responsible for the Passover Massacre in Netanya. The apprehension and termination of some of the leading commanders of Hamas did not bring back any of the victims killed in bombing attacks, nor did it advance the cause of peace.

And, as they had after Ayyash's killing six years earlier, many in Israel realized that Hamas would simply dispatch more suicide bombers to Israel to exact revenge for the deaths of so many of their senior operational commanders killed during the Intifadah and then later during Israel's military incursion into the West Bank.

But the State of Israel remains steadfast and undeterred in its policy to eradicate those who view the murder of many as a source of pious celebration. The region is doomed to destruction if such individuals are allowed to survive and flourish.

The legacy of Yehiya Ayyash is the current debacle of endless violence. For that legacy to disappear once and for all, politicians in the Middle East—from kings to Israeli prime ministers—must realize that the Arab-Israeli conflict, especially the dimension involving the Palestinians, can only be solved by a political process fueled by good faith, fairness, and security.

Both sides need responsible leaders who can offer the first glimmers of hope for a peaceful future for the generations to come.

Unless that vision is realized and realized soon, the fanatics who massacre worshippers in a mosque or who cold-heartedly send confused teenagers into restaurants wearing explosive belts will win out, and future generations will be condemned to a future of hatred, death, and hopelessness.